FIVE THOUSAND YEARS OF URBANIZATION: THE PUNJAB REGION

Five Thousand Years of Urbanization: The Punjab Region

Edited by

REETA GREWAL

INSTITUTE OF PUNJAB STUDIES
CHANDIGARH

MANOHAR
2005

First published 2005

ISBN 81-7304-614-X

Published by
Ajay Kumar Jain for
Manohar Publishers & Distributors
4753/23 Ansari Road, Daryaganj
New Delhi 110 002

Typeset by
Kohli Print
Delhi 110 051

Printed at
Lordson Publishers Pvt. Ltd.
Delhi 110 007

Distributed in South Asia by
FOUNDATION BOOKS
4381/4, Ansari Rorad
Daryaganj, New Delhi 110 002
and its branches at Mumbai, Hyderabad,
Bangalore, Chennai, Kolkata

Contents

Foreword

The phenomenon of urbanization is as old as the functioning of organized societies. In the Indian subcontinent the Indus valley, with its characteristically riverine civilization, was the first to experience this development almost five thousand years ago. Based on irrigation farming mainly, towns grew along the river as centres of marketing agricultural produce, management of irrigation works, supply of essential articles, handicrafts and administration. The evidence of this early urbanization is found in the ruins excavated in the early twentieth century. These were planned towns, morphologically well laid out, with interrelated internal functions and external association with the surrounding areas. However, 'cities do not grow up of themselves. The countrysides set them up to do tasks that must be performed in central places.' Many of these towns perished with the disruption of the irrigation system and shifts in the river's course. This statement by Mark Jefferson emphasises the point that rural and urban places do not exist exclusive of each other. They are interrelated and interdependent in many ways. At the same time, the factors stimulating urban development have varied from time to time and rural-urban relationships have also changed.

During the medieval period towns were generally centres of political activity, civil administration and magnets for artisans and the elites, apart from being important military headquarters. In the modern context also, major industry, commerce, administration, education, health and a variety of services are instrumental in promoting the process of urbanization. The morphological and structural outlines of each major historical period have their own characteristic features. All the surviving old cities bear the imprint of each period they have passed through. The process of urbanization, therefore, requires to be looked upon through temporal as well as spatial perspectives for a wholesome understanding of its significance in all details.

The 'Punjab Region' having a long history of urban development, from the Harappan civilization to the present, is eminently suited for a study of the multifacted phenomenon of urbanization.

Though a number of well-known cities existed and were of decisive significance in the innovation of human culture and civilization, but they did not account for more than a small fraction of the region's total population. It is only in modern times (mostly from the nineteenth century onwards) that urbanization has acquired a real demographic significance. Nevertheless, a comprehensive knowledge of the processes of urbanization would warrant studies of urban development covering the whole range of the time factor.

With about 26 per cent of its total population living in urban areas according to the census of 1991, India is among the less urbanized countries of the developing world. In the north-western part of the Indian subcontinent, a major part of which is the 'Punjab Region', the situation is hardly better. On the Indian side, in the present states of Punjab and Haryana urban population is only 29.7 per cent and 24.8 per cent respectively. But it is changing fast, with significant spatial patterns emerging in each state.

A look at urbanization in a wide spatial perspective reveals that the differences between urban and rural areas is not simply of degree. It reflects the development of a distinct way of life which involves the contrast in the character of the people—'the city slicker' and the 'country yokel'. More than the differences in density of population and size of settlement. It also includes the differences in values, attitudes, aspirations and socio-economic attributes of the people. Disparities in the mode and quality of life in rural and urban areas continue to be wide, though they have shown signs of narrowing in recent years, particularly since the availability of electricity, expansion of education and the development of modern communication systems. The present Punjab is a leading example of this transformation. The people of the urban and rural areas are gradually coming closer as a consequence of these technological advances. Studies of urbanization should invariably include such questions.

The pattern of urbanization is closely related to the nature of economy. In a commercial agricultural economy, as in Punjab and Haryana, the pattern is of 'multi-nuclear territories', while large-scale industrialization, specially in the Indian context, leads to the formation of 'uni-nuclear regions'. Wherever the two types of economies are combined, the uni-nuclear pattern is superimposed on the multi-nuclear territory. The size and spacing of urban centres and their functional inter-relations alongwith the transport network in which they work, should also draw the attention of scholars.

The determinants of growth of urban population are natural increase and migration (both rural-urban and urban-urban). It is important to know who are coming into towns and cities and what are their objectives. The changing ethnic composition of urban population in these regions, and its implications, should be of equal interest to the scholars. What is the impact of migration on areas from where the people are pulling out, and on areas into which they are moving? The pace of urbanization is accelerating in the developing world, though in varying degrees, and bringing about several kinds of changes in human life. The study of urbanization in all its dimensions will, therefore, become increasingly important in the years to come.

The study of urbanization is an interdisciplinary theme par excellence. The present volume which is the product of a seminar on 'Five Thousand Years of Urbanization: The Punjab Region', is an excellent example of such an enterprises. It drew eminent scholars from History, Economics, Sociology, Geography, Political Science, Anthropology, Literature and Town Planning. Its discussions across all these allied areas of studies were most enriching and enlightening, leading to a fusion of ideas on various issues and an outcome far beyond its multi-disciplinary character.

The organizers of the seminar, Profs. J.S. Grewal and Indu Banga, Honorary Director and Secretary respectively of the Institute of Punjab Studies, richly deserve our warmest compliments for arranging such an unusual academic meet, bringing the best of scholars to interact on all these important themes and ultimately coming out with such an outstanding volume, edited by Dr Reeta Grewal with meticulous care.

G.S. Gosal

Preface

The Institute of Punjab Studies is an interdisciplinary forum for comprehensive studies of the people of the geographical region called the Punjab in a broad historical and comparative perspective. The Institute organizes seminars and symposia and disseminates their findings through publications. The papers in the present volume were presented at a seminar on urbanization held in 1997 and have since been revised and updated. I am sure that like our previous publications the present volume would also be well-received.

I wish to thank Dr Reeta Grewal for cheerfully editing the volume. I also thank Mr Mohan Singh from the Department of Geography, Panjab University, who prepared the maps and Dr Surya Kant for guiding him. The Manohar Publishers have been extremely accommodating in preparing this volume for the press and producing it in a short time without compromising on its quality. In the organization of the seminar on urbanization the Institute received financial assistance from the Indian Council of Historical Research, New Delhi, and a subsidy from the Urban History Association of India, now based at Chandigarh. I am thankful to the Department of History, Panjab University for their collaboration.

I am thankful to Prof. G.S. Bhalla, the distinguished economist, for inaugurating the seminar. Its organization and the publication of this volume would not have been possible without the advice and involvement of Prof. J.S. Grewal, Honorary Director of the Institute. The Institute is indebted to Prof. Gurdev Singh Gosal, its present Chairman, and an eminent geographer, for graciously agreeing to contribute a meaningful Foreword to this volume.

INDU BANGA

Contributors

ATIYA HABEEB KIDWAI: Centre for the Study of Regional Development, Jawaharlal Nehru University, New Delhi.

G.S. BHALLA: Professor Emeritus, Centre for the Study of Regional Development, Jawaharlal Nehru University, New Delhi.

G.S. GOSAL: Professor Emeritus, Department of Geography, Panjab University, Chandigarh.

GOPAL KRISHAN: Sr. Professor and Hony. Director, Population Research Centre, CRRID, Chandigarh.

INDU BANGA: Secretary, Institte of Punjab Studies; presently at Department of History, Panjab University, Chandigarh.

IQBAL HUSAIN: Centre of Advanced Study, Department of History, Aligarh Muslim University, Aligarh.

J.K. GUPTA: Advisor, Town Planning, Punjab Urban Development Authority, Mohali, Chandigarh.

J.S. GREWAL: Life Fellow, Punjabi University, Patiala; and Honorary Director IPS; formerly at Department of History, GNDU, Amritsar.

J.S. RAHI: Formerly at School of Punjabi Studies, Guru Nanak Dev University, Amritsar.

JAYA MENON: Department of History, Aligarh Muslim University, Aligarh.

K.K. TRIVEDI: Centre for Historical Studies, Jawaharlal Nehru University, New Delhi.

KUMKUM ROY: Centre for Historical Studies, Jawaharlal Nehru University, New Delhi.

KUSUM CHOPRA: Formerly at Centre for the Study of Regional Development, Jawaharlal Nehru University, New Delhi.

REETA GREWAL: Department of History, Panjab University, Chandigarh.

RENU THAKUR: Department of Ancient Indian History, Culture and Archaeology, Panjab University, Chandigarh.

SUBHASH MARCUS: Development Alternatives, Chanakyapuri, New Delhi.

SURAJ BHAN: Formerly at Department of Ancient Indian History, Culture and Archaeology, Kurukshetra University, Kurukshetra.

SURYA KANT: Department of Geography, Panjab University, Chandigarh.

VEENA SACHDEVA: Department of History, Panjab University, Chandigarh.

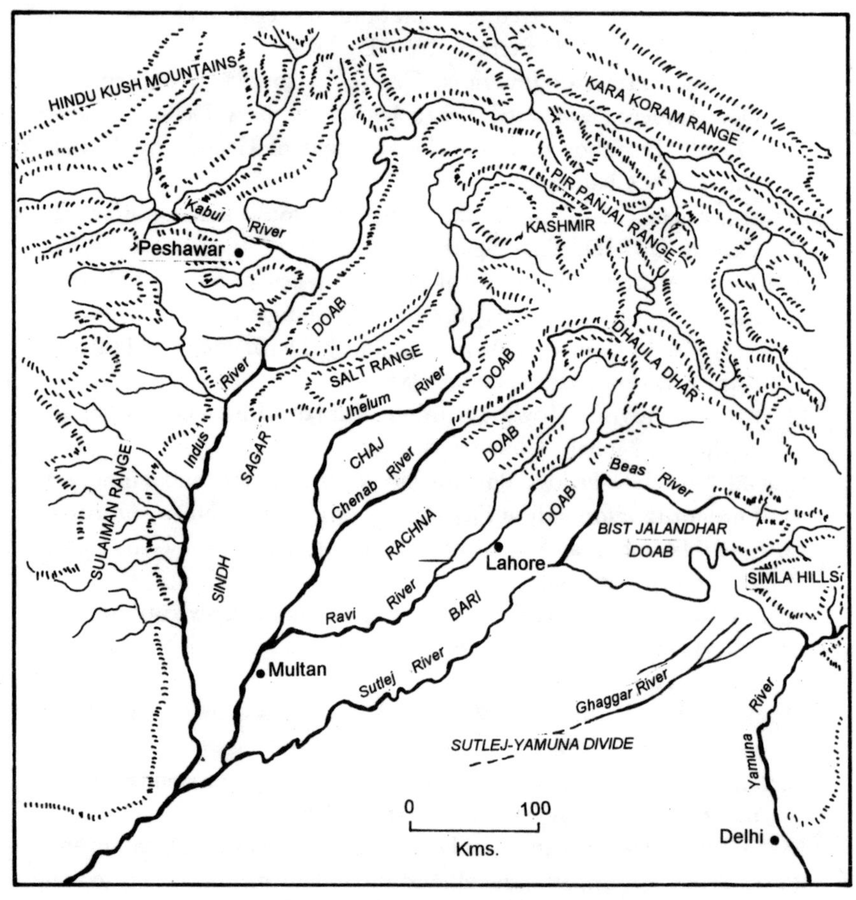

Map 1: The Punjab Region

1

Introduction

REETA GREWAL

The Punjab has been one of the highly urbanized regions in Indian history. The fifteen contributions to this volume trace its long history from the third millennium BC to the present. They do not provide a continuous narrative of the entire north-western region but represent all the important developments in the history of urbanization from the pre-historic to the contemporary times, stretching upto 2001. Approaches vary from author to author who write from the diverse but related perspectives of archaeology, history, geography, economics, development studies, town-planning and literature. Richness of perceptions and information is common to all of them which makes it difficult to capture their full texture in a brief statement. I hope to outline the major thrust in each case, beginning with the inaugural address which is of broader relevance.

I

In his inaugural address, G.S. Bhalla underlines the crucial importance of industrialization in accelerating the process of urbanization. There were urban centres before the industrial revolution, not only in the middle ages but also in the ancient period. However, the scale of urbanization remained limited due to the inbuilt constraints of agrarian economies. The demand for food is inelastic but the demand for manufactured goods is highly elastic. Industrialization created the possibility of a large-scale economy and changed the pattern of consumption and the basic pattern of life. Centres of trade, finance, legal services, education as well as goverance came up. Creative pursuits in art, science and technology also flourished in the new conditions. However, urbanization is not an unmixed blessing. Segmentation on the basis of power relations, economic status, religious affiliations, racial identities became apparent. Organized crime also became naked in the city.

In India, the nature of urbanization changed under the colonial regime. The older 'medieval' cities declined and new cities came up as instruments of exploitation. Through them, the surplus extracted from the rural hinterland was pumped to the metropolis. The pace of urbanization, however, remained sluggish due to the absence or slow pace of industrialization. Though the workers were attracted to the cities in search of employment, the cities remained marked by unemployment. Moreover, the city life was marred by poverty and religious fanaticism which led to social tension and even riots.

After Independence the pace of urbanization became rapid but even today India is one of the least urbanized countries in the world. In absolute numbers, however, it is next only to China, with 217,200,000 Indians living in urban centres according to the census of 1991. Nearly one-third of the urban population of India lives in 23 mega cities with more than a million population. If we turn to class I cities with a population of over 100,000, we find that two-thirds of the urban population is living in nearly 300 centres. This leaves over 3,300 towns of small and medium size with a population of only about 25 per cent. Such settlements have thrived more in Punjab and Haryana than anywhere else. This pattern of urbanization has however, failed to meet the needs of a predominantly agrarian economy. What Punjab and Haryana need is both modernization and diversification of agriculture to initiate a process of agriculture-based industrialization in these habitats. The real challenge is to accelerate the process of sectoral diversification at the lower level. So far, the investment in urban infrastructure in all classes of settlements has remained inadequate. Particularly in view of globalization, large-scale investment will have to be undertaken in areas like water supply, roads and communications, sanitation, sewerage and slum clearance.

The second paper relates to proto-historic Punjab in the context of a debate between 'revolution towards urbanism' and 'gradual development', suggested respectively by the metaphors of the 'step' and the 'ramp'. Jaya Menon in her paper emphasizes the relevance of the study of craft production for this debate since it enables us to study occupational differentiation, social stratification, and the role of political institutions all of which have a close bearing on early urbanism.

In this context, Jaya Menon believes that the fact that inscribed tokens appear for the first time in the Mature Harappan period, is of great significance especially when we know that there was a gradual transition from the Early to the Mature Harappan. Other 'innovations' relate to craft objects. The seals and weights used earlier, attained standardized forms. Though the basic technologies continued, elaborations occurred only in the Mature Harappan phase. The obvious examples are the production of stoneware, the making of miniature steatite beads and the etching of carnelian beads. There are stylistic differences too. An elaborate exposition of how skills are transferred from one generation to another reveals that the craftsmen, by and large, have a conservative attitude primarily due to the imitative character of apprenticeship. Thus, change in typology, technologies and tools, reflects 'new requirements', presumably, of the people in power, or the people of wealth.

Apart from demonstrating the relevance of the study of craft production for understanding the nature of early urbanism, Jaya Menon also develops a fascinatingly consistent and sophisticated argument in support of a 'threshold' for the Mature Harappan culture.

Suraj Bhan studies Harappan urbanism in the Sutlej-Yamuna Divide with a general statement on urbanization, based on his long experience as an archaeologist and deep reflection on the subject. He postulates four stages in the sequence of cultures in this region. The first phase was from about 2600 to 2300 BC, which can be characterized as chalcolithic peasant-pastoral colonization; the second was from about 2300 to 2200 BC, which marked pre-Harappan integration; the third was marked by Harappan expansion from about 2200 to 1700 BC; and the fourth stage, from about 1700 to 1000 BC, can be characterized as that of Harappan disintegration.

Carefully assessing the artifacts from a number of sites, Suraj Bhan outlines the major features of each stage, especially the first three. He comes to the conclusion that the second stage or the pre-Harappan culture made a considerable advance over the earlier culture in terms of growing specialization in crafts and social integration. Although social organization with the power-elites based in the fortified central sites had emerged, the level of social differentiation was rather low and there was no long distance trade supported by writing, inscribed seals or standard weights.

During the Harappan stage, a centralized authority, akin to that of territorial state emerged as, reflected in the twin mound pattern, elaborate fortifications, and trade. The elitist culture of this phase had no local roots in the pre-Harappan. It appears that intruders from the western parts of the Punjab brought with them the urban pattern of life, with its economic and political institutions. The possibilities existing in the region could sustain them for nearly 500 years. Significantly, they did not move into the Kurukshetra region which, according to Suraj Bhan, was not yet occupied by peasant communities.

Kumkum Roy takes up Taxila in the context of the Mauryan empire since it held a peculiar significance from the viewpoint of the empire. With her focus on interactions between the centre and province, she imparts a new dimension to the study of Taxila itself. Inscriptional evidence cited by her suggests that though efforts were made to establish an equivalence amongst all the provincial capitals in terms of administrative functions, it was never achieved. The use of Armaic, the north-western Prakrit, and Kharoshthi script in Ashokan inscriptions shows the complexity of interaction between the imperial and the provincial centre.

The variation between the centre and the province was not confined to language and script only; it was extended to the vocabulary used in the inscriptions as well. The terms *mahalaka* and *vudha*, in place of *thaira*, suggest that the category was broadened from a Buddhist elder to any old man. Similarly, the term *putra* or son was replaced by *praja* or offspring in general. There was hence a shift from a specific to a general category. The patrilineal descent embodied in the terms *putra, potra* and *prapotra* was also replaced by an inclusive descent by using variants on *nati* and *pranati* which had a wider connotation and included matrilineal descent. The term *spasa* replace *bhagini.* Kumkum Roy suggests that *spasa* was indicative of a more egalitarian relationship between brothers and sisters than *bhagini.* Another example is the use of variations on *stri* for woman in place of *abakajana* or *mahida.*

The use of the terms *brahmana* and *shramana* is equally significant. In the first place, they are bracketed in spite of the fact that they represented two opposing categories. Furthermore, whereas *brahmana* generally precedes *shramana,* the Shahbazgarhi and Mansehra inscriptions, give occasional precedence to *shramana.* The compound *dasa-bhataka* (slaves and servants), on the other hand, is uniformly used. Kumkum Roy suggests that the higher categories in the social order were possibly more fluid. Hence, in the case of Taxila, redefinitions operated not only at the level of script and language but also at the level of vocabulary. It is likely that such redefinitions were the outcome of alliances between local, predominantly urban elites and the imperial authorities. The references in the Buddhist sources to revolts at Taxila have to be viewed in this context.

Turning to archaeological evidence, Kumkum Roy draws attention to the absence of any radical change in the existing town at Taxila. Either there was no need to transform the urban centre or the imperial authority could not go too far in modifying the city. Resources were probably transferred from the provincial capital to Pataliputra but there is no archaeological evidence for it.

While some, such as the punch-marked coins can be viewed as direct indication of contact with Pataliputra, other objects could be attributed to internal transformation generated partly by the incorporation of Taxila within the imperial framework. Large storage jars could be symbolic of a new distribution system. While manufacture of textiles represented continuity, writing probably acquired greater importance and visibility. A progressive increase in the use of copper indicates the growth of a relatively richer material culture. The use of stone vessels was probably confined to the urban elite and iron tools and weapons perhaps confined to craftsmen and warriors. However, iron as a substitute for copper pottery and bone perhaps made it accessible to the common people in their daily lives. Though the use of semi-precious stones was probably confined to the urban elite, imitations of these beads suggest the presence of other groups who called into question the status claimed by the elite. The coins and seals of Taxila represent the penetration of imperial influence at one level and the continuation of local practices at another. The Dharamarajika stupa at Taxila, founded probably by Ashoka, thus has a peculiar significance of its own.

Renu Thakur takes up urban centres in the north-west of India during the early medieval period. For the role of local state formations, expansion of agriculture, intra-regional and inter-regional trade, and temples and guilds in the development of urban centres, she refers to the work of B.D. Chattopadhyaya and R. Champakalakshmi. She tries to grapple with the terms *pura, nagara, adhisthana* and inscriptions, which suggest not merely the existence of urban centers but also their basic function and hierarchy. Most of her information relates to the town of Pravarasenapura (Srinagar), Pratapapura, Parihasapura, Avantipura and Samkarpattana in Kashmir; Brahmapura (Bharmaur), Chamba, Kangra and Kiragrama in Himachal Pradesh; Pehowa and Thaneshvara in

Haryana; and to Ropar and Ghuram in Punjab. All the information about agrarian and natural produce, manufactures and trade, markets and customs, coinage, wealth and splendour, architecture in general and temples in particular, sculpture, artificats, features of morphology, the people in general and the merchants and traders in particular, is meant to suggest that urbanization was a recognizable phenomenon in the north-west. By implication, Renu Thakur modifies the hypothesis of de-urbanization during the early medieval period.

For the medieval period there are two papers, both on individual cities: Lahore and Sirhind. These can be appreciated only in the context of the general process of urbanization. The foundation of these towns was laid in the early medieval period; they began to develop further under Turko-Afghan rule and experienced maximum expansion under the Mughals. While Lahore served as the headquarters of a province, Sirhind came to serve as the headquarters of a *sarkar*. As administrative centres, both came to have some monumental buildings, both of them were on the main route for internal and external trade and both developed as centres of trade and manufactures. Sirhind however began to decline earlier than Lahore, primarily due to political reasons.

Medieval Lahore is examined by K.K. Trivedi as a centre of production and trade. From this perspective he is keen to point out that Lahore became known for its products during the eleventh and twelfth centuries under the Ghaznavids. The establishment of the Delhi Sultanate accentuated this development in two ways: the resources and the needs of the new administrators increased the production and it developed better linkages with the other parts of the Sultanate. The commercial activity of the Multani merchants was conducive and the craftsmen who migrated to this city in the wake of Mongol invasions added to its skills. New towns also developed in the province to serve as the hinterland. This process was reinforced by trade between India and the countries beyond its north-western frontiers. Sher Shah's interest in building roads and *sarais* was equally important in making Lahore the premier centre of production and trade in the north-west.

The rise of Agra as the most important centre of exchange in north India during the sixteenth century overshadowed Lahore but it continued to be a great centre of trade and manufactures, especially textiles, carpet and shawl weaving, metal work, weaponry, boat building, wood carving, enamelling and engraving, gold damascening, and painted and glazed pottery. Well known for trade in indigo, Labore was considered to be the best in the subcontinent for sugar products. Through its riverain trade, it used to send 12,000 to 14,000 camel-loads of merchandise to Persia early in the seventeenth century. The rich merchants of Lahore dealt with 'the whole of India' besides Persia and Central Asia. Its population appears to have risen to six figures by the end the sixteenth century.

According to Iqbal Husain, medieval Sirhind began acquiring importance in the fourteenth century when Firuz Shah Tughluq made it the headquarters of a separate division (*shiqq*). The *shiqq* was enlarged in the early fifteenth century and the town attracted a large number of Afghan settlers. It suffered a setback during the transition from the Afghan to Mughal rule but again started flourishing in the reign of Akbar. A number of administrators took particular interest in developing the city as a beautiful place and were encouraged by Akbar, Jahangir, Shah Jahan as well as Aurangzeb. Sirhind survived a great flood in 1586 and a severe epidemic in 1616. Contemporaries continued to refer to its trade and commerce, markets and manufactures, cotton goods, its large size and separate residential localities, besides, school of medicine, copper mint, Muhammadan Oratory, gateways and *sarai*, the royal palace and orchards, flowers and odoriferous herbs, the large number of *sarrafs* and eminent professionals, and its pious and learned men. Iqbal Husain gives an impression that Sirhind did not have a planned development even during the Mughal rule, except for its gardens. The city suffered badly in the Mughal-Sikh conflict after the death of Aurangzeb.

J.S. Grewal and Veena Sachdeva address themselves to the process of urbanization in the province of Lahore from the reign of Akbar to Ranjit Singh, a period marked by long intervals of both peace and political revolution. A number of new urban centres came up during this time. Some of the older towns also gained in size and importance due to the convergence of various political and economic factors. By the second quarter of the eighteenth century, however, most of these centres began to decline and suffered further in the third quarter. However, some of the old centres were being revived and a number of new towns were coming up in the wake of political change. This process continued for over half a century. A careful comparison of maps of the Mughal period and the early nineteenth century leaves no doubt that though urban centres increased considerably in number, but not necessarily in size. The change in the pattern of urbanization was much greater in the upper Doabs under Sikh rule than in the lower Doabs under Afghan rule. It was minimal in the hills under the Rajput rulers. Grewal and Sachdeva attribute this difference primarily to the political processes which gave rise to the successor states.

The population of urban centres in the early nineteenth century ranged from less than 5,000 to over 100,000. Amritsar emerged as the largest city. Two other new towns of this period which survived conspicuously into the colonial period also, were Gujranwala and Rawalpindi, the headquarters of two Sikh chiefs of the eighteenth century. In the processes of urbanization, de-urbanization and re-urbanization from the reign of Akbar to Ranjit Singh, it emerges that it is difficult to say whether the share of urban population in the province of Lahore was larger towards the end or was smaller.

Indu Banga concentrates on a sub-region of the *suba* of Lahore from the perspective of rural-urban interaction from the mid-sixteenth to the end of the nineteenth century, covering the Mughal, Sikh and British rule in the Punjab. She takes into account more than a dozen urban centres in the north-estern corner of the Bari Doab which is regarded as a valid sub-region by the geographers. Changes in the distribution and relative importance of the urban centres are well brought out in the first part of the paper. It is explicitly stated that the closest interaction between the rulers and the ruled took place during the late eighteenth century under Sikh rule. The major change which the British administration introduced was in the area of justice. The courts at the district and tahsil headquarters came to be thronged by litigants of several kinds, while the judicial officers, pleaders and petition writers of several grades mediated between the new legal system and the people, largely to their disadvantage.

Despite shifts in the relative importance of the urban centres and a certain degree of change in the patern, all the towns functioned as centres of collection and distribution for the villages in their neighbourhood. Manufactures complemented trade as the economic backbone of the towns and as means of integration between the town and the countryside. Different towns in the sub-region came to specialize in various products made largely from the locally available materials. Within two or three decades of the annexation, the manufacturing activity of these towns was substantially reduced or re-oriented. The urban craftsmen began producing mainly for the local market and the countryside. A few sugar refineries, distilleries and breweries were set up by the

British. A woollen mill was established at Dhariwal in 1882. Till the early 1920s, the rate of population growth in the towns in the subregion was equal only to the rate of natural growth. Thereafter, 30 to 40 per cent increase in population was recorded in Pathankot, Adina Nagar, Gurdaspur, Dhariwal and Batala. The other towns remained in a state of protracted decline.

While the villages were linked with towns by cartable stretches, most of the towns were also inter-linked. By the 1870s the region became linked with the ports of Calcutta and Bombay by rail via Amritsar and Delhi. Virtually every wheat producing village in the sub-region became linked with the global market through the mediacy of brokers and *arhtias* of the grain markets of the towns. Imported goods, consisting largely of cotton goods, iron and steel, sugar, gunny bags, dyes, tans and petroleum products, began to be distributed through Batala, the major town of the sub-region, while the small towns continued to serve mainly as collection centres.

Batala proved to be the most resilient urban centre of the sub-region throughout its history. Located at the centre of a fertile tract, Batala had road linkages with Lahore and Amritsar, and was located on the railway line from Amritsar to Pathankot. It also had enterprising business communities of Khatris and Khojas and a number of craftsmen from the earlier times. The survival and growth of Batala illustrates the strength of the organic relationship between the town and the countryside which provided it with economic viability to withstand political and administrative changes and economic adversity. Though the headquarters of a tahsil under the British, it remained more important as an urban centre than Gurdaspur, the district headquarters.

Indu Banga points out that exploitation of the countryside became rather relentless under colonial rule. The bulk of the peasantry, artisans, labouring classes, and the men of piety and traditional learning were dislodged from their traditional roles and economic security in the society. This raises the question of the nature of the relationship between the town and country. The simple assumption of the town *versus* the country has to be discarded. Both the town and the country had their privileged and unprivileged segments, and the exploitation of the country in favour of the town affected these segments differently. There was an unconscious alliance between the urban elite and the landlords and other privileged sections of the countryside, i.e. the rural elite. Furthermore, a tenuous balance between what the town received and what it returned, had to be perpetually adjusted. However, the relationship did not become equal, mutuality does not necessarily mean parity.

Urbanization under colonial rule is taken up by Reeta Grewal and J.S. Grewal. They start with the information provided by Ganesh Das in the province of Lahore at the beginning of the British rule. There were a wide range of urban centres as indicated by him by using the various terms for a small town, an average town, a large town, a small city, an average city, and a large city. The population of these urban centres ranged from less than 5,000 to over 100,000. Ganesh Das also makes a clear distinction between a village and a town. His *baldah* as a large city is also a clear category. Trade and manufactures were the hallmarks of an urban centre. However, the distinction between the town (*qasba*) and city (*shahr*) is not always clear.

The British census commissioners considered non-agrarian occupations as the principal criterion for determining a place with population of 5,000 persons or more as an urban centre. But they also included cantonments, municipal areas and princely state capitals in their list though the population could be less than 5,000. They also classified urban centres into cities and towns. The towns were divided into class II (50,000–99,999), or large towns), class III (20,000–49,999) or medium towns, while class IV (10,000–19,999), class V (5,000–9,999) and class VI (less than 5,000) were regarded as small towns.

Reeta Grewal and J.S. Grewal look at the changes in the pattern of urbanization under colonial rule in terms of the four well defined zones in the region. In the Himalayan zone there was only one class IV town (Simla), four class V towns (all capitals of princely states), and about half a dozen class VI towns which included cantonments and hill resorts created by the British as well as some old capitals of princely states. In 1941, the number of urban centrers in this zone was over a score. This increase was due to a large number of class VI towns created by the British for various purposes. The old towns, however, were generally on a decline. In the sub-Himalayan zone there were about fifty towns in 1881. Only one of these was new. In 1941, more than a dozen towns were new, but about a score of the old had lost their urban status. Three of the old towns became cities; obviously, the towns became larger in size and smaller in number. They were more evenly spread and spaced now. In the eastern plain the total number of urban centres increased a little by 1941. The number of small towns (class IV–VI) decreased by eight and the number of class VI towns by thirty. The upward movement at all levels is more clearly demonstrated here than in the case of the sub-Himalayan zone. In the western plain, there was no city in 1881. In 1941, there was one city in the western plain, two towns in class II and seven in class III. The number of small towns rose to eighty-two. The majority of these were new urban centres. The total number of urban centres in the western plain rose from less than fifty in 1881 to more than ninty in 1941. Nearly two-thirds of the latter were new urban centres.

In the Punjab as whole, a large number of old urban centres declined; many new towns came up and there was an upward movement in the size of population from class VI to class I, with the exception of the Himalayan zone. In the Himalayan zone and the western plain, most of the new towns remained in class VI; but in the other two zones, the majority of the new towns rose to class V and class IV. In the Himalayan zone, the new towns served as cantonments and summer resorts whereas in the western plain they served as markets.

The change in the pattern of urbanization is explained by the authors largely in terms of the politico-administrative measures of the rulers, their economic and cultural policies and the new means of communication and transportation they introduced. The inevitable link between the town and the countryside is shown by the developments in the Lower Chenab Colony in which villages and towns sprang up together. Administration, canals, railways, roads and markets, agrarian production and trade were all meshed together in the colony. Its main town, Lyallpur, took raid strides as an urban centre just as the colony as a whole became increasingly productive. The intimate link between the town and the country is illustrated further by Reeta Grewal and J.S. Grewal with special reference to a particular village in the tahsil of Lyallpur.

J.S. Rahi turns to Punjabi fiction in search of the social realities of Amritsar in the early decades of the twentieth century. This city has been the locale of many novels but only in the novels of Surinder Singh Narula, the first important novelist of the realistic tradition, can we perceive the tangibility of Amritsar in terms of its physical features, the character of its middle class, the dynamics of local administration, and the city's underworld. For the purpose of this analysis, two novels of Narula are taken up: the *Peo Puttar*, published in 1946 and its sequel, the *Sil Aluni*, published in 1965. Hira Singh, signifies the emergence of a new middle class preoccupied with their personal prosperity. His father was a *vaid* resigned to a simple living, but he aspires to become a *patwanta*, an elite of the city.

The novel reveals that entry of the Nauhriyas of Bikaner into Amritsar became an agent of change. Originally goldsmiths, they captured the textiles market by selling on credit, which the Banias of Amritsar could not afford to do. The Nauhriyas purchased houses and shops and gradually pushed out other businessmen. Their style of living influenced others. Women began to imitate the Nauhriya women who used a conspicuous make-up, wore costly jewellery and richly embroidered, heavy *ghagaras*. Hira Singh and his wife started saving money for interior decoration, which was never dreamt of before.

People of Amritsar began to be drawn into the political movements related to the Kamagata Maru and the Gurdwara Reform. In the *vadda hasptal* where *angrez* doctors were suspected of evangelical designs, the compounder Narinder Singh zealously attends to the injured brought in from the Akali Morcha and yet gets the reports published against himself that he maltreats the Akalis. There are other paradoxes which figure in J.S. Rahi's analysis, giving rare insights into the social life of Amritsar. The city emerges as a centre of paradoxes in the early decades of the twentieth century due to the impact of colonial rule.

Ironically, Amritsar figures nowhere in the paper on the urbanization process in the undivided Punjab by Kusum Chopra, Atiya Habeeb Kidwai and Subhash Marcus. This is due to their approach and methodology. They start with a benchmark in Irfan Habib's *Atlas of the Mughal Empire* which makes no reference to Amritsar. In any case, the place was called Ramdaspur during the Mughal period. This benchmark is compared by the authors with the urban centres of 1881 to identify seventy-five towns which were common to both the Atlas and the Census of 1881. Their interest then is to pursue the fortunes of these towns in 1931 and 1991. Some important points about continuity and change emerge from this analysis.

Furthermore, the authors argue that urban growth in the Punjab took place in the context of low levels of urbanization and there is no evidence of de-urbanization during the colonial period. During the colonial period more than 50 per cent of the towns were in the size category of 5,001–10,000. After Independence, growth took place in the size category of 10,001–20,000. The higher size categories of 50,000 plus gained importance only after the Green Revolution. Part of this growth could be due to the development of regional economy. The impact of the Green Revolution, therefore, demands special attention.

The Punjab did not have a strong industrial base and yet it developed a trading web, commercial centre and an urban hierarchy which remained more or less stable. The history of the region thus indicates that the earlier developments made it possible for Punjab to become the cradle of the Green Revolution in the country. The levels of agricultural development in 1929–30, 1962–3 and 1992–3, signifying three significant phases, are represented in maps. The authors tell us that some important patterns can be seen by superimposing these maps. However, they do not say anything more.

Surya Kant examines the process of urbanization in Himachal Pradesh from 1901 to 2001 in terms of size, growth, site and functional characteristics. He divides the century into two broad periods divided by 1941. The pace of urbanization remained sluggish during the colonial period and the number of towns did not appreciably increase. Hill stations and cantonments came up largely on the hilltops, but the pre-British towns in the valleys either went down or remained almost static. The number of towns and the percentage of urban population increased after Independence as a result of the influx of refugees in 1947, grant of full statehood in 1971, and the administrative and developmental policies. But, even so, no more than 9 per cent of the people of the state live in its fifty-seven towns. Shimla has become a class I city and has more than one-fifth of the total urban population. There is no class II town. Mandi and Solan have become class III towns. All the remaining towns are small and the new towns are in class VI. The degree of urbanization in Himachal Pradesh in 2001 is still the lowest in all the states and union territories. Urbanization has also been uneven and marked by intra-regional disparities. Most of the towns are mono-functional. Significantly, the valley towns have become more important again as administrative centres and market towns, while the old cantonment towns are declining.

Surya Kant righly points out that mountainous areas are not comparable with the plains. Like other hilly regions in the country, Himachal Pradesh has a low degree of urbanization and its own context of size hierarchy. Employment potential of urban economic base is limited due to poor industrial base of towns. Urban centres, in general, are either growing slowly or stagnating also because rural-urban interaction in the state remains quite weak.

Gopal Krishan concentraes on the social parameters of Punjab urbanization since Independence. He points out that Punjab is popularly perceived as an agricultural-rural state in the light of the strides it made in the Green Revolution since its formation in 1966. However, as indicated by the Census of 2001, it is well on its way to becoming an urban majority state in not too distant a future. Over one-third of the state's population is already in urban places and urban growth rate is picking up fast. The urbanization process in the state since Independence has passed through a number of successive phases, resulting in a significant transformation of its social scene. The initial phase was that of a complete replacement of the Muslim population almost anywhere by the displaced non-Muslim population (mainly the Hindus and the Sikhs) from Pakistan on the eve of the Partition of the subcontinent in 1947. This was followed by a phase of dispersed urbanization in the form of dynamic market or agro-based industrial towns as a positive outcome of agricultural development. Another phase is represented by the post-1966 period which witnessed a gradual increase in the proportion of the Sikh population in Punjab's towns and cities, and this process was more noticeable during the 1980s when the growth rate of Sikhs was two times that of the Hindus. Meanwhile, the scheduled castes, traditionally overwhelmingly rural, are gradually urbanizing and now over one-fifth of their total population is urban based as compared with one-eighth in 1961. It is equally significant that a substantial portion of the urban population is living in slums.

The most visible feature of the urban scene today, according to Gopal Krishan, is the corridor development, manifest in extensive physical growth of towns along the Ludhiana-Amritsar, Ludhiana-Chandigarh, Ludhiana-Rajpura, Ludhiana-Malerkotla, and Amritsar-Pathankot transport routes, in particular. By 2020, nearly half of the Punjab population would be living in towns. The maximum growth is likely to take place along the roads connecting the cities. The cities like Ludhiana, Jalandhar and Patiala would continue to grow at a fast pace, with planned urban estates within them or on their periphery. In the areas adjoining Chandigarh also the pace of urbanization is likely to be rapid.

Unlike Gopal Krishnan, J.K. Gupta is unhappy with the process of urbanization in the state of Punjab. In the first place, Urbanization *per se* is not an index of development. Urbanization becomes a catalyst for economic development only if urban settlements can offer substantial non-agricultural employment and absorb persons moving out of agricultural economy. Alleviation of rural poverty should also be an essential objective of urbanization. This objective has not been achieved anywhere in the country, including Punjab. However, percentage of urban population in Punjab is higher than the national average. In 2001 every third person in the state is an urbanite as against the all India average of one out of four persons. Metros and class I cities are growing at the cost of smaller centres and rural areas.

Analysing the growth of urban and rural population from 1901 to 2001, Gupta underlines a number of features of this growth in order to evolve a perspective on the future. It is absolutely necessary in his view, that agricultural production should diversify and intensify. The land-man ratio in rural areas should not be allowed to go down drastically with the increase in total population. A massive programme of industrialization should be undertaken by the state. A balanced and dispersed growth of urban centres, which is a must, cannot be ensured without active intervention of the government and large investment in infrastructures. The near defunct Improvement Trusts need to be revived. The planning and development inputs have to be increased. In the long run, only the local agencies can ensure an orderly growth within individual centres. They should be empowered to play this vital role. The slums need a special policy for their containment and eventual elimination. A consciously evolved urbanization policy alone can ensure that urban and rural settlements grow in tandem and not at the cost of one another. Futher urbanization pattern should be people and community oriented and environmentally sustainable, J.K. Gupta pleads.

As a whole, through its fifteen contributions, this volume covers all the broad phases of Indian history—proto-historic, ancient, medieval, colonial and contemporary, with some of the contributions cutting across conventional periods. Specifically, they relate to the Harappan, Mauryan, Rajput, Turkish, Mughal, Sikh, British and post-Independence periods. Some papers study the north-western region while others focus on its well recognized sub-regions like the Sutlej-Yamuna Divide (Haryana), upper Bari Doab and Himachal Pradesh. The individual urban centres studied are Harappa, Taxila, Lahore, Sirhind, and Amritsar. The approaches used are equally varied as authors base their findings on excavations, field work, quantitative data, literary evidence and analysis of literature as social document. Contemporary problems and prospects are the concern of a third of the contributors. This volume breaks fresh ground in the history of the Punjab on both sides of the international border, and provides insights into the processes of urbanization as well as the specificities of the Punjab region.

2

Urbanization: Some Basic Issues

G.S. BHALLA

There is a general consensus among the social scientists that rapid urbanization is a concomitant of industrialization. This is borne out by the unprecedented increase of urban population in most of the developed countries after the industrial revolution of the eighteenth century. This does not mean, however, that towns and cities did not exist before the advent of industrial revolution. It is well known that numerous towns and cities flourished since ancient times. According to Braudel, however, these cities in the ancient regimes were essentially 'parasitic'.

During the middle ages, numerous cities and towns flourished with their distinctive characteristics. The most important among these were, of course, the capital cities with their courts and courtiers, the army and administration. The palaces stood out from the modest habitats and housing clusters, reflecting the luxurious living made possible by surplus from agriculture, petty manufactures and trade. In addition to the capital cities, there were commercial cities in Europe where there was a flourishing trade during the mercantilist period. Indeed, Braudel points out that 'Capitalism was Cuckoo's eggs laid in the comfort nests of the medieval towns'. Trading centres were also quite important in some other parts of the world, including India and China. Then there were pilgrimage centres.

Nevertheless, in the pre-industrial ages, there was only a limited growth of cities because of the limited quantum of surplus that could be generated with low technology and inadequate division of labour, particularly from agriculture. Most of the population lived in rural areas and was essentially dependent on agriculture. There was a greater concentration of population around river beds, deltaic regions and other fertile areas where the yields from land were higher. Population was

*Inaugural Address to the Seminar on Five Thousand Years of Urbanization in the Punjab.

sparsely distributed in the infertile areas fed only by rain. According to Boserup and Ishikawa the population distribution followed a 'Rectangular Hyperbola' pattern in which high agrarian productivity was associated with low land-man ratio and vice-versa. With the coming of the industrial revolution, important changes took place in the habitation pattern, leading to urbanization on an unprecedented scale. Kuznets regards, urbanization as largely a product of industrialization (although the former may occur without the latter and the latter does not fully account for the former).

It is important to analyse why rapid industrialization and urbanization are intrinsically related. Urbanization reflects a drastic shift in occupational structure from predominantly agricultural to non-agricultural employment in manufacturing and services. This, in turn, is related to several technical (economic), technological and managerial factors.

Technically, the most important reason for urbanization is a drastic decline in the share of agriculture in the total national income. This share declines because of both demand and supply factors. On the demand side the main reason is often described as Engel's Law. This states that whereas there are limits to the demand for food and other agricultural commodities, since humans can eat only a certain amount of food, the demand for manufactured goods and for services is unlimited. While the demand for food is inelastic, the demand for manufactured goods and services is highly elastic. As incomes grow, people spend increasing proportion of their incomes on numerous non-food items like manufactured goods, consumer durables and services.

On the supply side, there are limits to growth in agricultural production due to limited land area. In fact, the classical economists felt so much concerned about the lack of growth in food grains that some of them, like Malthus, predicted large scale famines, assuming that the food supply could never match the increasing demand of a rising population. Even the more optimistic ones, like Ricardo, talked of a 'stationary state' on the assumption that the amount of agricultural output required for meeting a rapidly growing demand would increase the cost of production. This pessimistic scenario was changed by technological changes, mechanization and other biotehnological innovations which made it possible to increase production from a limited area. Simultaneously, these innovations enabled fewer hands to produce the desired quantum of foodgrains and other agricultural commodities, which made it possible for labour to be withdrawn from agriculture.

Unlike agriculture, economies of large-scale exist in non-agriculture pursuits. These are made possible, first, by technology that separates production process from land area and secondly, by optimum use of transportation, communication and more effective organization. Management leads to large corporations, public utilities and larger government and public sector. All the three increase those areas where in Kuznets' view, 'free enterprise in the usual sense must give way to complete or partial monopoly'.

Urbanization goes beyond the optimum scale in commodity production in the development of highly specialized functions feasible in large cities. With economic growth, centres of trade, finance, education, legal services and government also grow. Along with other sources of urban concentration, like manufacturing and retail trade, their location makes urbanization a necessary corollary of economic growth.

Urbanization leads to transformation of the basic pattern of life as changes take place in the pattern of consumption. To agricultural produce are now added manufactured goods and services. The most spectacular aspect of the new situation is the growth of service industries. Furthermore, health facilities become available for larger populations. As wage earning, salaried and educated groups become dominant, and the small and independent entrepreneurs decline, there is an emphasis on individual attainment through training. Cumulatively, as noticed by demographers, these factors lead to a higher standard of living and a lower birth rate.

The process of 'revolution' in the pattern of life and cardinal changes in the relative power and position of various groups in population inevitably overcome the resistance of a whole complex of established interests and values. Agglomeration and concentration of talents tend to lead to interpersonal relationships and conditions for intense intellectual activity. According to Kuznets, urbanization provides not only the sole economical way to affect industrialization, in a deeper and more important sense, it also provides the conditions under which a new way of life can grow and creative pursuits in art, science and technology can flourish. The urban centres become in a sense the outposts of modernity and liberty.

The 'urban' can have a number of referents: it may refer to a spatial form (city as opposed to country), to a cultural pattern (urbanism as opposed to ruralism as ways of life), or to a structural form (e.g. the city as a source of control in an urban hierarchy). Castells, however, rejects the cultural or the spatial definition. For him urbanism is the cultural expression of 'capitalist industrialization', the emergence of 'market economy' and the process of rationalization of 'modern' society.

The reality of the city is segmentation on the basis of economic status, religious and racial identities and indigenous and migrant populations. As migration takes place, these segmentations tend to become more pronounced, leading to serious tensions and conflicts.

The city mirrors the capitalist development process in the historical growth of national and per capita income through unprecedented growth in productivity made possible by the introduction of revolutionary technological changes. This process is accompanied by uneven growth, income inequalities, recurrent fluctuations in output and income, inflation and unemployment. Under inflation, it is the poor in the city who suffer the most; under depression, the unemployment affects the urban youth and women the most. Cities also tend to become centres of organized crime and extortions. All disparities in the pattern of capitalist development, not only in terms of income but also educational levels, cultural attainments, housing and other physical and social amenities, become naked and palpable in the cities.

II

The nature and pattern of urbanization is quite different in semi-industrialized economies where agriculture has a predominant or very significant role. Quite often, dualistic pattern of development, which is often perpetuated by colonial powers, leads to a habital pattern in which the cities stand in splendid isolation from the country. On the one hand, the process of de-industrialization and decline in the power and glory of princely states leads to the decay of medieval cities. On the other hand, some new port cities emerge with peculiar characteristics. An outstanding example is a city like Calcutta which was meant to house the foreign rulers and their allies, the zamindars and the other local elite, to pump the surplus forcibly extracted from the rural hinterland to the Metropolis.

In India, it was only during the inter-war period that there was some development of local industries, leading to the formation of a working class. In the beginning the migrant labour had strong links with their rural habitats, near or far and worked during the lean agriculture season to go back to their villages during the harvesting season. It was only gradually that a stable working class was formed in cities like Bombay, Calcutta and Ahmedabad.

Though quite often it was not the push but the pull migration that took place, the level of urban income, higher than rural income, was still so low as to force the migrants to live in slums and squalor. Braudel observed that 'A town would probably cease to exist without its supply of new people. It has to attract them. But they often come of their own accord towards its lights, its real or apparent freedom and its higher wages.' In the case of Indian cities, however, their lights often turned out to be dim and their freedom was more apparent than real.

In the colonial period, cities gradually emerged as living entities with all the problems of regional, religious, communal, ethnic and caste identities. The conflicts got exacerbated by unemployment, poverty and religious fananticism which was often fuelled by populist and opportunistic leadership and led to serious communal riots.

As India is predominantly an agrarian country with a slow rate of industrialization, the pace of urbanization has also been sluggish. This was particularly so during the British period when industrial output registered a very slow growth. Thus, by 1891 only 11 per cent of India's population was living in urban areas. This percentage increased to 17 by 1951. Although the growth rate of Indian economy accelerated during the post-Independence period, industrial output hovered only around 6 per cent per annum. This pace was not sufficient to create a strong impulse for diversification of the economy and rapid urbanization. Even by 1991, the share of urban population in the total population had increased only to 26 per cent. This is one of the lowest levels of urbanization in the world. The available data indicate that in 1990 the level of urbanization was 45 per cent for all countries of the world taken together and more than 70 per cent of the total population in Europe and North America was living in urban areas.

During 1951–91, the growth rate of urban population accelerated to 3.17 per cent compared with 1.77 per cent during 1901–51. The share of urban population in the total population rose from 17.3 per cent in 1951 to 25.7 per cent in 1991. It is significant that in spite of variations in the inter-decadel growth rates, there was a continuous increase in the rate of urbanization during 1951–81. Urban population recorded a high growth rate of 31.73 per cent during 1971–81. However, in 1981–91, the rate of 28.90 per cent showed a slowing down of the process of urbanization for the country as a whole.

Despite the slow growth, India has a large urban population in absolute numbers. The urban population increased from 25,800,000 in 1901 to 62,400,000 in 1951; it rose to 217,200,000 in 1991. Next to China, this is the largest population living in urban areas. Because of low per capita income even in the big cities and lack of adequate infrastructure in housing, transport, roads, water and sewerage and telecommunications, urbanization in India is beset with several socio-economic problems. Another matter of serious concern is the highly unbalanced distribution of its urban population. In 1991, nearly two-thirds of the total urban population was living in 296 class I cities of above 100,000 population. Among them, nearly one-third urban dwellers were concentrated in 23 mega cities with a million plus population. On the other hand, only 25 per cent of urban population lived in 3,313 medium and small towns and rural townships. Excessive concentration of urban population in large cities, combined with low per capita income has led to increasing socio-economic problems. Since large cities have generally a low level of linkages with the rural hinterland, such a pattern of urbanization has failed to meet the needs of a predominantly agricultural economy. Understandably, prevention of excessive concentration of urban population in big and mega settlements and bringing about an integrated development of small and medium towns for strengthening the rural urban networks has been the avowed objective of policy makers in India.

Indeed, policies have been initiated for a gradual deconcentration and relocation of industries and location of new industries outside the metropolitan regions. Various Five Year Plans have made provisions for resources for development of infrastructure like market yards, shops, warehouses, service centres, industrial sheds and transport services for the small and medium towns. Further emphasis has also been laid on their integrated development and the setting up of Urban Infrastructural Development Finance Corporation.

These policies have succeeded in developing new towns outside the network of big cities. But the dynamics of industrial development has simultaneously led to agglomeration. Furthermore, very little influence could be brought to bear on the private sector. Therefore, urban centres at the lower levels have grown more in response to the overall pattern of economic development. In areas of high agricultural growth, like Punjab and Haryana, small and medium size settlements have thrived. On the other hand, city size distribution continues to be highly imbalanced in states like West Bengal and Maharashtra. Industries, by and large, have preferred to make use of the agglomeration economies in the large cities. It is the small settlements of less than 20,000 population that are gradually losing their important place. This is mainly because the process of occupational diversification at the rural level has been extremely slow. The real challenge that policy makers face is that the process of sectoral diversification at the lower level is yet to be accelerated. The investment in urban infrastructure in all settlements is still inadequate.

Notwithstanding the economy recording a higher growth during the decade, and the trends towards globalization of the economy and entry of multinationals in the 1990s, lack of infrastructure in general, and urban infrastructure in particular, remains one of the major constraints in the way of large foreign direct investment in India. Therefore, large investments will have to be undertaken in slum clearance, sanitation, sewerage, water supply and roads and communications in the cities. Adequate infrastructural investment would have to be undertaken in small and medium towns also. With the revolution in telecommunication and informatics, the small and medium cities can also benefit from the economies of scale so far monoplized by large agglomerations. Because of the inadequacy of resources for investment at the local level, the development of small and medium towns is gradually ending up in extension of dirty villages and perpetuation of squalor and unhygienic conditions on a much larger scale. For a proper and decent pattern of habitation, both in rural and urban areas, there is no alternative to huge infrastructural expenditure on their renewal and upgradation. This implies both moderniztion and diversification of agriculture to initiate a process of agricultural led industrialization in small and medium habitats along with rapid exogenous industrialization in big cities and metropolises.

REFERENCES

Braudel, Fernand, *Afterthoughts on Material Civilization and Capitalism*, tr. Patricia M. Ranum, Baltimore: Johns Hopkins University Press, 1997.

Boserup, Ester, *The Conditions of Agricultural Growth*, London: George Allan & Unwin, 1965.

Ishikawa, Shigeru, *Economic Development in Asian Perspective*, Tokyo: Kinokuniya Book Store Co., 1967.

Kuznets, Simon, *Economic Growth and Structure*, New York: Norton, 1965, p. 96.

Castells,.Manuel, 'Theory and Ideology in Urban Sociology', in C.G. Pickvance (ed.), *Urban Sociology—Critical Essays*, London: Tawistock, 1976, pp. 60–84.

3

Urbanism in Proto-historic Punjab: Significance of Craft Production

JAYA MENON

There has been a difference of opinion amongst archaeologists and scholars regarding the beginning of urbanism and urban centres in the north-west of India in the third millennium BC. Some emphasize a long period of development which finally culminated in what we now call the Mature Harappan. The conception of a long gestation period for the Indus civilization was conveyed by the idea of a ramp, first put forward by Braidwood and Willey in 1962. By contrast, others entertain a short period of time, literally 100–50 years, within which the first urban centres were set up. The metaphor of a step conveys the idea of a sudden change, a revolution towards urbanism. Most of the studies in *Courses Toward Urban Life* edited by Braidwood and Willey deal with the approach to the threshold of urbanism but not with the phenomenon of the threshold itself.

We are concerned with the threshold itself. However, before we deal with this issue, we need to understand what is meant by urbanism in the Bronze Age context. Archaeologically, ten criteria were set forth by V. Gordon Childe to characterize the earliest cities: density of population, occupational specialization, presence of an agricultural surplus, monumental buildings, a ruling class, systems of recording and exact sciences, the invention of writing, naturalistic art, long distance trade and a state-ordered society. Childe perceived the urban revolution primarily in economic terms, a new economic stage accompanied by growth in population and change in social organization.

*My deepest thanks to Professor Shireen Ratnagar for her comments and suggestions on an earlier version of this paper.

In our view, the impact of nucleation of population lies in the socio-economic and political spheres. With density of population, citizenship becomes based on residence rather than kinship (Carter 1983: 2). The loss of autonomy of kin groups results in unequal relationships among individuals living in a city. Politically dominant groups base their power on differentiating themselves from the others. This distance assumes social undertones and gets represented archaeologically in spatial segregation of population, restricted use of wealth or elite goods, clear occupational differentiation and so on. Adams holds the view in fact that changes in social institutions primarily, 'precipitated changes in technology, subsistence and other aspects of the wider cultural realm' (Adams 1966: 12). There is hardly any doubt that the core trends of social stratification, political differentiation and craft specialization are relevant for the issue of urbanism.

An urban situation reveals occupational diversity as a result of population nucleation and involvement of people in non-subsistence activities. The role of agricultural surplus is important but more important are the institutions required for its collection. In an urban context, the potential for trade and craft production increases due to the density of population. The potential for exchange increases due to the differentiated groupings in society and the specialized demands of the elite.

Urban centres require political institutions to exploit the skills of the population and to organize non-subsistence activities. It is useful to understand the necessity of controlling a heterogeneous population. Political control is established through institutions in which kinship may not play a significant role. The control over the written medium can also have political implications.

Archaeologically, our information for the Mature Harappan is obtained through settlement morphologies, the pattern of Harappan settlements and crafted objects. It is not craft production *per se* that is significant, but the specialization of production. Archaeological indicators for specialization may lie in the provision of separate workshop areas, the performance by different individuals/groups of separate processes within each craft, the knowledge of diverse technologies, the manufacture of a diversity of objects, the control of production and the support of specialists.

Craft production, may provide us with the opportunity to study occupational differentiation, social stratification and the role of political institutions—all of which are integral to early urbanism. Till recently, the beginning of urbanism in the Indus valley was associated with the Harappan culture. However, with the excavation and delineation of early Harappan sites and cultures, the relation between the Early and the Mature phase has become an important issue. The idea of a 'genetic' relation between the two cultures was suggested by similarities in certain forms of artifacts.

The conception of the Early Harappan as constituting a formative stage of the Mature Harappan culture emerged from Mughal's study of 1970. It was reinforced by his later study of the excavated material from the site of Kot Diji. Certain artificats earlier thought to be solely associated with the Mature Harappan, such as terracotta toycart, frames and wheels, terracotta cakes, cones and pottery objects like offering stands and certain painted designs on pottery, were found to occur in the Early Harappan levels also (Mughal 1990: 186). The Early Harappan according to Mughal, constituted a long and slow process which began from the middle of the fourth millennium BC. In fact, cultural processes involving social stratification, complexities of architecture, inter-regional contacts and communication, craft-related activities and availability of economic surplus appear to have begun to emerge even earlier, perhaps by the fifth millennium BC (Mughal 1990: 187). These, for Mughal, constitute the first phase of development while the Early Harappan constitutes the second. Mughal emerged as the strongest advocate of the ramp approach to urbanism. Indeed, the Early Harappan as considered by Mughal (1990: 190) was not as a pre-urban but an early urban period.

The step approach to urbanism was emphasized by Shaffer and Lichtenstein (1989: 123–4) after Wheatley noted in 1971 the rapidity of the process of emergence of urban agglomerates in the Indus Valley. Shaffer and Lichtenstein postulated that the onset of the Mature Harappan period saw the fusion of previously separate ethnic groups, as represented by the Early Harappan cultures, into a predominant ethnic group, reflected in the uniformity of artifact styles. Thus, they looked upon the beginning of the Mature Harappan period as marking a distinct step. Relying on radiocarbon dates, this 'step' in cultural development took place within a century, However, the possibility of conflicts between groups and the reasons for fusion itself have not been investigated and in fact the role of a state structure for the fusion of distinct groups has been negated.

The idea of a 'revolution' was reinforced by Possehl (1986, 1990) in his conception of the onset of the Mature Harappan. Differentiation in terms of size, public monumental architecture, drainage system, grid plans, evidence for social stratification and differentiation, systems of writing and mensuration, and the oft-cited cultural homogeneity were some of the features present in the Mature Harappan but not in the Early Harappan.

The continuity approach tends to obliterate the difference between the Early and the Mature Harappan as 'archaeological cultures'. In archaeological context 'culture' should consist of definable attributes or entities. Mughal maintains (1990: 187) that 'more "Harappan" traits' appear at most Early Harappan sites, which eventually crystallized by the middle of the third millennium or in the Mature Harappan period. This conception makes the identification of Early and Mature Harappan diffused and arbitrary. The continuity approach fails to demarcate the Mature Harappan if its traits are considered to begin in the Early Harappan period itself.

What needs emphasis are the features that constituted a marked change. The original Kot Diji report by Khan (1965) discusses only the ceramics and barely mentions other antiquities, while Mughal traces a continuity of minor objects from Early to Mature Harappan levels. We note from Mughal's data that stone balls, chert blades, and chert cones are found in Kot Diji at the Early Harappan levels. In the transitional level between the Early and the Mature Harappan these continue along with grinding stones and pestles, terracotta cakes, cones, bangles, animal figurines, cart frames and wheels, terracotta beads, shell bangles and beads and two steatite seals. All these artifacts are found in the Mature Harappan levels too. But what is not apparent from Mughal's study is the typology of the animal figurines, shell bangles and steatite seals in Kot Diji at the Mature level. For example, are the steatite seals of the square stamp variety carved with motif and script which are typical of the Mature Harappan?

Thus, as Ratnagar has pointed out, we 'expect domestic artifact forms and basic technologies to continue to function, or to develop, even in the presence of a major political change, unless entire populations were wiped out' (1991: 82). Technologies for the cutting of steatite and for the production of stone beads were known from the neolithic levels of Mehrgarh in the Kachi plain. What is important for an archaeological analysis of continuity and change is the typology of artifacts. Changes should represent new requirements in the Mature Harappan period as for example the steatite stamp seals and the stone weights. There is no evidence for writing in the Early Harappan which appears in developed form in the Mature Harappan on the steatite stamp seals (Ratnagar 1991: 88; Parpola 1994: 52–4).

II

Our purpose now is to study the evidence for continuity or discontinuity between the Early Harappan and Mature Harappan, taking the area of the undivided Punjab as a case study. In this region, there are two Early Harappan cultures, the Kot Diji and the Sothi/Siswal or Kalibangan I cultures. Major sites in this area are Mitathal, Banawali, Kalibangan, Jalilpur, Harappa and Sarai Khola. Our major focus will be on Harappa.

Despite the poor structural preservation of Harappa, various factors account for the importance of this site within the Harappan culture. The history of the discovery of Harappa and the diversity of its material assemblage indicate its special role in the Punjab. While focussing on Harappa, we are focussing on the socalled 'core' of the culture. With the recent excavations we are in a better position to understand the Early Harappan phase of occupation at this site. Primary occupation levels of the Early Harappan have been found in the north-western portion of Mound E constituting the Lower Town where hearths and mudbrick walls were recovered. In addition to Kot Diji-related ceramics, there are grey fired bangles, stone blades of dark greyish-black chert, a stone celt, various types of stone beads and human figurines that are unlike Mature Harappan types (Kenoyer 1991a: 44).

The new periodization of Harappa indicates Period 1 as Early Harappan, Period 2 as transitional between Early and Mature Harappan, Period 3 as Mature Harappan, Period 4 as transitional to Cemetery H and Period 5 as belonging to the Cemetery H culture. Period 3 is subdivided into 3A, 3B and 3C, in order to delineate phases of urban growth and decay. Excavations on Mound E show that there was no break or hiatus between Periods 1 and 2 or between 2 and 3. In the north-western corner of Mound E, baked brick walls are seen to follow the same course as Early Harappan Period 2 mud brick retaining or revetment walls. Brick dimensions of a ratio of 4:2:1 are the same in both periods. In the southern part of Mound E, superimposed hearths show continuity of occupation from Period 2 to 3. However, in the eastern portion of Mound E, Period 2 houses lie outside the Mature

Harappan perimeter walls, covered with debris in Period 3 (Meadow and Kenoyer 1994: 459). Specific ceramic types, figurines, triangular terracotta cakes, terracotta toys and red fired bangles continue from Period 2 into 3 (Kenoyer 1991a: 47).

The gradual transition between Periods 1 and 2 and between Periods 2 and 3 prompted Kenoyer (1991b: 349) to accept a gradual development of urbanism for the core region sites of the Harappan culture—Naushara, Rahman Dheri and Ghazi Shah. However, to understand this issue in the context of Harappa, we have to understand the changes that appear in the Mature Harappan. The first to be noted is the appearance only from Period 3 of any kinds of written material. In Period 3A on Mound E, we first recover a steatite intaglio seal fragment along with terracotta bull figurines with conjoined legs (Kenoyer 1991a: 50, 55), an archaic type of figurine pointed out by Vats in his excavations at Harappa (1940: 69–70, 182). It is only in the 3B Period that the tiny inscribed steatite tokens and moulded faience tokens are found which were so common in the lowest levels of Mound F of Vats' excavations. Other new varieties of artifacts listed are distinctive figurines, terracotta cones, toys and painted pottery as also the use of fired bricks (Kenoyer 1991a: 50). The presence of seals and weights at only a particular juncture is enough to indicate the significant change that was wrought in society at that particular time.

Kenoyer (1991a: 47, 56; 1991b: 357) also notes the localization of production in Period 2 continuing into Period 3. The Period 2 kiln was unusual since the upper half of a large pot was placed in the centre of a circular mud-brick structure. The pot as also another vessel found inside the kiln were Early Harappan types. The pot comprising the kiln had its inner walls turned black due to reduction while the outer walls were oxidized (Dales et al. 1991: 230). The Early Harappan kiln was only 50 ′ 60 cm in diameter and about 40 cm in height. Kenoyer (1991a: 47) suggests that the kiln may have been used to produce the thin grey fired bangles which are common to Early Harappan sites. But what is significant is that this firing structure is quite unlike the Mature Harappan kilns which were of teardrop shape with a distinct opening for the fuel. One large Mature Harappan kiln was found at Harappa near a similar one. The large kiln measured 2 ′ 3 m and was probably used for firing pottery and other ceramic objects. The objects found in the vicinity included terracotta bangles, pottery and figurines (Dales and Kenoyer 1988: 31, Fig. 16). Thus, we note that despite pottery being fired in the same area in Periods 2 and 3, the shape of the kilns in the two occupations differed. This indicates a technological change in the later period.

Harappa does not present us with the kind of contextual evidence for craft production in the Mature Harappan period that is available from Mohenjodaro. However, we do get evidence about craft production from raw materials, tools and unfinished objects. It is evident that metallurgy, stone bead production, shell working, production of seals and weights, and the working of steatite were practised at Harappa.

If we look at the Early Harappan and the Mature Harappan purely as archaeological cultures, we notice the absence of a stratigraphical break between the two occupations and a continuity of forms between the two. There are transtitional phases at most sites in the Punjab, except for Sarai Khola and Jalilpur (where there are no Mature Harappan occupations) and Kalibangan and Sandhanwala (where there are clear stratigraphical breaks in occupation) (Mughal 1970: 101–2). But at sites like Mitathal, the transitional phase is thought of as one where the Mature Harappan appears as an intrusion into the earlier culture. This is possible, considering that the Mature Harappan here is chronologically later than in Sind or western Punjab and may represent an actual eastward movement of the Harappans. This is not the case at Harappa where the Mature Harappan is not an intrusion. Out of all the sites, Harappa is the most significant as it is in the Mature Harappan period that it appears to be clearly urbanized.

On the issue of the continuity of forms and features between the two occupations, we notice that terracotta cakes, toycarts and wheels, certain ceramic forms, like the dish on stand, and certain ceramic designs continue into the Mature Harappan. But the continuity of these features has no real meaning in socio-cultural terms. At Sarai Khola, which has no Mature Harappan occupation, were found stone beads, the use of copper/bronze, steatite, shell and faience. What is important from our point of view is not the presence of these objects but their typology. For example, shell is rare; only one bangle piece was found in the Early Harappan occupation and that too does not appear to be *Turbinell pyrum* (Halim 1972: 23), the favoured shell species of the Mature Harappans. Special Harappan stone beads such as etched carnelian beads or long barrel-cylinder beads are completely absent in Sarai Khola as are stone weights and steatite seals.

The archaeological evidence for the Mature Harappan culture provides us with major clues to study urbanism. As noted earlier, technologies for the production of stone beads, cutting of steatite, making of faience and metallurgy were known prior to the Mature Harappan. The Early Harappan material assemblage from our region illustrates the knowledge of craft technologies. But what we do notice is the production of basic types which do not require major expenditure of time or skill. The existence of specialists may be inferred archaeologically from the scale of output as well as the diversity of products. This diversity of products within each craft is in fact one of the innovations that we observe in the Mature Harappan period. Etched carnelian beads, long barrel-cylinder beads, zoned beads and composite beads being produced in stone have been found. Faience is no longer used for producing only beads and bangles but also miniature jars, sealings, animal figurines, spindle whorls, numerous kinds of ornaments, games, inlay, box covers, plaques, cones, dice, etc. Similarly, shell was used to make tools, small vessels and accessories and ornaments. In most cases, the same raw materials that were utilized in the Early Harappan are used in the later period to produce a wide variety of artifact types, reflecting the widening consumption in the Mature Harappan period. Production of typologically similar artifacts in different raw materials, some more exotic and valuable than the other may give us a good idea of social stratification in the Mature Harappan period.

Many of the innovations that we notice in the Mature Harappan period are not only the increased demand for crafted objects from heterogeneous urban population, but also demand for special-purpose objects that could have political implications. Objects like steatite stamp seals and cubical stone weights have no Early Harappan precursors and were produced in a standardized form only in the Mature Harappan. Their particular role is indicated by the need to maintain supervision over and standardization in their manufacture. These are what may be called technological innovations (Costin et al. 1989) that employ known technologies to produce objects with very specific, different functions.

The Early Harappan in the Cholistan Desert showed a marked change from the preceding Hakra Wares period in the almost 33 per cent increase in settlements with craft facilities (or kilns) and the decease in camp sites from more than half (i.e. 52.52 per cent) to 7.5 per cent. But the most significant change is in the Mature Harappan period, where 45.4 per cent of sites are purely industrial in nature, contrasted with the Early Harappan where not a single site was purely industrial in character (Mughal 1982: 92). In the same context we can mention the particular locations and functions of sites like Chanhudaro, Lothal, Shortughai and Nageshwar. If there was a particular purpose for their location, the rationale for it was absent in the Early Harappan period. In fact, we have scarce evidence for craft production in our region in the Early Harappan period.

III

If we accept that there were differences between the Early Harappan and the Mature Harappan, we may try to answer another set of questions. If the changes introduced were technological or stylistic in nature, then in what manner and for what purpose were they introduced and what could have been their role?

On the one hand, we find basic technologies continuing from the Early Harappan and on the other, elaboration of the same technologies during the Mature Harappan: such as the etching of carnelian beads, the making of miniature steatite beads, the production of stoneware bangles, the production of faience and so forth. Stylistically too there are differences in the Mature Harappan which indicate the cultural connotations of the period.

At a number of sites, there are no clear stratigraphical breaks. The question thus arises as to how the innovations in technologies and artifacts were introduced. Even to start answering this question we have to depend on ethnographic evidence in the absence of any written material in the protohistoric context. We have to know how craftsmen learn and how traditions are developed.

In most cases we find that the basic method of passing on craft instruction is through a period of apprenticeship. The apprentice learns best through observation and copying. In the village of Ratadi in Saurashtra, apprentices in various crafts worked at simple tasks repeating them continuously till they were perfected. Only then could they proceed to more complicated stages. There is constant supervision in the initial stages, especially where raw materials are expensive (Fischer and Shah 1970).

Craft is conceived of as a number of operations which occur in a sequence. These operations or processes do not occur in isolation but are integrally joined to each other. This sequence has been termed as a 'path' or as a '*chaine operatoire*' (Sigaut 1994; Vidale et. al. 1992). Thus, 'it is generally possible to infer the position of the preceding and the following elements' in the sequence (Vidale et al. 1992: 183). This has direct implications for our discussion. Since 'tool sequences are organized like strings of beads and learned by observation and memorisation, apprenticeship is essential' (Wynn 1994: 147). The process of learning is structured: the apprentice proceeds from stage to stage from the preparation of raw material to its working.

The passing on of craft tradition was very likely to have been within the family. In most ethnographic cases, we find that the children of craftsmen learn the craft within the family. For example, in a potter's family, a child may for years undertake unskilled jobs such as collecting firewood instead of being taught the craft. But craft learning was mainly through absorption of craft techniques, through observation and constant exposure. 'Watching, imitating and experimentation' constitute the process of learning (Fischer and Shah 1970: 118). Due to the graduated method of learning, the period of apprenticeship could take as long as 15, 20 or 25 years for a potter to learn the craft; the length of apprenticeship could also depend on the learning skill of the individual student (Choksi 1994).

There are known examples of apprentices who were not family members (Nadel 1942: 257). According to Nasel (1942: 266), among the Beni blacksmiths of Bida, former apprentices were regularly taken and they were not necessarily relatives. They came from villages near Bida and returned home as professional artisans. In the Bida glass industry, apprentices were regularly taken where formerly slaves were trained for the tasks. Interestingly, apprenticeship also entailed adoption into the kinship group as the apprentices were expected to marry within the new group (Nadel 1942: 278). Among the Mayan villages too, persons not necessarily related also played a considerable role in passing on craft skills (Hayden and Cannon 1994: 344–9). Similarly, studies of ceramic training in Hipi Mesa villages of north-eastern Arizona (Stanislawski and Stanislawski 1978) revealed that teaching of a particular style is not restricted to only relatives or clan members. Pottery styles do not function to maintain boundaries. About 60 per cent of the known teaching models are in-clan cases while 40 per cent are cross-clan cases. The 'spread of information thus occurs simultaneously to kin and non-kin, determined mainly by *ad hoc*, non-corporate local work groups, nearest neighbours or frequent visitors (Stanislawski and

Stanislawski 1978: 75). Thus, attempts to indicate that particular styles represent particular ethnic social groups in society need not be valid.

The introduction of material innovations could also be direct through the actual movement of craftsmen. We may think in terms of a direct form of diffusion which refers to the processes whereby an idea or information is communicated through specific channels within a specific social context over time (Davis 1983: 55). In most cases this would call for extended interaction between 'donors' and 'adoptors' (Davis 1983). In certain cases, even with little interaction between craftsmen, designs can diffuse easily (Friedrich 1970: 337). There could however be adoption also at an individual level, as noted by Nadel (1942: 271) in the case of a Bida brassworker who produced a certain style of figurine. The inspiration for the particular style came from information provided by a travelling Indian trader who showed him pictures of the model and explained the concept to him. In this case, the craftsman did not actually obtain knowledge through watching and imitating. This medium, we may add, can result in the replication not always being a faithful one, as there is no 'teacher' to correct errors or changes in design.

Thus, the transfer of craft information can be through different media. Hayden and Cannon (1984) identified six different modes of learning behaviour ranging from the family centred to cooperative forms and finally to the more structured and formal specialist mode. The modes were largely differentiated on the basis of the social distance between the persons involved and also the number of learning sources that the individual could be exposed to.

The important issue in innovation is the particular climate surrounding the adoption of innovations. Anthropologists and sociologists agree that a new idea or technique may well be known but not necessarily adopted unless there was social acceptance of the innovation. Thus, according to Lemonnier (1993: 13) 'in order to be inserted in a technical system, a new element must be compatible and must meet some "requirement" . . . the mental processes on which the production and use of a new technical feature are based must be consistent with the already existing representations of technology or run the risk of being rejected'. In the context of diffusion too, Davis (1983: 58) noted the importance of factors such as symbolic value or prestige associations in the acceptance or rejection of innovations. Thus, for example,

Saraswati (1978: 71) noted that even after two centuries, there was little absorption of Telangi or Kathiawadi potters in Maharashtra. The non-Maharashtrian potters continued to use their own type of wheel which was different from the local potters' wheel.

The conservative approach of the craftsmen helped them to perpetuate their own craft traditions. This conservative attitude was primarily due to the imitative character of apprentices during their period of craft study (Childe 1978 [1942]: 87). Tried and tested techniques were followed even in the face of new, perhaps technologically superior, processes. Thus, the Anga in Papuan society use a traditional type of arrow despite the fact that they have knowledge of a much deadlier type of arrow made by their neighbours (Wynn 1994: 154). For innovations to be accepted, a particular socio-cultural climate was needed. An important motivation for acceptance of innovations could be political.

We find a dramatic change in the type and production of objects used to distinguish elite status from the pre-Inka to the Inka period. We find a distribution of elite items by the state as also the production of elite items in established state styles (Earle 1991: 95). Though there are no real developments in technology from the pre-Inka to the Inka period, there are innovations in artefact styles, particularly in bronze casting, which evidently were 'requirements' of the elite (Costin et al. 1989).

In the Mature Harappan context, some of the material innovations in the forms of artifacts are special-purpose objects like stone weights and stone seals. Even though the relevant technologies were known in the earlier periods, the specific objects manufactured during the Mature Harappan are clearly the result of a distinct social requirement. Similarly, though the technology of bead manufacture was known from neolithic times in this region, the special 'styles' of beads are perhaps valuable objects in view of the complicated techniques involved. In the same context, the production of a specific type of bangle made from the *Turbinella pyrum* species, decorated with one particular motif, also appears to be a special requirement in the Mature Harappan period. The Early Harappan period at a site like Balakot in Sind shows no evidence of shell working, in marked contrast to the Mature Harappan where we notice the use of molluscs for both dietary and craft purposes. The extensive use of steatite and faience to produce a variety of artifacts is also an innovation of the Mature Harappan period. Which was characterized by the burgeoning of craft traditions.

The change was heralded also by innovations in tools and technologies. Craft working is usually considered conservative. New types of tools and new types of artifacts indicate favourable conditions for the introduction of innovations. In this context we can appreciate the introduction of the copper/bronze saw for the production of shell bracelets (Kenoyer 1983), the firing of steatite to make steatite ornaments and objects white and harder, and the introduction of a complex technology for the production of stoneware bracelets. The desire to transform known materials into new forms is a distinct feature of the Mature Harappan (Vidale 1989), with concomitant changes in the organization of production (Wright 1993).

Though we are not entirely clear regarding the reason for change in craft traditions, the political factor does appear to be a possibility. On the one hand, we have several distinct 'styles' of artifacts being introduced in the Mature Harappan period and on the other, the vast geographical area covered by particular artifact types. Even if craftsmen were working largely in family centred enterprises, the artifacts they produced were specifically required to be in a particular 'style'. These could indicate specific functional requirements in the Mature Harappan period.

The urbanism that we note in the Mature Harappan period does seem to have a threshold. The Cholistan Desert with its profusion of camp sites provides us with the evidence of the Early Harappan as a period when there was large-scale settling down of people of the earlier Hakra Wares period. However, the nucleation of population with all its impact in the social, economic and political spheres in all probability occurred in the Mature Harappan period Apparently, refinements in craft production, with changes in tool types for craft purposes and a considerable elaboration of the artifact styles from intrinsically basic types, underlay the Harappan urbanism.

REFERENCES

Adams, R.M., *The Evolution of Urban Society*, Chicago, Aldine, 1966.

Braidwood, R.J. and G.R. Willey (eds.), *Courses Toward Urban Life*, Edinburgh: University Press, 1982.

Carter, H., *An Introduction to Urban Historical Geography*, London, 1983.

Childe, V.G., *What Happened in History*, Penguin, 1978 rep.

———, 'The Urban Revolution', rep. G.L. Possehl (ed.), *Ancient Cities of the Indus*, New Delhi: Vikas, 1979, pp. 12–17.

Choksi, A., 'An Ethnoarchaeological Study of Pottery Manufacture in Kutch', unpublished Ph.D. dissertation, M.S. University of Baroda, 1994.

Costin, C., T. Earle, B. Owen and G. Russell, 'The Impact of Inca Conquest of Local Technology in the Upper Mantaro Valley, Peru', in S.E. van der Leeuw and R. Torrence (eds.), *What's New? A Closer Look at the Process of Innovation*, London: Unwin Hyman, pp. 107–39.

Dales, G.F. and J.M. Kenoyer, 'Preliminary Report on the Third Season (January–March 1988) of Research at Harappa, Pakistan', University of California at Berkeley and University of Wisconsin at Madison, 1988.

Dales, G.F., J.M. Kenoyer and the staff of the Harappa Project, Summaries of Five Seasons of Research at Harappa (District Sahiwal, Punjab, Pakistan), in R.H. Meadow (ed.), *Harappa Excavations 1986–90: A Multidisciplinary Approach to Third Millenium Urbanism*, Madison: Prehistory Press, 1986–90, pp. 185–262.

Davis, D.D., 'Investigating the Diffusion of Stylistic Innovations', in M.B. Schiffer (ed.), *Advances in Archaeological Method and Theory*, vol. 6, New York: Academic Pess, 1983, pp. 53–87.

Earle, T.K., 'Toward a Behavioral Archaeology', in R.W. Preucel (ed.), *Processual and Postprocessual Archaeologies: Multiple Ways of Knowing the Past*, Carbondale: 1991, pp. 83–95.

Fischer, E. and H. Shah, *Rural Craftsmen and Their Work*, Ahmedabad, 1970.

Friedrich, M.H., 'Design Structure and Social Interaction: Archaeological Implications of an Ethnographic Analysis', *American Antiquity*, vol. 35, 1970, pp. 332–43.

Halim, M.A., 'Excavations at Sarai Khola-Part II', *Pakistan Archaeology*, vol. 8, 1972, pp. 1–112.

Hayden, B. and A. Cannon, 'Interaction Inferences in Archaeology and Learning Frameworks of the Maya', *Journal of Anthropological Archaeology* vol. 3 (4) 1984, pp. 325–67.

Kenoyer, J., 'Shell Working Industries of the Indus Civilization: An Archaeological and Ethnographic Perspective', University Microfilms International, Ann Arbor, Michigan, 1983.

Kenoyer, J.M., 'Urban Process in the Indus Tradition: A Preliminary Model from Harappa', in R.H. Meadow (ed.), *Harappa Excavations 1986–1990*, Madison: Prehistory Press, 1991a, pp. 29–60.

———, 'The Indus Valley Tradition of Pakistan and Western India', *Journal of World Prehistory*, vol. 5, 4, 1991b, pp. 331–85.

Khan, F.A., 'Excavations at Kot Diji', *Pakistan Archaeology*, vol. 2, 1965, pp. 11–85.

Lemonnier, P., 'Introduction', in P. Lemonnier (ed.), *Technological Choices. Transforamtions in Material Cultures Since the Neolithic*, London and New York: Routledge, 1993, pp. 1–35.

Meadow, R.H. and J.M. Kenoyer, 'Harappa Excavations 1993: The City Wall and Inscribed Materials', in A. Parpola and P. Koskikallio (eds.), *South Asian Archaeology*, Helsinki: Suomalainen Tiedeakatemia, vol. II, 1994, pp. 451–82.

Mughal, M.R., 'The Early Harappan Period in the Greater Indus Valley and Northern Baluchistan (c. 3000–2400 B.C.)', University Microfilms International, Michigan: Ann Arbor, 1970.

———, 'Excavation at Jalilpur', *Pakistan Archaeology*, vol. 8, 1972, pp. 117–24.

———, 'Recent Archaeological Research in the Cholistan Desert', in G.L. Possehl (ed.), *Harappan Civilization: A Contemporary Perspective*, New Delhi: Oxford and IBH, 1982, pp. 85–95.

———, 'Further Evidence of the Early Harappan Culutre in the Greater Indus Valley: 1971–90', *South Asian Studies*, vol. 6, 1990, pp. 175–99.

Nadel, S.F., *A Black Byzantium: The Kingdom of Nupe in Nigeria*, London, 1942.

Parpola, A., *Deciphering the Indus Script*, Cambridge: Cambridge University Press, 1994.

Possehl, G.L., 1986, *Kulli: An Exploration of Ancient Civilization in South Asia*, Durham: Carolina Academic Press, 1986.

———, 'Revolution in the Urban Revolution: The Emergence of Indus Urbanization', *Annual Review of Anthropology*, vol. 19, 1990, pp. 261–82.

———, 'Meluhha', in J. Reade (ed.), *The Indian Ocean in Antiquity*, Kegan Paul International in Association with the British Museum, London, 1996.

Ratnagar, S.F., *Enquiries into the Political Organisation of Harappan Soceity*, Pune: Ravish Publishers, 1991.

Saraswati, B., *Pottery-Making Cultures and Indian Civilization*, New Delhi: Abhinav Publications, 1978.

Shaffer, J.G. and D.A. Lichtenstein, 'Ethnicity and Change in the Indus Valley Cultural Tradition', in J.M. Kenoyer (ed.), *Old Problems and New Perspectives in the Archaeology of South Asia*, Wisconsin Archaeological Reports vol. 2, 1989, pp. 117–26.

Sigaut, F., 'Technology', in T. Ingold (ed.), *Companion Encyclopaedia of Anthropology: Humanity, Culture and Social Life*, London and New York: Routledge, 1994, pp. 420–59.

Suraj Bhan, *Excavation at Mitathal (1968) and Other Explorations in the Sutlej-Yamuna Divide*, Kurukshetra: Kurukshetra University Press, 1975.

Vats, M.S., *Excavations at Harappa*, 2 vols., Delhi, 1940.

Stanislawski, M.B. and B.B. Stanislawki, 'Hopi and Hopi-Tewa Ceramic Tradition Networks', in I. Hodder (ed.), *The Spatial Organisation of Culture*, London: Duckworth, 1978, pp. 61–76.

Vidale, M., 'Specialized Producers and Urban Elites: On the Role of Craft Industries in Mature Harappan Urban Contexts', in J.M. Kenoyer (ed.), *Old Problems and New Perspectives in the Archaeology of South Asia*, Wisconsin Archaeological Reports, vol. 2, 1989, pp. 171–81.

Vidale, M., J.M. Kenoyer and K.K. Bhan, 'A Discussion of the Concept of "Chaine Operatoire" in the Study of Stratified Societies: Evidence from Ethnoarchaeology and Archaeology', in A. Gallay (ed.), *Ethnoarchaeologie, Justification, Problemes, Limites*, France: Juan-les-Pins, 1992, pp. 181–94.

Wheatley, P., *The Pivot of the Four Quarters*, Chicago: Aldine, 1971.

Wright, R., 'Technological Styles: Transforming a Natural Material into a Cultural Object', in S. Lubar and W.D. Kingery (eds.), *History from Things: Essays on Material Culture*, Washington and London: Smithsonian Institution Press, 1993, pp. 242–68.

Wynn, T., 'Tools and Tool Behavior', in T. Ingold (ed.), *Companion Encyclopaedia of Anthropology: Humanity, Culture and Social Life*, London and New York: Routledge, 1994, pp. 133–61.

4

Harappan Urbanism in the Sutlej-Yamuna Divide

SURAJ BHAN

The growth of urbanization marks the beginning of a new socio-economic and cultural stage in society. Cumulative changes in the economic structure and social organization of communities accompanied by concentration of heterogeneous segments leads to the growth of population towns and cities. Conceived in the hopes and aspirations of the affluent classes emerging from the distribution system and control of the means of production, the production and acquisition of the surplus is in fact the corner-stone of the growth of urban centres. Social contradictions emerging in a class-based society demand mechanisms for their resolution or control. This results in the rise of a centralized state, well-defended settlements to conduct the economic, administrative and cultural enterprises and functions and to ensure safe and comfortable life in residential buildings.

The accumulated surplus, results in the rise of specialists producing quality goods, scientific ideas, techniques, arts, beliefs and rituals and the long distance trade facilitated by the invention of script, standard weights and measures and transport. The beginning of urbanization thus results in the release of energy and growth of productive forces, new cultural values and cultural hegemony of the new ruling classes through economic and political expansion. The urban centres thus develop into islands of prosperity, quality life conditions and the elitist ruling class ideology and ethos in contrast with the general conditions of paucity, heterogeneity of traditions and the deepening inequalities. The kind of urbanism that grows depends upon the socio-economic formation and its political economy working in the world historical context rather than merely on natural or environmental and ecological

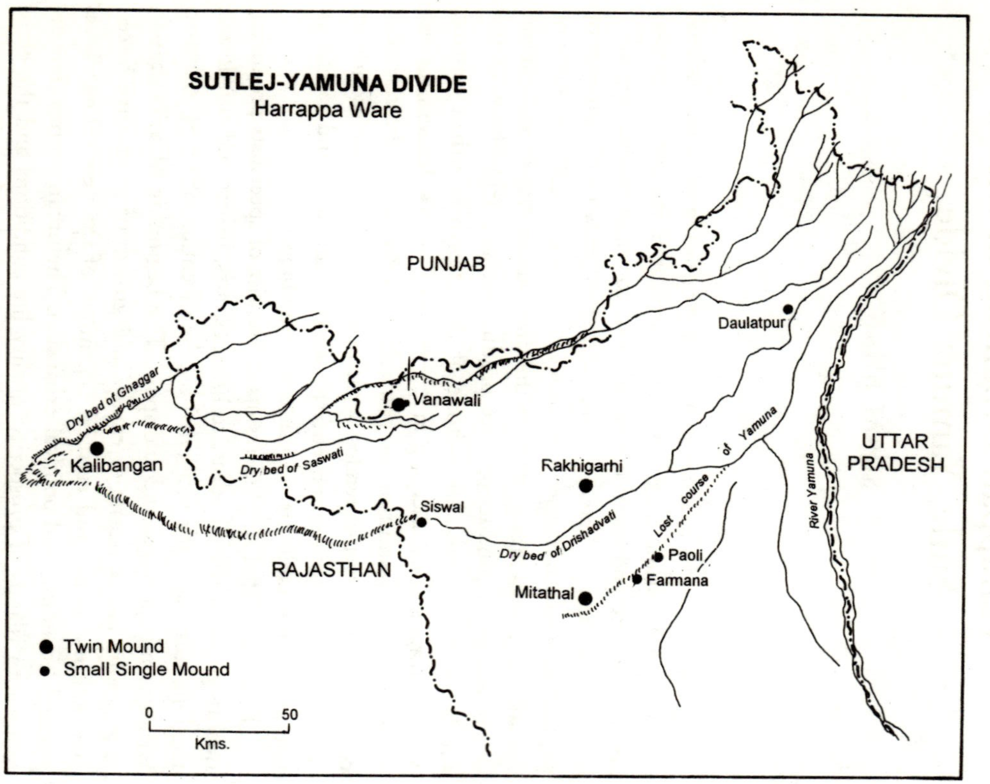

Map 4.1: Sutlej-Yamuna Divide—Harappa Ware

condition. The material culture of the pre-Harappan and the Harappan stages appears to bear this out despite many a gap in the information and its scientific analysis.

II

The Sutlej-Yamuna Divide is a wide open terrain bordered by the Shivaliks in the north, the sandy tract of Bagar in the south and the Aravalis in the south-east. These alluvial plains of Punjab and Haryana stretch between the Yamuna in the east and the Sutlej in the north-west. The region is mainly drained by the Ghaggar and its tributaries which originate in the Shivaliks. There is no clear datable evidence to suggest that the Sutlej or the Yamuna flowed through the Ghaggar bed in the proto-historic period. On the whole it is a semi-arid tract with tropical climate and insufficient rainfall. There are no mineral deposits known. Deposits of iron ore, lime stone, slate and semi-precious stones however, occur in the Aravalis.

Nearly 800 sites have been explored in the Ghaggar basin. More than two dozens of these have been excavated. As a result, the following sequence of cultures has been reconstructed:

Stage I: Chalcolithic peasant-pastoral colonization (*c.* 2600–2300 BC).
Stage II: Pre-Harappan integration (*c.* 2300–2200 BC).
Stage III: Harappan expansion (*c.* 2200–1700 BC).
Stage IV: Harappan disintegration (*c.* 1700–1000 BC).

The chalcolithic peasant-pastoral culture marked the first stage of colonization in the region. It is represented by open settlements at Kunal IA and Banawali IA (IA stands for the first phase of the Early Harappan). It is marked by the use of circular dwelling pits and bichrome painted pottery bearing affinities with the Hakra Ware of Pakistan. The people used bone tools, copper arrow heads and fish hook, chalcedony micro-blades, micro-beads, and the potter's wheel. Banawali IA, another open site of this early phase, is distinguished by the use of rectangular structures laid north-south and made of mud bricks of 1:2:3 ratio in size. The culture is represented so far only in the Rangoi bed along the Ghaggar. In Punjab a comparable pottery is recovered from the ancient sites of Bhudan IA near Malerkotla and Faridkot.

The life conditions of the people as judged from the nature of their dwellings and artifacts reflect a differentiated society comprising settled agricultural and semi-nomadic tribes. The various products such as copper and bone artifacts and the earthen wares suggest the existence of limited division of labour and exchange. The absence of fortification perhaps hints at a tribal status. The cultural affinities of their pottery with further west in the Punjab (both eastern and western) and its absence from the Chautang basin hints at the movement of the Hakra-related people from the Punjab into the Ghaggar basin.

In Stage II the pre-Harappan culture of Banawali IB is distinguished by the emergence of a fortified settlement and rectangular and mud brick (1:2:3 ratio) houses. In pottery all the six fabrics of Kalibangan I are met with. A similar pottery has been reported from Siswal A, Rakhigarhi (lower levels), Rohira, Balu I and Lohata. Besides these a number of smaller sites have been discovered at Bhudan I, Mahorana IA and others not yet excavated. By now the pre-Harappans seem to have advanced beyond the peasant-pastoral stage. The division of work is indicated by the growth of limited specialized crafts, like the wheel-made pottery, copper working, and bead making. The hierarchy of two tier settlements and structures mark the growth of differentiated society. The use of fortifications reveals the emergence of socio-economic integration beyond the egalitarian tribal stage and perhaps suggests a social organization of the level of chiefdom.

The pre-Harappan groups occupied different ecological niches within a bigger fortified central site. Some of the tribes now appear to have moved into the Kantli valley and initiated copper working in northern Rajasthan. Some others moved into parts of the Bagar tract in Bhiwani-Mahendragarh districts.

The advent of the Harappans marked a new stage in Banawali IC, representing the third phase of the Early Harappan. It reflected drastic changes in the settlement plan, architecture, ceramic industry and artifacts. The entire settlement was planned and constructed *de-novo*. The settlement has a citadel perched on the top of the pre-Harappan fortified settlement. The lower town extends beyond it on the north, east and west. The orientation of the houses differs at several places as also the radial street pattern. The houses are now made of mud bricks of the Harappan size (1:2:4 ratio). Terracotta triangular cakes, chert blades, beads of steatite, chalcedony and clay, and bangles of clay with circular section are typical finds of the Harappan culture. But the characteristic Indus seals, standard weights and script have not been found so far. Some of the pottery forms reveal imperfect adaptations of Harappan norms side by side with slightly more evolved pre-Harappan ceramic corpus and artifacts.

Kunal IC too reveals a similar layout of the houses in a composite cultural millieu. But no citadel has been traced here so far. Mitathal I and Siswal B also represent more or less a similar interaction with the Harappan cultures.

The hierarchy of settlements represented by the central sites with citadels and village sites, the nature of the architecture, pit silos, standardized production of copper artifacts, gold and silver ornaments, lapislazuli and chalcedony beads indicate long distance trace in addition to specialized crafts and class character of the culture not so well marked in the previous stage. A change is discernible in the social organization. Perhaps a centralized Harappan state had emerged in the region and influenced the pre-Harappan settlements on the Rangoi bed on a scale greater than in the Chautang valley. The discovery of uninscribed steatite and shell seals, silver headgear, gold ornaments and lapislazuli beads from Kunal IC perhaps attests to a special status for the site. The discovery of a cluster of classical Harappan sites in Sangrur and Bhatinda districts on the other side of the Ghaggar might throw a significant light on the nature of the early Harappan expansion into the Sutlej-Yamuna Divide and its interaction with the Kunal IC and Banawali IC.

The Harappans soon established themselves in the Sirhind drain, Naiwal, Chautang and Sabi valleys and reached upto the Shivalik foothills and the Bangar tract of Hissar, Jind, Bhiwani, Rohtak and Karnal districts. The Harappans occupied only a small tract of the Rangoi believed to be the dry bed of the Rigvedic Saraswati. They did not colonize the holy Saraswati in the Kurukshetra region, the seat of Vedic culture. The village settlements retained the pre-Harappan tradition of the material culture. The satellite towns too revealed lesser Harappan influence.

The relationship of the Harappan ruling class with the preceding pre-Harappan elites on the one hand and with the pastoral agricultural settlers of the Bagar tract on the other, demands explanation. The more elaborate nature of the citadel and the township in Banawali IC, superimposed upon the pre-Harappan fortified settlement, the drastic change in the settlement plan, the dominant use of Harappan bricks for structures and typical pottery types, copper artifacts, chert blades, beads and bangles perhaps reflect the intrusive character of the Harappans to subjugate and control the wheat-barley-cotton zone and to extract the surplus from the non-Harappan peasant communities of the Ghaggar basin.

The peak of Harappan expansion was reached in Rakhigarhi, Banawali II (transitional period between the early and Mature Harappan), Rohira II, Mitathal IIA, Balu II, Augand (further up on Chautang) and Lohat (on Sabi) as others on the Sirhind drain. This is evident from the settlement plans, architectural remains, artifacts and pottery found from the excavations and surface explorations.

Rakhigarhi and Mitathal IIA are laid on typical twin mound pattern, so characteristic of Kalibangan II, Mohenjodaro and Harappa city sites. Banawali II, Rohira II and Balu II reveal a bipartite settlement plan comprising the citadel and the adjoining fortified lower town. The layout of Banawali II citadel is horse-shoe shaped, while the streets of the lower town show radial arrangement unlike those at Balu II and Rohira. The fortification walls as well as the structures are made of moulded mud bricks (1:2:4 ratio). Drains and a few houses are constructed with burnt bricks of similar size at Banawali II as at Rakhigarhi. The discovery of seals, sealings and weights and the luxury items like gold and shell ornaments, beads of lapislazuli, copper, carnelian, steatite and faience attest to long distance trade.

The introduction of the plough, copper implements such as celts and hoes, and irrigation facilities enhanced the efficiency of labour and agriculture. The surplus extracted supported specialized craftsmen and the ruling classes. The class character of the social organization is reflected in the segregation of citadel and the lower town; hierarchy of settlements represented by cities, towns and villages; brick architecture and insignificant hutments of wattle and daub and in the Harappan and pre-Harappan pottery traditions and artifacts found side by side.

The Mature Harappan settlements were distinguished by impressive and well-planned fortified towns replacing the earlier moderate sized settlements of the pre-Harappans. They were supported by plough agriculture, irrigation canals, specialized craftsmen and long distance trade facilitated by inscribed seals, standard weights, transport facilities (such as beasts of burden and bullock carts), and served as the administrative and trade centres of a centralized state. The pottery styles and forms of the artifacts represent a composite character of the culture, with elements of both the elitist Harappan and the pre-Harappan traditions. While the Harappan elements dominate the town sites, the pre-Harappan tradition survives predominantly in the village sites. The phase marks the advent of a new wave of Harappans as conquerers along the Ghaggar and the Drisadwati valleys. The course of Saraswati above Jakhal and large part of the Kurukshetra region were still under the forest. The ruling class did not need to expand further north into a region which was not yet occupied by peasant communities.

III

It is evident from the above that the pre-Harappan culture of the second stage in the Ghaggar basin did make an advance over the Hakra culture by growing specialization in crafts, and social integration. A social organization, with power-elites based in the fortified central sites, had emerged. But the absence of long distance trade supported by writing, inscribed seals, standard weights and the lower level of social differentiation hardly justify any urban and state based social status for the pre-Harappans.

The Harappan stage reveals a clear evidence of the growth of cities and satellite towns in the region. A centralized authority not less than a territorial state is reflected in the evidence of the twin mound pattern, elaborate fortifications and trade. The Harappan elitist culture of urban centres had no local roots in the pre-harappan sub-stratum. They appear to be intruders into the region from the western Punjab. They brought with them the urban pattern of life and economic and political institutions. But the possibilities existing in the region could sustain them for nearly 500 years. The subjugation of the pre-Harappans seems to have distorted the local pattern of social development in the course of Harappanization of the non-Harappans who constituted the mass of the people.

REFERENCES

Agrawal, D.P., *The Archaeology of India*, London: Curzon Press, 1982.

Allchin, Raymond and Bridget Allchin, *The Rise of Civilization in India and Pakistan*, New Delhi: Penguin Books, 1996.

Dani, A.H., *Indian Palaeography*, Oxford, 1963.

Fairservis, W.A., *The Roots of Ancient India*, London, 1971 (2nd edn).

Gordon, D.H., *The Prehistoric Background of Indian Culture*, Bombay, 1958.

5

Taxila in the Mauryan Empire

KUMKUM ROY

Taxila has acquired a certain centrality in the discussions on early urbanism. It is perhaps the only early historical city which has been subjected to relatively large-scale horizontal excavation. Hence, we know more about Taxila than about cities like Pataliputra. What is perhaps more important in this case is the evidence of a long historical sequence of settlements. Even if one ignores the prehistoric archaeological cultures in the area, the evidence from the historical period, ranging possibly from Achaemenid level to what is regarded as the early medieval period, is rich and varied. While the nucleus of the settlement seems to have shifted, from the Bhir Mound to Sirkap and still later, to Sirsukh, the importance of the locality as a whole is evident from its continuous occupation for at least a millennium.

The strategic location of Taxila has been frequently remarked upon. It evidently owed its importance to the convergence of routes from Bacteria to the north-west, Kashmir to the north-east, and the Gangetic plains to the south-east (Marshal 1975: 1–2; Fussman 1993: 84). It is situated near one of the major fords on the Indus. At the same time, there were other geographical advantages: the Potwar plateau, where Taxila is located, is a well irrigated area, facilitating both fruit-cultivation and agriculture.

While the data from the site can be examined from a variety of perspectives, we propose to explore a specific problem pertaining to political structures in early India. The problem relates to the nature of early empires such as that of the Mauryas. There was a tendency to regard to empire as uniformly and consistently centralized, but this has been called into question in the last decade or so (Thapar 1987). This has complicated our understanding of imperial structures and processes. In place of the homogenous model of the empire as a monolithic structure which was imposed from above, we are now required to take into account the possibility of more complex interactions between the central and the provincial authorities and the differences amongst provinces as well.

Some of these complexities can be traced by examining the inscriptional and archaeological evidence pertaining directly and indirectly to Taxila. In a sense, these pertain to different levels of political, social or economic interaction. An awareness of their coexistence is a prerequisite for understanding their inter-relationship, if any.

The Ashokan inscriptions where Taxila is mentioned are the separate rock edicts found at Dhauli and Jaugada in the present-day Orissa. Ashoka instructs his officers located in regional centres such as Tosali, Ujjain and Taxila, that they are to undertake periodic tours of inspection, to ensure the enforcement of justice in particular and paternalistic rule in general. The famous campaign against Kalinga is not mentioned. The administrative centres in Kalinga, located within the Mauryan imperial framework, are accorded as much importance as other provincial centres such as Ujjain and Taxila. Thus, at one level there is an attempt to establish an equivalence amongst these centres, at least in terms of their administrative functions.

This equivalence is something which was probably attempted rather than achieved. Apart from their distinct geographical locations, a survey of approximate settlement size (Allchin 1995: 207) would suggest that Tosali, the largest of the three centres, identified with Sisupalgarh, was probably thrice the size of Taxila, whereas Ujjain may have been twice as large. Incidentally, Tosali is probably the only provincial capital which may have been planned and constructed by the Mauryas. In the case of Ujjain and Taxila, the Mauryan presence was located within the context of pre-existing settlements.

There are Ashokan inscription in and around Taxila. At Taxila itself, we have, from Sirkap, a fragmentary marble inscription. This evidently summarized the contents of Rock Edict IV, meant to impress and convince the subjects about the importance of *dhamma* and includes general prescriptions for courteous social behaviour. This may have been part of an entire series of inscriptions, which have not been discovered as yet. What makes this inscription unique is the use of Aramaic which was evidently introduced into this area during the Achaemenid period. In fact, this marks the eastern limit of Ashok's Aramaic inscriptions, some of which have been recovered from Afghanistan.

Two other better known and more complete versions of the major rock edicts have been found at Shahbazgarhi and Mansehra, both of which would have been within the ambit of Taxila. Interestingly, while the language used in these inscriptions is a form of Prakrit, the script is Kharoshti, considered peculiar to the north-west of the subcontinent. In a sense, these variations in language and script can be viewed as symptomatic of the complex interaction between the imperial and provincial centre. While the content of the inscriptions may have been determined by the former, the form was obviously influenced by local considerations. In this respect Taxila presents a contrast with other provinces where there is a consistent use of the Brahmi script and varieties of Prakrit.

There is another indication of the somewhat unique status of Taxila. The Ashokan inscriptions contain lists of peoples and kings, who are represented as being more or less friendly recipients of the emperor's benevolent activities and missions. What is interesting is that references to kings occur exclusively in the context of the north-western frontiers of the realm and beyond. These include the *yonaraja* or Greek king Amtiyoka mentioned in Rock Edict II, and Turamaya or Ptolemy, Amtekina or Antigonas, Maka or Magas, and Alikasumdara or Alexander, who are mentioned in the longer list in Rock Edict XIII. Almost all of these have been identified as rulers of the successor states which emerged after the collapse of the Macedonian empire in West Asia and beyond.

The mention of kings along a single frontier of the empire may reflect a political reality. Monarchs may not have existed in other parts of the subcontinent. The proximity to more complex political systems enhanced the significance of Taxila as a centre for mediating relations between contemporary kings and may account for its importance and relative autonomy.

The distribution of Ashokan inscriptions is by now fairly well-established. Broadly, the rock edicts (especially the major rock edicts) occur in the provinces, whereas the pillar edicts (with a few exceptions such as Sanchi) tend to be concentrated in and around the mid-Ganga valley. This distinction is useful in focussing on the questions we started with.

Generally Ashokan inscriptions have been analysed in terms of variations in their script and grammatical structure, and not the vocabulary. A means for elucidating the emperor's policies, these can be located within a broad, humanistic framework. These inscriptions also touch on specific social categories to whom administrative policies are addressed. It is this group which is of interest because reference to social categories tend to be less standardized than those to administrative personnel. These variations can provide us with an entry point to explore whether the relative importance of such categories, or even their existence, varied from region to region.

We may also stress that, given their function, the inscriptions were placed in areas where diverse peoples would have congregated, which, in most situations, would have implied proto-urban or urban settlements. These would have been situations of social complexity. While some of the issues arising out of such complexity were addressed in the inscriptions, not all of them were necessarily acknowledged.

Amongst the social categories the inscriptions recognize are the old, ideally venerable, but obviously vulnerable members of the society. Respect towards them, as well as ensuring their welfare, is the ideal subject. One can speculate as to whether this insistence on caring for the aged had something to do with stresses within kinship structures, which may have customarily provided support to old kinsfolk. Such stresses, in turn, may have been more likely in an urban situation. The terminological variation in this context are also interesting.

The old are referred to as *thaira* (Sanskrit *sthavira*) in the Girnar inscriptions. However, versions of the edicts from Dhauli, Kalsi (Uttar Pradesh), Shahbazgarhi and Mansehra, use terms such as *mahalaka* and *vudha* (Rock Edicts V, VIII). *Thaira* could be interpreted as a Buddhist elder, or senior monk, as opposed to a more universal category of the old.

The vocabulary of the Girnar inscriptions tends to correspond most closely with that of the inscriptions from the mid-Ganga valley, it is likely that the central formulation, which emanated from Pataliputra may have contained the word *thaira*, with its specific connotation. However, the formulation seems to have been modified and broadened in the course of its transmission to other regions. This modification may have been undertaken by local administrative authorities or elites, who probably undertook the actual task of communication.

Other variations are discernible in the treatment of kinship terminology. Rock Edict IX refers to rituals which are commonly performed in order to obtain progeny. While the term *putra* or son is used in the Girnar inscription in this context, the other regions show a preference for the term *praja* which, while occasionally synonymous with son, could also mean offspring in general. As in the case of defining elders, there seems to be a shift from a specific to a general category.

This variation extends to the notion of patrilineal generations. Some of Ashoka's inscriptions (e.g. Rock Edict IV) end with the hope that his sons, grandsons, and great grandsons would follow the *dhamma* promulgated by him. Interestingly, while the Girnar version mentions the *putra*, *potra* and *prapotra* in this context, the other versions, including those at Shahbazgarhi and Mansehra replace *potra* and *prapotra* with variants on *nati* and *pranati* which have a wider connotation, including matrilineal as well as patrilineal descendants. In other words, while the emperor may have intended to delimit his legitimate succesors, the closely structured potential genealogy was generalized and opened up in regional contexts.

In Rock Edict V, the emperor mentions the *mahamatras* he has despatched to work amongst his sisters and brothers. While the term for the latter is broadly uniform (*bhata* and its variants) the term for sister in Shahbazgarhi and Mansehra is *spasa* (derived from *svasr?*) as opposed to the term *bhagini* used in other regions. Elsewhere (Roy 1994: 249) we have argued that the term *svasr* represented a more egalitarian relationship between brother and sister than *bhagini* and that the former was probably typical of the early Vedic situation. If this is true, its use in the north-west may point to the continued existence of distinctive kinship relations in the area.

Not surprisingly, women seem to have proved most resistant to terminological uniformity. Rock Edict IX elaborates, among other things, on the futility of rituals performed by women, advocating *dhamma* as an alternative. Here, while the term *mahida* is used in Girnar, the inscriptions of Kalsi and Mansehra contain the term *abaka jana*, while variations of *stri* are used at Shahbazgarhi and Dhauli. While the significance of such variations requires exploration, their existence points to the social heterogeneity of the empire. What is interesting is that when *mahamatras* were appointed to look into the affairs of women, their official designation was relatively standardized, consisting of variants of the term *ithidhiyakkha* (Sanskrit *stri-adhyaksa*, Rock Edict XII).

Other socio-religious categories mentioned routinely in the inscriptions are the *brahmanas* and *shramanas*, i.e. priests and representatives of heterodox sects respectively. While Ashoka advocates a uniform attitude of respect towards both categories (e.g. Rock Edict VIII), the dual compound of *brahmana–shramana* is in fact one which is fraught with tension, given the divergent values upheld by each category. Broadly, while the latter were more preoccupied with ensuring the well-being of themselves and their supporters in this world, the former laid greater emphasis on renunciation. At another level, *brahmanas* were obviously implicated in and explicitly upheld the notions of social stratification associated with *varna*, whereas *shramanas* either denied the validity of social differences, or, alternatively, advocated other criteria for social differentiation (Chakravarti 1983). Yet in spite or perhaps because of these differences, *brahmanas* and *shramanas* can be envisaged as competing for social patronage. While the inscriptions from Girnar uniformly accord primacy to the *brahmana*, those from Shahbazgarhi and Mansehra, as also those from Dhauli, at least occasionally give precedence to *shramanas* (e.g. Rock Edict VIII).

As opposed to this, the other dual compound which figures in the inscriptions, the *dasa-bhataka* (slaves and servants), is invariable. This would suggest that the status of the slave or servant was regarded as being relatively stable. While this may be an accurate reflection of social reality, it may also point to the marginality of this category from the perspective of those by whom the inscriptions were written and those for whom they were intended. It is likely that the categories higher in the social order was more fluid and could vary in different regions. According primacy to *shramanas* in some regions, including Taxila, may have been one means of coming to terms with this fluidity.

It is evident then that while administrative designations throughout the empire reflect a certain degree of uniformity and centralization, the social contexts within which the administration functioned were evidently less amenable to homogenization, and even apparently universal categories were subject to redefinition. In the case of Taxila in particular, we have seen how such redefinitions operated not only at the level of vocabulary, but also at the level of script and language. It is likely that such redefinitions were the outcome of alliances between local, predominantly urban elites and the imperial authorities.

It is in this context that one can look afresh at the somewhat stereotypical stories about the Mauryas and Taxila which occur in Buddhist sources such as the *Divyavadana*. These represent the citizens of Taxila as rebelling against imperial control. Almost invariably, the crown prince is sent to quell the rebellion. However, this proves to be somewhat superfluous, as the citizens inform him that their grievance was against the oppressive local governors rather than against the apparently benevolent but distant emperor. The story and its resolution though obviously coloured by the complex relationship between Buddhism and Ashoka, points to the tensions amongst different socio-political categories located within the imperial framework. Although the stories suggest a single resolution that the existence of the empire was essential for the citizenry of Taxila, there are indications that other resolutions were also possible.

II

The archaelogical evidence of the Mauryan presence at Taxila is derived substantially from the Bhir Mound. The shape of the existing mound is somewhat irregular. Its greatest length being about 1,200 yds, whereas its width is about 730 yds. As Allchin (1995: 207) observes, it is relatively small in comparison with other contemporary settlements. For instance, while Pataliputra is placed in Grade I in his settlement size hierarchy, with an area of 340 hectares, Taxila is in Grade 5 (sites between 31 and 60 hectares). While the straightness of the edge of the mound in some parts of the settlement may point to the existence of a mud rampart, there does not seem to be any obvious evidence for it at present.

Stratigraphically, the evidence from Bhir Mound has been interpreted in terms of four periods. The earliest of these (Stratum IV) pertains to the sixth and fifth centuries BC, the second to the fourth century BC, the third to the Mauryan period, and the fourth to the post-Mauryan period.

More recently, these strata have been assigned slightly different dates. In one instance, Stratum III and not Stratum II has been regarded as Mauryan whereas in another, Stratum III has been ascribed to the early Mauryan and Stratum II to the late Mauryan phase (Allchin 1993). In spite of varying emphases, the broad sequence seems to be fairly well established. Besides, it is likely that there is no neat coincidence between archaeological strata and dynastic changes. This is especially true in the context of the Mauryas, who are not associated with the wholesale destruction of populations and settlements (with the possible exception of Kalinga). Hence, given the nature of the Mauryan political intervention, the settlement was probably not radically altered from the pre-Mauryan to the Mauryan period, or even subsequently.

The excavated data on the structural remains from the Bhir Mound are not particularly coherent. Most of these pertain to Stratum II. House plans are not clearly differentiated and the evidence for town planning appears limited. Most streets and lanes tend to be narrow and winding. Waste disposal was probably organized through bins and soakwells rather than drains. There do not seem to have been any wells within the city. As such, water for daily needs was probably drawn from the adjoining Tamra river or from wells along its banks.

The almost inevitable comparisons with Harappan settlements have, not surprisingly, underscored the inferiority of the civic amenities in Mauryan Taxila. However, we can also view the problem somewhat differently. The nature of the interaction between Pataliputra and Taxila may not have required the transformation of what may have been a pre-urban or proto-urban settlement. Alternatively, the vitality of pre-existing traditions of settlement in the area may have precluded any dramatic intervention from the imperial capital.

It is in this context that we focus on the items recovered from the excavation, classified as 'minor antiquities' by Marshall. These range from pottery to a variety of stone, bone, and metal artifacts, beads, coins, and seals. While many of these have been examined at length earlier, little attention has been given to the conjunctures and disjunctures between Strata III and II.

It is obvious that each of these types of artifacts were generated in distinct contexts and represent different kinds of historical processes. One of these could be the interaction between the imperial centre and the province. At one level, one would expect evidence of resources being transferred from the provincial centre to the capital. Unfortunately, there are no explicit epigraphic references to such transactions. The only mention of taxation in Ashokan inscriptions, for example, comes from the Rumminidei Pillar Inscription in Bihar, which mentions exemptions rather than impositions. Given the specific nature of the inscription, this does not preclude the possibility of resources being transferred from other areas. We also need to remember that some of the produce brought into the capital may have been perishable, or in the form of raw materials, which may have been processed in Pataliputra. As such, these transactions would not be visible in the archaeological record. The limited problematic archaeological evidence from Pataliputra does not allow us to identify the produce which was siphoned off from the provinces.

What we do have is the stratified material from Taxila itself. While some of the evidence (e.g. punch-marked coins) can be viewed as direct indication of contact with Pataliputra, the other data (e.g. beads, metals) may point to transformations within the settlement which were probably generated, in part, by the context of its incorporation within the imperial framework, while in yet other instances, there may be continuity from pre-Mauryan to Mauryan levels and beyond.

If we examine the data on pottery, it appears that large storage jars are found within the settlement for the first time in Stratum II. One can speculate on their use to store grain and other produce to meet the requirements of the population concentrated in the urban centre. In other words, they may be symbolic of a new distributive system being put into place. What can be tentatively suggested is that with the emergence of Taxila as a regional political centre, distributive networks in the region may have tended to be drawn into and through Taxila to a greater extent than before. In other words, the incorporation of Taxila within the imperial framework may have altered the relationship of the settlement to its hinterland and sharpened socio-economic difference between Taxila and the adjoining areas. Yet, the degree of change should not be overestimated: large storage jars do not constitute a centralized granary.

In other instances, there is a relative proliferation of pottery types. These include small vessels, perhaps for liquids such as oil or wine, lids, and stoppers, bowls, saucers, waterpots, and handled and spouted jugs. While the precise significance of such finds may elude us, it is obvious that they are representative of a richer, more complex material culture.

Other uses of pottery are evident in ring wells and drains, which appear in the Stratum II. These are clearly related to the provision of civic amenities. While some of these were in the nature of public facilities, associated with squares, which have been compared to the present-day *chowks* (Dani 1986), others were meant for private use. As such, they do not seem to be indicative of close central control or planning either at the local or at the imperial level. Nevertheless, the existence of these structures points to the growing importance of long-term residence within the urban centre, and the concomitant need to provide relatively permanent facilities.

What is also interesting is that soak wells evidently disappear in the post-Mauryan Indo-Greek city of Sirkap (Marshall 1975: 202). Obviously, other systems of garbage disposal were devised. It is also likely that the ringwells were adopted from the example of Gangetic settlement and with the collapse of the imperial network and the incorporation of Taxila within a more westerly sphere of influence, the older sanitary arrangements went out of fashion.

In other instances, such as the use of bone and ivory objects, there appear to have been shifts rather than any noticeable increase in their importance. The greatest range of bone objects has been recovered from the earliest levels of the Bhir Mound. Some of these, such as beads, pendants and hair pins, do not occur in the otherwise rich Stratum II, probably because of the greater use of metal and or bone substitutes. Other objects, such as draughtsmen or counters for games, and arrowheads, styli and spindle whorls, appear in Strata III and II, reflecting three distinct and perhaps mutually exclusive activities of hunting, writing, and the manufacture of textiles.

In an attempt to locate the evidence within the imperial framework, we can suggest that some activities such as hunting may have continued relatively unchanged, whereas others, such as writing, may have acquired greater importance and visibility. The latter was probably connected with the exigencies of record keeping for administrative and economic transactions. At another level, the substitution of bone by metal or stone would point to greater access to the resources of more or less distant regions. This may be symptomatic of a reworking of existing channels of communication in the interests of the population of Taxila. What is more, the ability to acquire and use substitutes for bone ornaments may have served as markers of social status both within the settlement and *vis-à-vis* outsiders. However, the argument cannot be pressed too far. The presence of spindle whorls, for example, cannot be taken to represent the introduction of weaving by the Mauryas.

As in the case of the use of bone, there is a shift in the use of stone. Leaving aside the evidence for semi-precious stone beads for the moment, we find that there is a proliferation of stone vessels, which would have been relatively difficult to make in Stratum II. These include dishes, saucers, cups, bowls and trays. Once again, the ability to use such vessels may have been confined to the urban elite. Like metal and stone jewellery which probably functioned as constituents of status.

There appears to have been a progressive increase in the use of copper. In all, 32 objects have been found, of which one bar of copper comes from Stratum IV, five artifacts from Stratum III and 26 from

Stratum II. These include bangles, pendants, various kinds of pins, needles, vessels, etc. The technology involved in producing these objects seems to have been fairly simple. Besides, these objects are not particularly spectacular in terms of number, quality or variety. Nevertheless, as in the case of the proliferation of pots and pans mentioned earlier, they seem to point to the growth of a relatively richer material culture as one moves from the earlier to the later strata.

Yet, this pattern is by no means uniform. Gold and silver artifacts (apart from punch-marked coins) are extremely rare in the Bhir Mound. Besides, most of these occur in Stratum III (including pendants, necklaces and amulets), while Stratum II, which is otherwise richer, has yielded only pendants. This may provide a useful corrective to attempts to trace a unilinear development.

At another level, one can speculate on whether the paucity of gold and silver had something to do with Taxila's status as a provincial centre. Probably its status of provincial centre ensured that some resources were directed towards and controlled by dominant groups whereas the most valued or prestigious, were regarded as the exclusive preserve of the imperial centre. Unfortunately, we have no means of testing this hypothesis.

The evidence of iron is more dramatic and tangible. Hence, the excavations from the earliest stratum are sparse, consisting of swords or daggers. Stratum III yields evidence for a few crafts tools, including adzes and knives, whereas Stratum II provides evidence for many more types of iron weapons, including spear heads or javelins, arrowheads, and an elephant goad. Craft tools such as axes, chisels, tongs, anvils, nails, iron hoe and household goods including bowls, spoons, sieves and a scale-pan. The scale-pan object probably had non-domestic uses as well.

Thus, on the one hand, the increasing use of iron can be linked to Taxila's position within the empire, on the other hand, the kinds of iron equipment produced and/or available suggests that this was intended to meet the requirements of specific social categories: warriors or soldiers and craftsmen. Additionally, one can suggest that iron was increasingly used as a substitute for copper, pottery and bone. In that capacity, it would have been available not only to the elite or specialist groups, but also to common people in their daily lives as well. In other words, while incorporation within the empire held different possibilities for different socio-economic categories, it was not necessarily a relationship of unmitigated exploitation between the ruler and the ruled.

The evidence from beads pertains to a different level of interaction, that of representing social status, indications which have been noticed earlier. As many as 1,763 beads have been recovered from the Bhir Mound. Of these 42 per cent are of semi-precious stones, 32 per cent of glass, and 14 per cent of shell. It is likely that different types of beads may have been used by different social strata, the use of semi-precious stones being confined to the urban elite.

Some of the most exquisitely finished beads at Taxila are associated with Stratum II. These include leech beads and pyramidal pendants of agate (Marshall 1975: 743–5), as well as triangular barrel beads and a range of amulets (ibid: 746). Marshall (1975: 731) suggests that beads of semi-precious stones may have been obtained from centres of production such as Ujjain, Vidisa, Bhrigukaccha or Nasik, whereas cheaper varieties may have been manufactured locally. If this is true, then access to these beads was probably related to incorporation within the exchange network created by the Mauryan Empire. At the same time, while certain bead types are not found in the post-Mauryan settlement of Sirkap, beads of semi-precious stones continued to be in use.

There is another facet of the distribution of beads which is worth noticing. While agate and carnelian occur in all three strata (IV–II), there is a sharp increase in their numbers from the earlier to the later strata. For example, while fourteen agate beads have been found in Stratum IV, the number increases to 104 in Stratum II. In the case of carnelian, there are only 34 beads from Stratum IV and as many as 224 from Stratum II.

If this points to the increasing availability and use of semi-precious stones, the situation is complicated by the growth in numbers of shell and glass beads as well. Forty-nine shell beads have been recovered from Statum IV, as opposed to 149 from Stratum II, while in the case of glass beads, the earlier stratum yielded 25 beads and the later one yielded 314. The glass beads in particular may have been meant as imitations of beads of semi-precious stones. As such, if the latter were symbols of status devised by the urban elite, the exclusive claims they represented could be called into question through such imitations. Thus, while the simultaneous proliferation of different kinds of beads may be explicable, their existence points to a fairly complex social interaction.

The other artifactual category where one notices a major shift in the evidence from the Bhir Mound is terracotta figurines. These are virtually absent in the lowest stratum. While a few types, including toy animals and *mithuna* figurines occur in Stratum III, we find many more female and male figurines, toy carts, wheeled animals, and pot-bellied figurines in Stratum II.

It is easy to classify some of these figurines as religious. Alternatively, one can locate them within the context of the empire. However, the relationship between political structures and art forms is notoriously complex. Without denying the possibility of such interpretations, we may for the present simply treat this as another instance of the growing and varied uses of a locally available material in a new political context.

While the evidence examined thus far constitutes implicit (and sometimes explicit) proof of various kinds of interaction, there are certain artifacts which evidently functioned as the medium of some of these transactions. These include coins and seals.

There are variations discernible in the punch-marked coins. The Bhir Mound has yielded 1,579 silver and copper punch-marked coins. Most of the silver coins have been found in two hoards, one, the apparently older hoard, consisting of 1,167 coins, and a second, evidently later collection, containing 116 coins. The repertoire of symbols used on these coins is evidently quite rich, with as many as 138 variants being recorded (Walsh 1975: 845).

As opposed to the silver coins, most of the copper coins (179) come from stratified contexts. These belong to a type which has been styled the local Taxilan coinage (Marshall 1975: 756). The bulk of the copper coins (134) found from the Bhir Mound come from Stratum II. Apart from distinct metals associated with different values, what distinguishes these two sets of coins are their symbols. Unlike the silver coins, copper coins are stamped with a more limited repertoire, including the typical Buddhist symbols like the *chaitya* or *stupa*, pillar and tree in railing (ibid: 757).

The coexistence of these two types (or, variants within a single system of coinage) probably represented the kinds of interactions between the Mauryan capital and provincial centres. Copper coins probably had a limited spatial range of circulation. However, they would have been used more intensively within the region for numerous small transactions. As such, it is probably significant that their issue does not seem to have been regulated from the relatively remote Pataliputra and they continued to be used even later, with as many as 502 being recovered from Sirkap (ibid: 756). Silver coins, on the other hand, had more in common with the coins found elsewhere in the empire and were obviously symbolic of a different kind of economic transaction. We are in no position to assess the volume of transactions conducted through one or the other medium. All that can be suggested is that the imperial apparatus did not or could not regulate exchanges beyond a certain level.

The evidence of seals from the Bhir Mound is also interesting. Two types have been identified: one, pyramidal, made of stones such as agate and carnelian, copper and glass, and the other scaraboid, made out of stone such as chalcedony and agate and glass. Apart from the material and shape, the techniques of seal-making, as well as representations on them, appear to have been distinctive (Marshall 1975: 674–7). The scaraboid seals indicate the use of a drill, whereas the pyramidal ones were probably engraved. While both represent mythical or ritual scenes, the scaraboid seals show a preference for mythical or real animals, including winged horses, whereas the pyramidal ones use symbols which can be traced in punch-marked coins and have parallels in Buddhist imagery. According to Marshall, the scaraboid seals are characteristically Persian, and as such represent contact with the west, whereas the pyramidal seals are more typically Mauryan.

As in the case of coins, it is likely that each of these seal types was used in distinctive transcations, although we may not be in a position to reconstruct their specificities at present.

A few terracotta sealings have been recovered from Taxila. These seem to bear some correspondence with the scaraboid variety both in terms of shape and representational motifs, the lion figuring in both. While the evidence is extremely limited (only seven sealings), this may suggest that such seals and sealings were particularly important for local transcations.

III

We have already suggested that an awareness of the imperial context may help us to arrive at a better understanding of the early historical Taxila. It is also likely that an awareness of both the uniqueness and commonalities of Mauryan provincial centres can enrich our perceptions of the polity.

One obvious axis of comparison is in terms of the other provincial centres named in Ashokan inscriptions. If Taxila is unique in being near other kingdoms, Suvarnagiri in the south may have had a different importance both on account of its proximity to gold mines and its interaction with possibly tribal peoples, like the Cholas, Pandyas, Satiyaputas, and Keralaputas (Rock Edict II). At another level, Sisupalgarh, located in a province which seems to have been more systematically annexed, may provide us with a different configuration. In the case of Ujjain, the evidence from pre-Mauryan settlements and its strategic location along important routes of communication between north and south India and between north and west India, may offer certain points of similarity with Taxila. While most of these sites may not provide us with comparable data, certain broad contours may emerge.

Another possible line of comparison is opened up by the Dharamarajika Stupa at Taxila. While the archaeological evidence is not particularly clear Marshall (1975: 236) suggests that the Taxilan stupa may have been constructed by Ashoka. Ashokan inscriptions refer to the enlargement of a single stupa, that of the Buddha Konakamana (Nigalisagar Pillar Inscription). The Buddhist tradition ascribes the construction of 84,000 stupas to the emperor, and there is more or less positive evidence for the nucleus of stupas being Mauryan in the case of Sarnath, Sanchi, and possibly Amaravati. If the core of the stupa at Taxila is indeed Mauryan, it would need to be located within the interesting frameworks of imperial and Buddhist geography.

Taxila can thus be situated in a variety of contexts—politico administrative, socio-cultural and, above all material. It is important for an understanding of the specificities of early historical urban centres, as it is for focusing on broader historical processes.

REFERENCES

Allchin, F. Raymond, 'The Urban Position of Taxila and Its Place in North-west India-Pakistan', in H. Spodek and Doris Meth Srinivasan (eds.), *Urban Form and Meaning in South Asia: the Shaping of Cities from Prehistory to Pre Colonial Times*, Washington: National Gallery of Art, 1993, pp. 69–80.

Allchin, F. Raymond, *The Archaeology of Early Historic South Asia: The Emergence of Cities and States*, Cambridge: Cambridge University Press, 1995.

Chakravarti, Uma, 'Renouncer and Householder in Early Buddhism', *Social Analysis Journal of Cultural and Social Practice*, vol. 13, 1983, pp. 70–83.

Dani, A.H., *The Historic City of Taxila*, UNESCO: The Centre for East Asian Cultural Studies, 1986.

Fussman, Gerard, 'Taxila: The Central Asian Connection', in H. Spodek and Doris Meth Srinivasan (eds.), *Urban Form and Meaning in South Asia: the Shaping of Cities from Prehistory of Pre Colonial Times*, Washington: National Gallery of Art, 1993, pp. 83–100.

Marshall, John, *Taxila: An Illustrated Account of Archaeological Investigation*, 3 vols., Delhi: Motilal Banarsidass, 1975.

Roy, Kumkum, *The Emergence of Monarchy in North India c. 8th to 4th Centuries BC, as Reflected in the Brahmanical Tradition*, New Delhi: Oxford University Press, 1994.

Thapar, Romila, *The Mauryas Revisited*, Calcutta: K.P. Bagchi, 1987.

Thaplyal, K.K., *Studies in Ancient Indian Seal: A study of North Indian Seals from c. Third Century BC to Mid Seventh Century AD*, Lucknow: Akhil Bharatiya Sanskrit Parishad, 1972.

Walsh, E.H.C., 'Two Hoards of Silver Punch-marked Coins found in the Bhir Mound at Taxila', in John Marshall (ed.), *Taxila: An Illustrated Account of Archaeological Excavations*, Cambridge: Cambridge University Press, 1951, vol. II, pp. 843–52.

6

Urban Centres in the North-West (*c.* AD 600–1200)

RENU THAKUR

In the light of the evidence of agrarian expansion and emergence of towns from north-western India, this paper examines the problem of urban decay during the early medieval period. Already, B.D. Chattopadhyaya and R. Champakalakshmi have worked on the growth and development of urban centres in early medieval India, unfolding many intricacies and answering various questions arising out of the hypothesis of urban decay in the post-Gupta period.[1] Chattopadhyaya holds the view that urban settlements were fairly common in India by the ninth century AD.[2] He has studied urban growth in north India especially with the help of epigraphic evidence and suggests that during the early medieval period large-scale local state formations led to the emergence of nodes in the form of political or exchange centres, or both. Proliferation of such nodes and linkages further resulted in inter-regional and intra-regional trade contacts.[3] However, he gives a rather sketchy information regarding the urban centres in the north-west, especially Kashmir, Himachal Pradesh, Haryana and Punjab.[4]

Champakalakshmi's study indicates that urbanization in south India was generated from within during the early medieval period through agrarian expansion and diverse economic activities.[5] Many *brahmadeya* and *devadana* settlements acquired the status of *taniyur* owing to increase in size, population and economic functions and formed a separate level of urban hierarchy performing urban functions.[6] Temples played a significant role in the development of urban settlements in early medieval south India.[7] A large-scale commercial activity gave impetus to the emergence and development of trade centres which resulted in organized trade through guilds.[8]

When we turn to the study of urban centres in the north-west during AD 600–1200, we find that sources like the *Vastusastras*, *Rajatarangini* and a few epigraphs from the adjoining areas, employ a number of epithets to denote urban settlements: *pura*,[9] *nagara*,[10] *adhisthana*[11] and *pattana*.[12] The *Samaranganasutradhara* alludes to three different types of *puras*, namely large, medium and small.[13] The *Aparajitaprccha* also mentions *puras* of varying dimensions, small, medium and large.[14] The *Manasara* refers to *pura* as a large city with gardens, dwellings of heterogenous population and frequented by sellers and buyers.[15] The terms *nagara* occurs in the *Aparajitaprccha* in the sense of a settlement smaller than a *pura*.[16] However, in epigraphs, *pura* and *nagara* have been used as synonyms.[17] Epigraphical evidence from Pehowa confirms that *adhisthana* was used to denote an urban settlement.[18]

Pattana figures in our sources quite frequently. According to the *Manasara*, *pattana* is situated close to waterways and has merchants.[19] It was a place at which different import and export transactions took place. The *Mayamatra*, a south Indian text, follows the *Manasara* and stipulates that the *pattana* is situated by the sea and is a place where products of other countries are found.[20] It is inhabited by the people of all classes. There are shops with abundance of merchandise such as grains, precious stones, fine cloth and perfumes. Inscriptions from other parts of north India confirm that the *pattana* primarily performed commercial functions. The records of AD 907 and AD 968 refer to Siyadoni in Jhansi district as *pattana*, with several *hattas* (markets) attached to the customs house (*mandapika*).[21]

Siyadoni town was a centre of exchange; it had contacts with other areas; and merchants from other areas used to deposit custom duties in its *mandapika*. The existence of special road for merchants (*vanijonijarathya*) further suggests that it was primarily a commercial town. Tattandapura identified as Ahar, situated on the western bank of the Ganga has been referred to as *pattana* in records ranging from AD 867 to AD 904.[22] The presence of merchants from Bhinmal, Mathura and Apapura (not yet identified), along with a number of roads in Tattandapura, suggests that it functioned as a commercial centre during the early medieval period.

We do not have any inscriptions from Kashmir which would have made easier for us to cross-check details regarding *pattana* stipulated in the *Rajatarangini*. A few inscriptions from Himachal Pradesh, which give us information on urban settlements during AD 600–1200, use epithets such as *pura* and *nagara*. The Pehowa inscription from Haryana also gives us valuable information. Excavations conducted at Ghuram in Patiala district and Rupar, suggest continuous habitation from earlier times.

Our study reveals that large-scale grants of land made to secular and religious beneficiaries resulted in agrarian expansion in the north-west of India. Several steps were taken to improve the productivity of land through irrigation. Special interest was taken by the authorities in the construction of irrigational canals and water wheels or *araghattas*.

II

Hiuen Tsang in the early seventh century, while giving general description of Kashmir, refers to it as a country where abundant fruits, flowers, saffron, medicinal plants, and horses of dragon stock were found.[23] Extension of agricultural land led to increase in agrarian production which is amply borne out by the fact that the average price of one *khari* of rice came down from 200 dinars to 36 dinars.[24] The growth in agriculture resulted in the establishment of a number of *hattas* or markets, which suggests brisk internal trade. Consequently, these market centres attracted traders from different regions and led to inter-regional and intra-regional trade. The hierarchical political order definitely led to the emergence of nodes in the form of politico-exchange centres which probably gave impetus to inter-regional and intra-regional movement of resources. The existence of *mandapika* in exchange centres also suggests outside trade contacts. Our sources acquaint us with a number of towns established by the royal family but they lack details about the exact planning and the extent of these settlements. How far temples influenced urban activity in the north-west during the early medieval period cannot be ascertained but large or small temples were a marked feature of these towns.

At the end of the sixth century, Pravarsena II founded a city called Pravarasenapura, identified with the present Srinagar. Kalhana describes it as situated at the confluence of two rivers with a hill in the centre. It had more than thirty-six lakhs of houses. Regularly arranged markets were a special feature of this town.[25] Bilhana, a writer of the eleventh century, refers to it as the principal city of Kashmir which surpassed all other cities in beauty.

The *Rajatarangini* refers to the establishment of Pratapapura, the present village of Tapar, by Durlabha Pratapaditya II of the Karkota dynasty in the seventh century. It is compared with the city of Indra, but no details are given.[26] The coming of numerous merchants to Kashmir from different directions however, confirms that it was a great centre of trade, owing to its proximity to north India, Tibet, Afghanistan and Central Asia.

The *Rajatarangini* also refers to the establishment of Parihasapura by Lalitaditya Muktapida in the first half of the eight century. It was located some 20 kilometres north-west of Srinagar on the left bank of the Vitasta (Jhelum). The king is credited with the construction of Brahmanical temples at his new capital.[27] The temples of Parihasakesava, Muktakesava, Mahavaraha and Govardhanadhara are mentioned in the *Rajatarangini.*[28] The remains of Buddhist edifices and temples confirm that it was an important urban settlement during the eighth century under the Karkota kings.

Excavations conducted by Daya Ram Sahni in the second decade of the twentieth century unearthed a monastery called Rajavihara and the remains of three buildings constructed by Lalitaditya.[29] Forty-four silver coins, belonging to Durlabhadeva, Muktapida, Jayapida, Vinayaditya and Vigrahtunga, were recovered from the excavation.[30] It was an important centre of cloth weaving in Kashmir. It had a big market where sale and purchase of livestock and other items was carried on.[31] Lalitaditya's queen is credited with the foundation of Kamalathatta in Parihasapura.[32] The establishment of *hatta* suggests that internal trade was carried on through regularly arranged markets, where different commodities were sold, These included wool, grapes, grapewine, rice, salt, pepper, asafoetida, horses, incense, sandal oil and clothes. The arrangement of markets within the various wards was a special feature of the town.[33] The regular visits of *desika* (local) traders to Kashmir suggest trade of Kashmir with other parts of India. Many hoards of coins of the eighth century, recovered from Aunjhar fortress in the Banda district of Uttar Pradesh and Rajghat in Benaras, indicate the wide circulation of coins struck in Kashmir. It is very likely that Kashmir had regular trade contacts with Uttar Pradesh.[34] Lalitaditya sent diplomatic missions to China, which suggests cordial relations with the Tang empire. Perhaps this could be one of the reasons of increase in Chinese maritime trade with India and the Middle East which led to the beginning of what has been called the 'first period of great oceanic commerce in the history of the world'.[35]

Lalitaditya is also credited with the building of the temple of Martanda along with a *pattana*, encircled with massive stone walls and ramparts. This *pattana* was intersected by lakes, rivers and mountains.[36] It was probably a great centre of pilgrimage and trade. The dearth of inscriptional evidence remains a major handicap in the reconstruction of its history as a commercial centre. But large-scale building of excellent temples suggests that expanding markets for goods definitely brought substantial revenues for the Kashmir ruler which enabled him to construct eloquent art edifices.

Avantivarman (AD 856–88) is credited with the foundation of the city of Avantipura which is represented by the present village of Vantipor, şituated on the right bank of the Vitasta.[37] The vast remains belonging to this city can by seen to this day. These remains consist of streets, houses, temples, images, terracotta objects, pottery and coins. The excavations conducted by Daya Ram Sahni recovered more than half a dozen temples.[38] The famous temple of Avantisvara built by Avantivarman figures in the *Rajatarangini*.[39] The chronicle informs us that prior to the foundation of Avantipura various steps were taken to improve the productivity of the area. Several embankments were built on the river Vitasta to control the flow of water to reclaim land on which numerous villages teeming with population were established.[40] The excavations conducted at this place yielded 108 copper coins 32 of which are completely worn out. The rest of these coins include twenty-two coins of Tormana, one coins of Samkarvarman, the successor of Avantivarman (AD 883–902), one coin of Queen Didda (AD 980–1003), three coins of Sangramaraja (AD 1003–28), two coins of Ananta (AD 1028–63), two coins of Kalasa (AD 1063–89), thirty-four coins of Jayasimhadeva (1128–49) and one of Vijaysuta Simhadeva (1287–1301).[41] Avantipura seems to have remained an important exchange centre from the ninth to the fourteenth century.

Samkarvarman (AD 883–902) founded the town of Samkarpattana.[42] It was famous as a centre of cloth-weaving and sale and purchase of livestock.[43] Probably numerous merchants visited this centre for better variety of wool, cattle and horses, which seems to be the major reason why this town could flourish even after Samkarvarman's reign.[44]

III

Pehowa in the Karnal district of Haryana has been called an *adhisthana* in an epigraph of AD 882–3 of the Gurjara Pratiharas. The inscription furnishes details of a fair held at Pehowa in which horses were bought and sold. The horse dealers came from nine different localities.[45] All these localities appear to be Indian. This suggests that Indians of the north-west acted as intermediary dealers in horse trade. This is confirmed by the *Rajatarangini* which refers to the *desika* (local) horse dealers visiting Kashmir for horse trade.[46] Regular purchase of horses was done in Kashmir where better breeds of horses from Afghanistan and Central Asia were available.[47] It is clear that north Indian merchants actively participated in horse trade. The restrictions imposed in contemporary Brahmanical texts against this trade lost their force in the face of huge profits. Pehowa was also an important pilgrimage centre where people came from distant lands for attaining spiritual merit. Probably this was the main reason for the development of Pehowa as a centre of activity. The networks of horse dealers of the north-west enabled them to supply horses to the kings and the local lords. Al-Idrisi refers to another city in Hary and Karnal (Atrasa), situated on the western frontier of the Ganges, as a large, well built and well-watered town.[48]

Thaneshwar, near Ambala, was another important town of early medieval India. It was noticed in the early seventh century as a densely populated place where the majority of the people pursued trade and only a few were agriculturists. Rare and valuable merchandise was brought to Thaneshwar from different places. The families living here were rich and led a luxurious life.[49] In the eleventh century, Al-Biruni also refers to Thaneshwar as an important city.[50] It appears to have remained an important urban centre throughout the early medieval period.

Ropar, some 60 miles from Ambala, on the river Sutlej, witnessed a succession of occupations from the Harappan to nearly the present times. Period V, commencing from about the ninth century and lasting for two or three centuries, reveals a spacious brick building neatly constructed. Three or four types of pottery, ivory bangles, and an ivory needle are some other artifacts unearthed from the site.[51] The habitational area of Period V remained confined to the southern part of the site now occupied by the present town. Explorations conducted in the adjoining area also indicate a similar pattern. The entire region was probably very prosperous during the early medieval period.

Ghuram in Patiala district was a fortified township during the under study period.[52] This place served as the official residence of the governor. The remains of sculptures, pillars and water channels for storing water for cooling rooms have been recovered. It was devastated in 1710 by Banda Bahadur.

IV

In Himachal Pradesh, Brahmapura (Bharmaur) was the capital of Meruvarman in AD 680.[53] Several remains in the form of imposing temples such as Mani Mahesa, Lakshana Devi, Ganesa and Narsimha are intact to this date. Innumerable land grants were made for the maintenance of these temples in Brahmapura which served as the capital till AD 920 when Sahilavarman shifted it to Champa or Chamba. The shifting of the capital from a remote area to a fertile land was favourable for the appropriation of revenue from the land-owning chieftains. Chamba was more intimately connected with the Punjab plains on the south. Sahilavarman beautified his new capital and built many temples. For carving sculptures for the newly-built temples, he sent his sons to the Vindhyas for procuring the best quality of marble.[54]

Kangra, the ancient Trigarta, was one of the leading hill states of the ancient and medieval Punjab. A part of the kingdom of Jalandhara, Hiuen Tsang's testimony confirm that the kingdom of Jalandhara existed in the seventh century. Utbi refers to Bhimanagar, and Firishta uses the epithet Nagarkot or Bhimkot for Kangra.[55] All accounts agree that Nagarkot was the same as Kot Kangra. The town was surrounded by the Ban Ganga, a tributary of the river Beas.[56] It was a strong centre of power under the Shahi rulers. Here they deposited heavy treasures when they were ousted from Kabul. This fort was plundered by Mahmud of Ghazni who carried away all its accumulated wealth: stamped coins amounting to 70,000 royal dirhams, gold and silver ingots amounting to 700 maunds in weight, soft and embroidered clothing, a folding house made of silver, and a richly decorated throne.[57] It is almost impossible that such vast wealth was amassed by the petty rulers of the Kangra valley. A large number of silver and copper coins of the horseman and bull types of the Shahis have been recovered from Kangra and its vicinity.[58] Nagarkot remained a centre of power of the Shahi rulers. This is confirmed by the information provided by Al-Biruni: a genealogical list of the Shahi rulers, written on a piece of silk, was found in the fort of Nagarkot.[59]

The Baijnath *prasastis*, discovered from Baijnath, 23 miles east of Nagarkot,[60] give important information regarding the towns of Susarmapura (Kangra), and Kiragrama, a frontier station in the beginning of the thirteenth century. Two headmasons, Nayaka and Thoduka, were called from Kangra to build a temple at Kiragrama, the seat of the *rajanaka* Lakshmana Chandra. This suggests that expert artisans usually lived in large towns and were paid handsome amount when they were called to build imposing edifices in other areas. Lakshmana Chandra granted 6 *drammas* daily for the maintenance of the temple from the custom house (*mandapika*). Two rich merchants got a temple constructed at Kiragrama and contributed for its maintenance income out of an oil mill, a shop (*panayasala*), and a piece of land in the neighbouring village of Navagrama.

The detail found in the epigraph shows that trade was carried on by *vaniks* who were rich enough to invest heavy amounts in the construction of excellent temples. This also reveals that articles for sale were kept in the *panyasalas*. The commodities obtained from outside were charged custom duties at the custom house (*mandapika*). This seems to imply outside trade contacts, which is further confirmed by a Jain inscription found in the same temple. It mentions two rich Gujarati merchants, named Alhana and Dolhana, who were responsible for the construction of Mahavira temple and dedicated a statue, consecrated by Duabhadra Suri, who was an adherent of one of the subdivisions of Kharataragachchha which arose at Anhilvadapattana in Gujarat. Remnants of old buildings and tanks and coins found in the vicinity of Baijnath from time to time indicate that it was an important settlement during the early medieval period.

The evidence cited in the foregoing paragraphs suggests that hierarchical political order resulted in the emergence of nodal points as exchange centres. The ruling elite took measures to improve the productivity of land by providing better irrigational facilities. They granted land to numerous beneficiaries, which resulted in the increase of arable land. Agrarian production could meet the demand for surplus. Trade relations developed between various regions and with some other countries. All these factors converged to make urban development a recognizable phenomenon in the north-west during the early medieval period.

NOTES AND REFERENCES

1. For the exposition of this hypothesis, see R.S. Sharma, *Urban Decay in India (c. 300–c. 1000)*, New Delhi: Munshiram Manoharlal, 1987.
2. Sharma postulates that mild urban renewal began in the eleventh century and its became a recognizable process by the fourteenth century. Ibid., p. 185.
3. B.D. Chattopadhyaya, 'Trade and Urban Centres in Early Medieval North India', *Indian Historical Review*, vol. 1, no. 2, pp. 203–19; 'Markets and Merchants in Early Medieval Rajasthan, *Social Science Probings*, vol. 24, pp. 413–40; 'Urban Centres in Early Medieval India: An Overview', in S. Bhattacharya and R. Thapar, *Situating Indian History*, New Delhi: OUP, 1986, pp. 8–33; *The Making of Early Medieval India*, New Delhi: OUP, 1994; 'State and Economy in North India: Fourth Century to Twelfth Century', in Romila Thapar (ed.), *Recent Perspectives of Early Indian History*, Bombay: Popular Prakashan, 1995, pp. 309–46.
4. Chattopadhyaya, 'Trade and Urban Centres in Early Medieval North India', p. 219.
5. R. Champakalakshmi, 'State and Economy: South India, circa AD 400–1300', in Thapar (ed.), *Recent Perspectives of Early Indian History*, pp. 288–90.
6. R. Champakalakshmi, *Trade, Ideology and Urbanization: South India 300 BC to AD 1300*, New Delhi: OUP, 1996, pp. 378–81.
7. R. Champakalakshmi, 'Growth of urban centres in India: Kudamukku-Palaiyarai, the twin city of the Cholas', *Studies in History*, vol. 1, no. 1, pp. 1–30.
8. This is also shown by Champakalakshmi, *Trade, Ideology and Urbanization.* Meera Abraham's study of *Medieval Merchant Guilds of South India* (New Delhi: Manohar, 1988) shows organized internal and maritime commerce as a significant feature of South India from the ninth century onwards.
9. *Rajatarangini: The Saga of the Kings of Kashmir*, tr. Ranjit Sitaram Pandit, New Delhi: Sahitya Academi, 1968, 8. 1054. *Epigraphica Indica* (*EI*), vol. 1, pp. 107 and 127.
10. *Rajatarangini*, 6.70. *EI*, vol. 1, pp. 1 and 107.
11. *EI*, vol. 1, pp. 184–90.
12. *Rajatarangini*, 4.10, 11 and 192.
13. *Samaranganasutradhara of Maharajadhiraja Bhoja* (*The Parmar Rulers of Dhara*) rev. and ed. by Vasudev Saran Agrawala, Gaekwad's Oriental Series No. 25, Baroda: Oriental Institute, 1966.
14. *Aparajitaprccha of Bhuvandeva*, ed. P.A. Mankad, Gaekwad's Oriental Series No. CXV, Baroda: Oriental Institute, 1950, 2.17; 72.1–2.

15. *Architecture of Manasara*, tr. P.K. Acharya, Manasara Series, vol. IV, rpt., New Delhi, 1980, 10.53–55.
16. *Aparajitaprccha*, 72.1–3.
17. In the Baijnath *prasastis* a town Susarma has been referred to as both Susarmanagara and Susarmapura.
18. Srinagar has been mentioned in the sources as *adhisthan* which would make it an urban centre during the early medieval period. Edward C. Sachau (ed.), *Alberuni's India*, New Delhi: Low Price Publications, 1989, p. 207. Gwalior or Gopagiri has been referred to as *adhisthana. EI*, vol. 1, pp. 154–62.
19. *Manasara*, 10.63–6.
20. *Mayamata: An Indian Traatise on Housing, Architecture and Iconography*, tr. Bruno Dagens, New Delhi: Sitaram Bhartia Institute of Scientific Research, 1985, 10.28–9.
21. *EI*, vol. 1, pp. 162–79.
22. Ibid., vol. 19, pp. 52–4.
23. Samuel Beal, tr., *Si-Yu-Ki: Buddhist Records of the Western World*; rpt, New Delhi: Oriental Book Reprint Corporation, 1983, p. 148.
24. *Rajatarangini*, 5.116.
25. Ibid., 3.358.
26. Ibid., 4.10.
27. Ibid., 4.194.
28. Ibid., 4.195–8.
29. *Archaeological Survey of India: Annual Report* (*ASI: AR*), New Delhi, 1915–16, pp. 56–60.
30. Loc. cit.
31. *Rajatarangini*, 5.162.
32. Ibid., 4.208; 3.358.
33. Loc. cit.
34. Andre Wink, *Al-Hind: The Making of the Indo-Islamic World*, vol. 1, New Delhi: OUP, 1990, p. 246.
35. John K. Fairbank, et al., *East Asia: Tradition and Transformation*, London: Houghton Miffin, 1973, p. 135.
36. *Rajatarangini*, 4.192.
37. Ibid., 5. 44.
38. *ASI: AR*, 1913–14, pp. 40–61.
39. *Rajatarangini*, 5.189.
40. Ibid., 5. 156.
41. *ASI: AR*, 1913–14, pp. 40–61.
42. *Rajatarangini*, 5.162.
43. Loc. cit.
44. Ibid., 5.211.

45. *EI*, vol. 1, pp. 184–90.
46. *Rajatarangini*, 8.493.
47. Ibid., 8.73.
48. H.M. Elliot and John Dowson, *The History of India as Told by its Own Historians*, Allahabad: Kitab Mahal, n.d., vol. 1, p. 91. Andre Wink, *Al-Hind*, p. 299.
49. Beal, *Si-Yu-Ki*, p. 183.
50. Sachau, *Alberuni's India*, p. 199.
51. *Ancient India* (*AI*), no. 9, pp. 123–6.
52. *Indian Archaeology—A Review* (*IAR*), 1976–7; pp. 44–5.
53. J.Ph. Vogel, *Antiquities of Chamba State*, pt. I, *Archaeological Survey of India, New Imperial Series* (*ASI, NIS*), vol. 36, Calcutta, 1991, *passim.*
54. J. Hutchison and J.Ph. Vogel, *History of the Panjab Hill States*, 2 vols, Simla: Department of Languages and Culture, Himachal Pradesh, 1933, pp. 279–80.
55. Elliot and Dowson, *History of India*, vol. I, p. 34 and note 1.
56. Ibid., p. 445.
57. Ibid., p. 35.
58. P.L. Gupta, *Numismatic History of Himachal Pradesh*, New Delhi: B.R. Publishing Corporation, 1988, p. 37.
59. Elliot and Dowson, *History of India*, vol. 1, pp. 10 and 410.
60. G. Buhler, 'The Two Prasastis of Baijnath', *EI*, vol. 1, 1892, pp. 97–118.

7

Medieval Lahore: Production and Trade

K.K. TRIVEDI

> People that are attached to the world will collect in towns, without which there would be no progress.

In these few words, Abul Fazl appreciates the dynamic role of towns in a society.[1] In the light of this general observation, we propose to study the city of Lahore as a centre of production and trade and its links with other urban centres in and outside the Indian subcontinent. The politico-administrative role of Lahore, already covered in a number of historical works,[2] does not fall within the scope of the present discussion.

Lahore was first noticed in the tenth century.[3] One source mentions the location of a fort there.[4] This suggests that various kinds of activities in this region had reached a level which prompted some superior authority to station itself for deriving maximum benefit out of the economic developments around it.

Another source depicts the yearning of an exile from Lahore for its products.[5]

When the Punjab region came under the control of the Sultans of Delhi, they introduced the *iqta* system from the very beginning to tighten their control. Large areas were placed under the charge of the *muqtis.* The new arrangement brought larger surplus into the hands of a few. Along with their contingents the *muqtis* had to station themselves at one of the most developed centres of the territory under their control. Lahore was one such centre. The *muqti,* his retinue and his contingent soon generated additional demands for goods and services, including new items of consumption. Lahore became an integral part of the Sultanate, making inter-regional interaction much more pronounced.

The turmoil created by the Mongol expansion resulted in the migration of people in large numbers to safer areas. Lahore was the major town on entry to the subcontinent from the north-west. The immigrants added to the population and the skills of the town, making it more important as a centre of production.

Historical works of the Sultanate period focus on the activities of the court and the ruling elite, and contain only incidental references to its economy. The observations of the travellers like Ibn Battuta, Shihab al-Din al-Umari and Marco Polo, combined with the stray references of the historians, provide some glimpses of production and trade in India. For instance, varieties of sugar products were available in sufficient quantities.[6] Indigo was produced in Gujarat and some other regions.[7] Slowly but progressively the trading activities noticed during the early medieval period developed India's trade relations with the regions on its north west.[8] Lahore being the major town on the route played an active role in this context. Enquiries received at Lahore for some of the items must have encouraged production of new items as well as expansion of the existing ones. Produce from remote areas must also have found encouraging response from Lahore. Slowly and steadily, Lahore developed into an important entrepot in long distance trade. Emergence of new centres of production in its vicinity was linked to this development. Since it was not possible for outside merchants to fruitfully interact with the producers, especially due to the language barrier, trading houses of Lahore arranged supplies for them and encouraged the producers to undertake manufacture of newer and finer varieties. Some of these items came to be known after the town from which these were normally obtained, like the 'Lahore indigo'.[9]

Indeed, Lahore sent products of the subcontinent far and wide in the international trade. Sher Shah was perhaps the first Indian ruler who took serious note of this fact and tried to give it further push by repairing and realigning a very long route, linking the north-west with as far a place in the east as Sonargaon in Bengal. This route established closer contacts with other production centres like Dariyabad, Khairabad, Jaunpur, Benaras and Patna.[10]

The fortunes of Lahore were affected in the sixteenth century by the emergence of Agra as the most important centre of exchange in nothern India.[11] The importance of Agra was noticed thus by Pelsaert:[12]

> All goods must pass this way, as from Gujarat, Tatta (or Sind); from Kabul, Kandahar, or Multan, to the Deccan; from the Deccan or Burhanpur to those places, or to Lahore; and from Bengal and the whole East country; there are no

practical alternate routes, and the roads carry indescribable quantities of merchandise, especially cotton.

However, Lahore continued to function as a vital link between the subcontinent and the other Asian regions. The accounts of the European traders indicate that Lahore developed into a big centre for the production of a variety of items and provided lucrative market for products from other trade centres leading to the growth of satellite towns in the region.

By the time the *Ain-i-Akbari* was written, Lahore had become renowned for its carpet weaving, woollen, silken and mixed fabrics, so much so that a Mughal imperial *karkhana* was established there to look after the royal needs.[13] Other establishments numbering around one thousand, according to the *Ain*, were actively engaged in this line of production. Shawl weaving was also undertaken in the imperial *karkhana.* On account of its fine variety and beautiful patterns, a kind of shawl called *miyal* (which had an admixture of silk in it) was used as a turban (*chira*) and as a band (*fota*).[14] Production was influenced by the demand generated by the upper sections of the society. The presence of a large number of shawl weaving establishments strongly suggests that inferior and coarser variety were also produced, including the varieties produced in the satellite towns, for local and outside markets.[15] Lahore remained on the list of the European companies for procurement of a variety known as painted cloth.[16]

A number of crafts that attained great perfection at Lahore are unfortunately not mentioned in the contemporary works. The tradition, however, continued and was noticed at a much later period. Important among these activities were enamelling, wood-carving, gold damascening, copper and brass-smith's crafts, stone-carving, lapidary work, seal engraving, precious stone-cutting and inlay stonework. Gold damascened matcholocks, shields, swords, *charaina* (set of armour) and similar other objects were made here. The potters (*kasahgars*) of Lahore were known for their coloured tiles and painted and glazed pottery. Many of these traditions survived till the early years of the twentieth century.[17]

The *Ain* mentions construction of large sea-worthy vessels at lahore which were floated down the river to the sea. Along with these, smaller barges were also constructed, with the carrying capacity of about 60 tons for regular ply over the river Ravi to Multan and Thatta which also carried merchandise brought from Kashmir.[18]

Construction of buildings was a large scale activity at Lahore. 'Once the builder is dead', says Pelsaert, 'no one will care for the buildings . . . everyone tries, as far as possible, to erect a new building of his own, and establish his own reputation alongside that of his ancestors'.[19] A growing population and changing fortunes acted as an additional factor for an active building industry. Babur testifies to the presence of large number of stone-cutters and 'numberless artisans and workmen of every sort in Hindustan'.[20]

Some of the surviving buildings at Lahore are: the fort, the Jami Masjid built by Raja Bhagwan Das, the Shahi Masjid which had cost Aurangzeb more than Rs. 500,000 and the mosque of Wazir Khan (a physician by profession) who constructed several houses and shops for its maintenance. Asaf Khan is reputed to have spent Rs. 2,000,000 on the construction of his mansion.

Lahore exercised tremendous influence on areas in its close proximity by providing an outlet for their products. Some of the satellite towns which greatly benefitted from Lahore were Sialkot (for embroidered and plain muslin, brocade, daggers and paper), Gujrat (for embroidered muslin), Sirhind and Sultanpur (for chintz), and Samana and Machhiwara (for calico).[21]

Production activities, especially the textiles, had a marked impact on the agricultural sector. The *Ain* records the cultivation of cotton and indigo in all the *sarkars* of the *suba* of Lahore.[22] However, it is difficult to say which of these received maximum advantage as a result of increase in demand. Manrique refers to the cultivation of indigo in the region between Lahore and Multan.[23] He notices the indigo produced at one particular place.[24] However the term 'Lahore indigo' was used for the indigo produced and processed elsewhere and marketed from Lahore.[25] For sugar products, both ordinary and candied, Lahore was considered to be the best in the subcontinent.[26]

Lahore was also important for the Multani merchants.[27] Their domination in the Delhi markets during the thirteen-fourteenth centuries is suggestive of their wide reach in the north Indian markets.[28] Perhaps the navigability of the river Ravi, between Lahore and Multan, was considered an added advantage for the frequency of travel between these two places and beyond. This was certainly a shorter and more hospitable route in comparison with travel to Gujarat, or north India, through Bikaner and Jaisalmer.[29]

How and when the local traders of Lahore assumed prominence is not clear.[30] Yet the annual transport of 12,000 to 14,000 camel-loads of merchandise from Lahore to Persia in the early years of the seventeenth century is a fair indication of their participation in trade on a large scale.[31] One cannot rule out the possibility that sometime under the Sultans of Delhi, the Lahore traders had started looking for shorter and alternate routes to directly reach the markets of Central Asia. On one of these, perhaps, Babur travelled to reach Lahore.[32] Perhaps the difficulties on this route induced Sher Shah to build a road upto Peshawar for directly reaching Kabul.[33] The availability of this route is borne out by the fact that Akbar preferred it when he constructed forts further on this route in the direction of Kabul.

On all major routes to Lahore, *sarais* (rest-houses) were constructed at regular intervals, both by the rulers and the nobles.[34] Separate arrangements were made not only for Hindus and Muslims but also for 'foreigners'. Many of these *sarais* were very large structures which could sometimes accommodate 2,000 to 3,000 persons at a time, together with their horses and camels.[35] Moreover, the volume and variety of items moving in an out of Lahore in different directions had become possible on account of the development of a complex monetary system. One could purchase a bill of exchange for any amount for any of the market centres of the subcontinent or even for regions outside India.[36]

The diverse production and intense commercial activity of Lahore, added to its role as the provincial capital and an important centre of Sufi saints. The opportunities available at such an active centre should also have attracted people of varied professional attainments in search of lucrative employment. At times the city was found incapable of providing shelter to all coming to it. Manrique observed that 'large as it appeared, there was not houses enough for the accommodation of the people, who were encamped on half a league outside the city'.[37] We have no information on the population of Lahore but it certainly reached six figures at the end of the sixteenth century.

Our study of Lahore shows that its origin goes back to the early medieval period. From its very initial stages it was involved in productive activities. Gaining much from the commercial activity of the Multani merchants, the city became an independent centre of trade, with its network of far-flung linkages. It own manufactures entered the trade.

As a contemporary observed: 'The city of Lahore is inhabited by great and rich merchants who deal with the whole of India, and it is the key to the kingdoms of Kabul, Balkh, Tartary, Kaṣhmir, Persia, Multan, Bhakkar aṇd Tattah'.[38]

NOTES

1. Abul Fazal, *Ain-i Akbari*, tr. H. Blochmann, Delhi, 1965, p. 232, Persian text of the *Ain-i Akbari*, ed. H. Blochmann, Calcutta: Bibliotheca Indica, 1872, p. 167.
2. For extensive references of the politico-administrative role of Lahore, see Hamida Khatoon Naqvi, *Urban Centres and Industries in Upper India, 1556–1803*, Bombay, 1968; *Urbanization and Urban Centres Under the Great Mughals*, Simla, 1972. Muhammad Habib, 'The Urban Revolution in Northern India', in K.A. Nizami (ed.), *Politics and Society During the Early Medieval Period*, vol. I, Delhi, 1974. M.P. Singh, *Town, Market, Mint and Port in the Mughal Empire*, Delhi, 1985. Tapan Ray Chaudhuri and Irfan Habib (eds.), *The Cambridge Economic History of India, c. 1200–c. 1750*, vol. 1, Delhi, 1984. Shireen Moosvi, *The Economy of the Mughal Empire, c. 1595: A Statistical Study*, Delhi, 1987. Stephen Blake, *Shahjahanabad: The Sovereign City in Mughal India, 1639–1739*, New York, 1991.
3. Muhammad Baqir, *Lahore, Past and Present*, Delhi, 1993, p. 1. Contemporary sources refer to the place variously as Lauhavar, Lahur, Lauhur, Lahavar, Lohor, and Lahor.
4. Gardizi, *Zainul Akhbar*, refers to a fort, while the earliest reference to a market at Lahore is available in the *Hududul Alam*: Baqir, *Lahore, Past and Present*, pp. 2 and 4.
5. Ibid, p. 8 Musud bin Sad Salman (d. 1121), a Punjabi poet imprisoned in Ghazna, yearned for Lahore and its products.
6. Shihab al-Din al-Umari, *Masalik al Absar fi Mamalik al-Amsar*, tr. Iqtidar Husain Siddiqi and Qazi Muhammad Ahmad, Aligarh, 1971, p. 34.
7. *The Travels of Marco Polo*, tr. R.E. Latham, London, 1958, pp. 261, 265 and 267.
8. B.D. Chattopadhyaya, 'Trade and Urban Centres in Early Medieval North India', *Indian Historical Review*, vol. 1, no. 2, pp. 203–19. V.K. Jain, *Trade and Traders in Western India*, Delhi, 1990, passim.
9. F. Pelsaert, *Jahangir's India*, Delhi, 1972, p. 30.
10. Nizamuddin Ahmad, *Tabaqat-i Akbari*, tr. B. De (rev. and ed. Beni Prasad), Delhi, 1990, p. 106.

11. K.K. Trivedi, 'The Emergence of Agra as a Capital and a City: A Note on its Spatial and Historical Background during the Sixteenth and Seventeenth Centuries', *Journal of Economic and Social History of the Orient*, vol. 37, p. 164.
12. Pelsaert, *Jahangir's India*, p. 6.
13. *Ain-i-Akbari*, pp. 101 and 104–6. Nicolao Manucci, *Storia do Mogor, 1656–1712*, tr. W. Irvine, London, 1907–8, vol. 2, p. 424. *English Factories in India, 1618–69*, ed. W. Foster, Oxford, 1906–27, (*1618–21*), p. 51. Pelsaert, *Jahangir's India*, p. 31.
14. *Ain-i-Akbari*, p. 104.
15. Ibid., pp. 105–11.
16. *English Factories* (*1618–21*), pp. 51–2. Pelsaert, *Jahangir's India*, p. 9. Manucci, *Storia do Mogor*, vol. 2, p. 424. Jean-Baptiste Tavernier, *Travels in India*, tr. V. Ball, ed. W. Crooke, Delhi, 1977, p. 4.
17. George Watts and Percy Brown, *Arts and Crafts of India: A Descriptive Study*, Delhi, 1979, pp. 25, 44–5, 87 and 89. Manucci, *Storia do Mogor*, vol. 2, p. 424.
18. Pelsaert, *Jahangir's India*, pp. 30–1.
19. Ibid., p. 56. For the ruinous condition of buildings for want of maintenance at Lahore, F. Bernier, *Travels in the Mughal Empire, 1656–1668*, tr. A. Constable, Delhi, 1972, p. 384.
20. Zahiruddin Muhammad Babur, *Baburnama*, tr. A.S. Beveridge, Delhi, 1970, rep., p. 520.
21. Sujan Rai Bhandari, *Khulasat-ut Tawarikh*, ed. M. Zafar Hasan, Delhi: 1918, pp. 66, 72, 75, 83 and 91–94. *English Factories* (*1618–21*), pp. 46–7 and 168; (*1624–9*), p. 149; (*1637–41*), pp. 134–5; (*1642–5*), pp. 204 and 301. F.S. Manrique, *Travels of Fray Sebastian Manrique 1629–1643*, tr. C.E. Luard, London, 1927, vol. 2, p. 182.
22. *Ain-i-Akbari*, p. 380.
23. Manrique, *Travels*, vol. 2, p. 221.
24. Jean de Thevenot, 'Relation de Hindostan, 1666–7', tr. A. Lovell, *The Indian Travels of Thevenot and Careri*, ed. S.N. Sen, New Delhi, 1949, p. 68. Manrique, *Travels*, vol. 2, p. 180.
25. Pelsaert, *Jahangir's India*, p. 30. The author knew that the 'Lahori indigo' which reached Europe in the earlier period was not produced in the Punjab.
26. *English Factories* (*1637–41*), p. 135. About extensive cultivation of sugarcane in the region, Ziauddin Barani, *Tarikh-i-Firuzshahi*, ed. Sir Sayyid Ahmad, Calcutta, 1891, p. 568; *Baburnama*, p. 388. Thevenot, *Indian Travels*, p. 85.
27. During this period, the Lahore region is mentioned as a dependency of the power centre at Multan. Baquir, *Lahore Past and Present*, pp. 2 and 5.

28. Barani, *Travels*, p. 120.
29. For these routes, Jean Delouche, *Transport and Communications in India Prior to Steam Locomotion*, 2 vols., vol. 1: *Land Transport*, tr. James Walker, Delhi, 1993, map opposite page 27. *Alberuni's India*, tr. Edward C. Sachau, Delhi, 1989, pp. 205–6.
30. Chetan Singh, *Region and the Empire: Panjab in the Seventeenth Century*, Delhi, 1991, pp. 173–203, *Tuzuk-i Jahangiri*, ed. Sir Sayyid Ahmad, Aligarh, 1863–4, p. 35.
31. Thomas Roe states that 20,000 camel-loads from Agra and elsewhere passed through Lahore annually, *Embassy of Sir Thomas Roe, 1615–19*, ed. W. Foster, London, 1926, p. 446.
32. *Baburnama*, pp. 238–9.
33. This was not an isolated case. Other important roads 'constructed' by Sher Shah include Agra to Burhanpur, Agra to Jodhpur and Chittor, and Lahore to Multan. On these, he had also built *sarais* (rest-houses). Abbas Khan Sarwani, *Tarikh-i Sher Shahi*, ed. Imamuddin, Dacca, 1964, pp. 216–17.
34. Strangely, only Thevenot mentions the *sarais* inside the Lahore city: *Indian Travels*, pp. 60–1.
35. Manucci, *Storia do Mogor*, vol. 1, p. 69. Thevenot, *Indian Travels*, p. 48.
36. *Letters Received by the East India Company from its Servants in the East, 1602–17*, 6 vols, vol. I, ed. F.C. Danvers, London, 1896, p. 106; vol. 4, pp. 196–7; vol. 6, p. 164. *English Factories (1618–21)*, pp. 85–6 and 181–2. Tavernier, *Travels*, vol. 2, p. 36.
37. Manrique, *Travels*, vol. 2, p. 191.
38. Manucci, *Storia do Mogor*, vol. 2, p. 424.

8

Medieval Sirhind

IQBAL HUSAIN

Tradition traces Sirhind to the early medieval period when Sahir Rao, the ruler of Lahore, is said to have founded the place.[1] This, perhaps, was meant to explain its earlier name of 'Sahrind'. It was believed to form the eastern limit of the dominions of Jaipal, the king of Ohind.

Tracing the origin of Sirhind, Raverty found that the *Tabaqat-i Nasiri* mentioned the place as Tabarhinda or Tabarhind, while the printed text refers to it as Sirhind.[2] In the *Tarikh-i Mubarak Shahi*, both Tabarhinda and Sirhind are referred to.[3] From a close reading of its printed text it appears that wherever Tabarhind is mentioned, it referred to the fort while Sirhind stood for the territorial limits of the *iqta* or the *khitta*.[4] 'Tabarhind' would of course be 'Sirhind' with dots added in the first part of the name in Arabic characters.[5] Sirhind seems to have gained importance during the reign of Feroze Shah Tughlaq who separated it from Samana and formed a separate division (*shiqq*) in 1359, appointing Zainul Mulk Shamsuddin Abu Raza[6] to hold its charge.[7] Thereafter Sirhind became an important urban centre and a populous place, an Afghan settlement grew here.[8] Later on Sunam was placed under Sirhind.[9] In 1447 Khizr Khan assigned Sirhind to Malik Sultan Khan Lodi. This accelerated the pace of Afghan migration to Sirhind.[10]

The process of urbanization in Sirhind seems to have suffered a setback due to Babur's invasion. Despite gallant resistance offered by the people, especially the Mundharis of *pargana* Kaithal, Sirhind had to face the brunt of the invading forces.[11] According to Bayazid, when Humayun reached Sirhind after his return from Persia, Sikandar Sur appeared on the scene with a strong force of 100,000 Afghans to check his advance.[12] Sikandar Sur was defeated and Humayun forced his way into Delhi. It is likely that Sirhind suffered a further setback in the reign of Humayun.

Humayun's rule, however, was short lived. His accidental death in 1556 and the accession of Akbar to the throne gave some respite to the people of Sirhind, especially the Afghans who were dominant there. It seems that the political transition and the recapture of power by the Mughals from the Surs did not affect the fortunes of the Afghan settlers at Sirhind.

After having consolidated his position at Agra, Akbar seems to have considered the Afghan concentration in the Punjab as a menace to his power. Abul Fazl provides justification for the dispersal of Afghans from the Punjab. Akbar told Raja Todar Mal that the Afghans settled in the towns and the villages of the Punjab as traders and husbandmen were oppressing the weak. Consequently he gave orders that the Afghans should be scattered. Todar Mal sent detachments to different provinces so that the people might obtain relief.[13] This dispersal of the Afghans from Sirhind probably depopulated the place.

Though Sirhind suffered from this policy of dispersal, it seems to have regained its former position with considerable development in trade and commerce. Credit for the revival of Sirhind also goes to Akbar. One of his *shiqdars*, Hafiz Rakhna, took a great interest in the development of Sirhind.[14] Khwaja Nizamuddin Ahmad says that while marching to Lahore to suppress the rebellion of Mirza Hakim in 1567, Akbar arrived at Sirhind. Applauding Hafiz Rakhna for his work, Akbar assigned him the *sarkardari* (commissionership) of Sirhind. Later on Hafiz Rakhna seems to have been raised to the position of the *karori* of Sirhind. His interest in promoting trade and commerce resulted in the establishment of new *bazaars* there.[15] Hence, at this time Sirhind emerged as an important urban centre.

Monserrate's description of Sirhind is noteworthy: 'The city is of great size and is divided into separate quarters, in which respect it resembles Memphis of Egypt'.[16] Monserrate further tells us that Sirhind had a famous school of medicine, from where physicians were sent out to all parts of the empire. Bows, quivers, shoes, greaves, and sandals were also made in Sirhind and exported to all the cities of the Mughal empire.[17] A mint had also been established here for minting copper coins.[18]

Hafiz Rakhna seems to have had a great sense of building beautiful gardens. Almost all the contemporary historians like Abul Fazl, Badayuni, Faizi Sirhindi and Nizamuddin Ahmad are full of praise for the beauty of the garden laid out and maintained under the supervision of Hafiz Rakhna at Sirhind.[19] From the chronogram *rashk-i jannat* (envy of paradise) given by Sirhindi, the garden appears to have been laid out in 1566–7. Monserrate, while appreciating the beautiful gardens at Sirhind, refers to a deep artificial lake on the southern side of the city which was filled during the rainy season by irrigation channels. He also refers to a tower in its middle which provided a pleasant view of the lake and the surrounding park and gardens.[20] This was open to the general public for enjoyment.

Sirhind however, seems to have suffered from natural calamities. According to Abul Fazl, there was an unusually heavy rain from 8 September to 11 September 1586. Consequently a violent flood came from the northern hills, and the water rose to three yards in the city. Outside, it was five yards. Nearly 2,000 houses were destroyed, and the fort wall was thrown down for 150 yards; 500 yards of the old garden were destroyed, 100 of the new one and much property was carried away by the flood water. One hundred persons and 2,000 animals were drowned. The high road to the capital was closed for some time.[21] The destruction was extensive and the market and houses suffered adversely. On Hafiz Rakhna's death in 1592 he was succeeded by a new *karori*, Abu Said.[22] On Akbar's desire to restore the damage caused by the floods, the new *karori* exerted himself and coerced people to furnish forced labour. Abu Said's efforts restored the garden, and some new buildings were raised but his harsh methods annoyed the people and the traders of Sirhind. They complained to Akbar on his arrival in 1598. The Emperor was expected to stay there for five or six days. But after making a brief halt, he left. Later on it was discovered that Akbar had been quite unhappy with the way in which the construction work was done, especially through the use of forced labour.[23]

Apart from Hafiz Rakhna, Mulla Sher Ali Danishmand appears to have rendered valuable services in the beautification of Sirhind. He built a beautiful garden which was greatly appreciated by Akbar. It seems that trees were planted in the adjoining land to create a pleasant green area. Some of Sirhind's prosperity stemmed from the large *madad-i maash* grants around the city. It may be interesting to note that on learning that Mulla Ali Sher Danishmand had been assigned 2,000 *bighas* of land by Shaikh Abdul Nabi, Akbar observed that a *khadim* need not have such a large grant and ordered its reduction to 600 or 700 *bighas*.[24]

Jahangir had old association with Sirhind since his princehood. Sirhindi refers to his *haveli* adjacent to the garden of Hafiz Rakhna where he was staying in 1598–9.[25] Jahangir took a keen interest in not only the maintenance of the garden but also in raising new buildings there. In order to get the necessary repairs done, he directed Khwaja Wasimi, an expert in agriculture and building construction, to proceed to Sirhind as *karori*.[26] In 1619, Jahangir visited Sirhind, went round the garden and found many old trees losing their old freshness. He ordered Khwaja Wasimi to remove the old trees, put in new plants, clean up the *arq-bandi*, repair the old buildings and raise new buildings in the shape of baths, etc. in suitable places.[27] On 13 January 1622, Jahangir revisited Sirhind and was much delighted to see the garden and the new buildings.

In 1616, the Punjab had to face a severe plague epidemic. People from Lahore to Delhi were the worst sufferers. Panic striken people took refuge in forests, abandoning their homes. Sirhind also suffered and a considerable number of people had to abandon it.[28]

Like his father and grandfather, Shah Jahan also took a considerable interest in Sirhind. He visited it on 9 April 1632. On 11 April, he directed Dayanant Khan, the *faujdar* and *diwan* of Sirhind, to construct beautiful apartments on one side and a tank on the other.[29] In 1634, Shah Jahan revisited Sirhind. On his orders, Mir Akbar, the *karori* of Sirhind, constructed new buildings. By 1650 several beautiful buildings were standing around the tank. It seems that by this time the garden of Hafiz Rakhna had become an imperial garden.[30]

Manrique who visited Sirhind during the reign of Shah Jahan gives an interesting account which is worth reproducing even though it is long:[31]

> It is a city which is filled with followers of the mercantile profession on account of the great store of various cotton goods made there. In this city also stands a most magnificent great reservoir, constructed of fine cut stone and full of spring water. From the centre rises in circular form the foundation of a round shrine of great beauty. This Maumetan (Mohammedan) Oratory is reached by a most beautiful bridge, built of the same hewn stone, and supported upon fifteen fine great arches. I took the opportunity to visit the royal garden at this place, belonging to the Mughal Emperor, which stood just over half league away from this fine placid reservoir. One passes to it along a most lovely road, or rather avenue, some forty feet wide and ornamented on both sides with fresh green willow, planted at regular intervals. Their shady branches meet above and, interlacing, from a green, leafy canopy, which resists the brilliant Planet, whose fierce rays, on encountering it, cannot pass below.
>
> Along one side of this pleasant avenue flows a rivulet, whose gentle stream and pleasant banks might well produce on a certain modern port the dreamy effects of African Lethe.

The avenue ends in a wide open plain, where the garden is situated. It was square in form, divided into equal sections each covering about half a league, the whole enclosed by a high massive wall of strong burnt bricks. Four lofty sumptuous gateways lead into this most pleasant fruit garden.

Each gate way, when open, gives a vista down a long, wide roadway, the four forming a cross; one could not see from one end to the other. These roads are ornamented at regular intervals by funereal obelisk-shaped cypresses which divide the garden into four sections; one section contains every kind of fruit tree; a second every kind of flower and odoriferous herbs in abundance; in the third section are eatable vegetables of all kinds, and in the last section a grand Royal Palace surrounded by a beautiful, well-designed Gallery, running along the top, of eight sets of rooms, the apartments of the royal concubines.

Aurangzeb visited Sirhind in the early years of his reign and enjoyed its beautiful gardens.[32] Sirhind continued to be a flourishing city with considerable trade and commerce. Khafi Khan tells us that it was a city 'glutted by the merchandise'; a large number of rich *sarrafs* and other professionals of eminence, gentlemen belonging to every community, especially the pious and learned men, lived in the city. However, Sirhind suffered badly in the post-Aurangzeb period owing to the growing Mughal-Sikh conflicts. Its *bazaars* were looted and a number of buildings, both secular and religious, were destroyed.[33]

Cunningham's description of Sirhind is interesting. Giving the details of Afghan architecture he refers to the monuments and buildings of the thread makers, butchers, painters, etc. Referring to the Mughal architecture he appreciates the big *sarai*:[34]

The *Sarai* of Sirhind is remarkable for its superior accommodation and additional buildings. The *Sarai* consists of a large enclosure with the royal apartments arranged on all four sides, and a tank in the middle of the square. The enclosure is 600 ft. by 280 ft. with a flight of eight steps on all four sides and an arched causeway or bridge passing through the middle of it. The principal apartments, which are on the north side, consist of a block 97 ft. long by 65 ft. and on the opposite side across the tank there is a *sheesh mahal* or a hall of mirrors for public audience. At the south-east and south-west corners there are *hamams* and private apartments, and on the east and west side there are suits for servants rooms and stables.

Cunningham does not identify the builders. It is clear from the above details, that the *sarai*, the buildings and the tanks were built during the Mughal rule under Akbar, Jahangir and Shah Jahan.[35] Its development during the reign of Feroze Shah Tughlaq finds little mention in the contemporary chronicles to enable us to know how Sirhind developed as an urban centre during its early phase. Unlike most of the Afghan settlements in the north, such as Farukhabad, Shahjahanpur and Shahabad,[36] Sirhind does not appear to have any planned development even during the Mughal rule, except for its gardens.

NOTES

1. *The Imperial Gazetteer of India*, vol. 22 (new edn.), New Delhi, 1971, pp. 20–1.
2. H.G. Raverty tr., *Tabaqat-i Nasiri*, vol. 1, Delhi, 1970, pp. 457–8n. Alexander Cunningham, *The Ancient Geography of India*, rep. Varanasi, 1963, p. 123.
3. Yahya bin Ahmad, *Tarikh-i Mubarak Shahi*, Calcutta, 1931, pp. 7, 9, 27, 28, 177, 178, 195 and 212.
4. Ibid, pp. 177, 185 and 190.
5. Ibid., pp. 186–7. Irfan Habib says that 'the original spelling Sirhind was altered to Sahrind, after the change in name promulgated under Shah Jahan': *An Atlas of the Mughal Empire*, New Delhi, 1982, p. 11.
6. Nizamuddin Ahmad, *Tabaqat-i Akbari*, tr. and ed. B. De, 3 vols., Calcutta: Bibliotheca Indica, 1913, vol. 1, p. 248.
7. In the *Imperial Gazetteer of India* (vol. 23, pp. 20–1) the re-foundation of Sirhind is attributed to Feroze Shah Tughlaq at the behest of his *pir*, Syed Jalaluddin of Bokhara in 1361. Cunningham dates the creation of Sirhind and its placement under the charge of Zia Barani, the historian, in 1366. *Archaeological Survey of India*, rep., Varanasi, 1972, vol. 2, pp. 265–6.
8. Sujan Rai Bhandari, *Khulasat ut-Tawarikh*, ed. Zafar Hasan, Delhi, 1918, pp. 34–5.
9. Iqtidar Husain Siddiqui, *Sher Shah Sur and his Dynasty*, Jaipur, 1995, pp. 132–3.
10. Yahya bin Ahmad, *Tarikh-i Mubarak Shahi*, pp. 195–6. Rizqullah Shirazi refers to large-scale migration of Afghans from Roh and their settlements at Ludhiana and Sirhind during Bahlol Lodi's reign: *Waqiat-i Mushtaqi*, B.M. Add 11633, folio 91a.
11. Zahiruddin Muhammad Babur, *Baburnama*, tr. A.S. Beveridge, rep., New Delhi, 1979, p. 706.
12. *Tazkirah Hamayun wa Akbar*, ed. M. Hidayat Hosain, Calcutta: Bibliotheca Indica, 1941, pp. 192–3.
13. Abul Fazl, *Akbarnama*, 3 vols., Calcutta: Bibliotheca Indica, 1873–87, vol. I, pp. 247–8.

14. Hafiz Rakhna came from Herat and settled at Bhakkar as a *faqir.* During Humayun's wanderings he entered his service by reciting touching verses. Rakhna rendered valuable serivice to Humayun during the latter's hard days. He appears to have gained the confidence of Akbar and served as the *shiqdar* and *karori* of Sirhind. He died in 1592. Jauhar Aftabchi, *Tazkirat-ul Waqiat,* tr. and ed. S. Moinul Haq, Karachi, 1955, pp. 75–6. Abul Fazl, *Akbarnama,* vol. I, pp. 223–42. Illhadad Faizi Sirhindi, *Akbarnama,* B.M. Ms 169, folios 148ab.
15. *Tabaqat-i-Akbari,* p. 323.
16. Fr. A Monserrate, *Commentry on his Journey to the Court of Akbar,* tr. and ed. J.S. Hoyland and S.N. Banerjee, Cuttack, 1922, pp. 101–2.
17. Loc. cit., Sirhind was a great market for exporting Samana white cloth to Lahore. *The English Factories in India, 1637–41,* ed. W. Foster, Oxford, 1912, vol. 6, p. 134. Samuel Purchas, *Purchas His Pilgrimages,* Glasgow, 1905, vol. 4, p. 267.
18. Irfan Habib, *An Atlas of the Mughal Empire,* Sheet 4B.
19. Abul Fazl, *Akbarnama,* vol. 1, pp. 2243–4. *Tarikh-i Humayun Shahi,* Cambridge University Ms, folio 46b. Sirhindi, *Akbarnama,* B.M. Ms 169, folios 185ab. Nizamuddin Ahmad, *Tabaqat-i-Akbari,* p. 323.
20. Monserrate, *Commentry,* p. 102.
21. Abul Fazl, *Ain-i-Akbari,* vol. 2, p. 501.
22. Sirhindi, *Akbarnama,* folios 244ab.
23. Sirhindi uses the phrase *mardum-i-bazaar,* loc. cit.
24. Ibid., folios 148a–9a.
25. Ibid., folios 244ab.
26. Jahangir, *Tuzuk-i Jahangiri,* ed. Syed Ahmad Khan, Aligarh, 1863–4, p. 283.
27. Rodgers and Beveridge find '*iraqbandi*' in the IO Ms. and '*iraqbandi*' in the BM Ms. *Tuzuk,* vol. 2, p. 113. It seems that the scribes of the Mss. used by Syed Ahmad Khan and Rodgers and Beveridge wrote '*ain*' instead of '*alif*', changing '*arq*' to '*iraq*' or '*irqa*'. In Arabic '*arq*' means canal, so that '*arq-bandi*' would be provision of channels for irrigation.
28. Khwaja Kamgar Husaini, *Ma'asir-i Jahangiri,* Aligarh, 1978, p. 222.
29. Abdul Hamid Lahori, *Padshahnama,* ed. Kabir al Din Ahmad et al., Calcutta: Bibliotheca Indica, 1866–72, vol. 1, pt. 2, pp. 8–9.
30. Ibid., pp. 115–16. Fray Sebastian Manrique, *Travels, 1629–43,* tr. C.E. Luard, London, 1927, vol. 2, pp. 182–3.
31. Ibid., p. 183.
32. Muhammad Kazim, *Alamgirnama,* ed. Khadim Husain and Abdul Hai, Calcutta: Bibliotheca Indica, 1868, p. 868.
33. Khafi Khan, *Muntakhab ul-Lubab,* ed. Kabir al Din Ahmad and W. Haig, Calcutta: Bibliotheca Indica, 1860–74, p. 654.

34. Alexander Cunningham, *Archaeological Survey of India*, rep., Varanasi, 1972, vol. 2, pp. 209–10.
35. Lahori, *Padshahnama*, vol. 2, pp. 115–16.
36. Cf. Iqbal Husain, *Rise and Decline of the Ruhela Chieftaincies in 18th Century India*, New Delhi, 1994.

9

Urbanization in the Mughal Province of Lahore (*c.* 1550–1850)

J.S. GREWAL AND VEENA SACHDEVA

What happens to urban centres in a political upheaval involving the fall of an empire? We propose to seek a partial answer to this question with reference to the Mughal province of Lahore beginning from the reign of Akbar till Ranjit Singh's reign.

The province of Lahore was equated with the Punjab during the seventeenth and eighteenth centuries.[1] This area witnessed relative peace and prosperity under Akbar, Jahangir and Shah Jahan. Soon after the death of Aurangzeb in 1707, it was thrown into political turmoil. The uprising of the Sikhs under Banda Bahadur was followed by Sikh insurgency before the Persian and Afghan invaders appeared on the scene. Mughal authority in the Punjab ended formally in 1752. Ahmad Shah Abdali though successful against the Mughals and the Marathas, was unable to contain the irrepressible Sikhs.[2] Before the end of the third quarter of the eighteenth century, a large number of Sikh chiefs were ruling over a large part of the province of Lahore. A large number of non-Sikh rulers were holding territories in the hills and the plains. They were all subjugated by Ranjit Singh in the early nineteenth century.[3] He reimposed political unity over the Punjab but did not revive the former province of Lahore as a politico-administrative unit. This new political scenario from the seventeenth to the early nineteenth century was bound to affect urbanization. We propose to concentrate first on the area which witnessed the largest degree of political change during the eighteenth century: the Bist Jalandhar and the upper portions of the Bari, Rachna, Chaj and Sindh Sagar Doabs.[4]

I

In his study of the seventeenth-century Punjab, Chetan Singh talks of 'a symbiotic relationship between town and country' and goes on to explain that the urban centres 'emerged and thrived' in the agriculturally developed north Punjab in two lines running roughly parallel to the hills. The first line was formed by the towns like Attock, Hasan Abdal, Jhelam, Gujrat, Wazirabad, Sialkot and Bajwara and the second by the towns like Eminabad, Goindwal, Sultanpur, Nakodar and Nur Mahal. Between these two lines and placed in the middle of the Bari and the Jalandhar Doab respectively, were the towns of Batala and Jalandhar. Just as Attock, Gujrat and Eminabad rose as urban centres in the reign of Akbar, Wazirabad, Goindwal, Nur Mahal, Phillaur and Rahon rose as urban centres during the seventeenth century. A role of some significance in this development was played by the Mughal aristocracy and religious grantees. But more essential for this development was agrarian production and international trade. Chetan Singh takes specific notice of the manufactures and trade of Lahore, Sialkot, Wazirabad, Gujrat, Batala, Jalandhar, Sultanpur and Bajwara. The silver mint at Lahore and the copper mints at Attock, Bhera, Sialkot, Kalanaur and Jalandhar are seen by him as both the markers and the agencies of commerce. Another non-agrarian industry specially important in the Punjab was the extraction of salt from the Salt Range in the Sindh Sagar Doab.[5]

Chetan Singh underlines that 'riverine trade was a normal feature of daily life in medieval Punjab'. Each town was linked symbiotically with its hinterland and the towns were intermeshed with one another through a network of trade routes. Goods produced in one town were often marketed to another. Trade and commerce facilitated the integration of Punjab economy with 'major trends in the world trade'. The inter-regional and international networks, thus, sustained urbanization in the Punjab. Any disruption in these networks could have adverse effect on its urban centres. In this context Chetan Singh attaches some importance to the fact that an element of uncertainty was introduced into the riverine trade in the Punjab by the increasing difficulty of navigating the Indus by large boats during the second half of the seventeenth century. Eventually, this resulted in complete disappearance of riverine trade in the Punjab before the end of the eighteenth century.[6]

Muzaffar Alam believes that the Mughal province of Lahore in the seventeenth century was among the most prosperous and rich territories of the Mughal empire. Lahore was regarded by some of the European travellers as the greatest city of the East, surpassing even Constantinople. It represented only the apex for there were many others also. The prosperity of the region was reflected in the enormous revenue collected from the *sair mahal*, which represented urban centres, numbering about sixty. This prosperity had a bearing on trade too. On the routes for external and internal trade there were a number of towns with 'merchants who specialized both in inland and foreign trade'. Any possible loss from the silting of the Indus was made up by trade with countries beyond the north-western frontier. The Punjab appeared to be in 'a flourishing state' even in the early eighteenth century. In the reign of Muhammad Shah, however, revenues began to fall sharply, especially from *sair mahal*. Before the middle of the century trade had begun to decline, resulting in the decline of urban centres. For several decades during the second half of the eighteenth century there was dislocation of trade. It was re-established only in the time of Ranjit Singh. Muzaffar Alam's study suggests that there was de-urbanization in the region during the last three quarters of the eighteenth century.[7]

II

Indeed, writing at the end of Sikh rule, Ganesh Das does refer to the decline of several urban centres during the late eighteenth century. About Attock, for instance, he says that, 'at present, the city is deserted but the fort is inhabited'. It was no longer an urban centre.[8] Similarly, Rohtas became an inhabited fort and not an urban centre.[9] The town of Sodhra, founded by Ali Mardan Khan in the reign of Shah Jahan, had been depopulated since 'the beginning of the Sikh rule'. With 'only a small number of people' it could not longer be regarded as a town.[10] Similarly, the town of Aurangabad, founded by Aurangzeb in his twentieth regnal year, had been 'lying deserted since the inception of the Khalsa rule'.[11] Khuhi Sialan, a large town at one time, was merely a village at the time of Ganesh Das.[12] There is hardly any doubt that the change from the Mughal to the Sikh rule had an adverse effect on the fortunes of some of the urban centres.

This, however, was only one side of the picture. Before the end of the eighteenth century contemporary observers began making positive comments on agriculture in the Punjab. Writing in the 1770s Polier observed that the possessions of the Sikh chiefs were 'exceedingly well cultivated, populous and rich'. A few years later, George Forster referred to the extensive and fertile territories of the Sikhs. James Browne also talked of 'a state of high cultivation' in the Sikh territories. Towards the end of the century, William Francklin referred to the abundance of sugarcane, wheat, barley, rice, pulses of all sorts, tobacco and various fruits produced in this region. Grain was also cheaper here than in any other part of India. As Veena Sachdeva points out, 'there was hardly anything in the last quarter of the eighteenth century in the Punjab which should necessarily have resulted in the decline of agriculture'.[13] Thus, agrarian production in the last quarter was much greater than in the third quarter of the eighteenth century.

There is enough evidence in support of manufactures in the urban centres of the Punjab during the late eighteenth century. Nakodar under Tara Singh Dallewalia was known for the manufacture of various kinds of cloth of which *chandeli* was famous. It was carried to Multan, Peshawar and Kabul. Several kinds of coarse cloth and vessels of brass, copper and bell metal were manufactured at Phagwara. Coarse cloth and chintzes were made at Sultanpur which was also known for its quilts during the Mughal times. Bows and arrows, silver wire and laces were made in Jalandhar. The Jalandhar Doab as a whole was known for its sugar.[14]

In the Bari Doab, the city of Lahore had revived some of its old manufactures such as arms, shawls and blankets, fine cloth and coarse piece goods. Amritsar was as important now as the city of Lahore; it was regarded as the grand emporium of trade for the shawls and saffron of Kashmir and of other commodities from the south and the east of India. It had its own manufactures of coarse cloth and inferior silks. The other towns in the Bari Doab, known for their woollen textiles, leather work and wood carving were Batala, Dinanagar, Pathankot, Sujanpur, Dera Baba Nanak and Sri Hargobindpur. In the Rachna Doab, Sialkot was known for its manufacture of paper. The village of Kotli Loharan was known for its manufacture of guns. Chiniot was known for its bow-makers, wood-carvers, painters and masons. Wazirabad retained its name for boat building, and manufactured a variety of hardware, metalware and knives. Gujranwala was known for its brass vessels, jewellery, shawl-edging and silk and cotton scarves. Sahiwal in the Chaj Doab was famous for its *salus* and metal work; Gujrat for matchlocks, swords and daggers in addition to shawls, embroidery, brass vessels, wood-work and shoes. Bhera was known for the excellence of its stone-cutters and its manufacture of arms, cutlery, felt, cotton cloth, iron, rice and sugar. In the Sindh Sagar Doab, Rawalpindi manufactured brass and copper articles. Cloth, blankets, packing bags, saddles, lacquered legs for bedsteads and low chairs were made in Pindi Gheb, Fatehjang and Dangli. Pind Dadan Khan served as the market for the salt mined from the Salt Range.[15]

The trade routes of the Mughal period were no longer operative. A new route from Delhi to Kashmir, through Bilaspur, Kangra and Jammu, was instead used. Francklin refers to a trade route within the Punjab from Amritsar to Patiala through Machhiwara. From Patiala there were two routes to Rajasthan and one to Delhi. Forster notices caravans, custom duties and bankers on this route. There are also references to the bankers and moneylenders of Amritsar and Lahore. The statement made by Forster on the Sikh chiefs becomes important in this context: 'Merchants of every nation or sect, who may introduce a traffic into their territories, or are established under their Government, experience a full protection, and enjoy commercial privileges in common with their own subjects'. Forster goes on to add that this privilege was not extended to 'foreign' traders who in case attempted to pass through this region were likely to be plundered. But immunities were granted to the merchants and traders who functioned in the Sikh dominions and imported wares for the supply of markets in territories of the Sikh chiefs. A certain degree of stability was thus achieved by the 1770s. Even goods from Murshidabad consisting of raw silk, cotton fabrics, and Chinaware came to Lahore through Patna.[16]

Revival of agriculture, manufactures and trade was reflected in the revival of old cities and towns and the foundation of new ones. Since the number of new rulers was very large, the number of their headquarters or capitals was also equally large. Veena Sachdeva has located about sixty capitals in the plains.[17] Some of these were old while others were new. The total number of urban centres at the end of eighteenth century was larger than at the end of the sixteenth or even the seventeenth century. However, to say that the number of urban centres increased is not the same as to say that there was greater urbanization. We have to take into account the size and population of urban centres in order to determine whether or not urbanization was on the increase.

There is hardly any doubt that many of the old towns were revived. We may start with the native city of Ganesh Das which was founded in the reign of Akbar, namely Gujrat. It was a flourishing city in the seventeenth century, but suffered the 'ravages of time' in the eighteenth century before it was devastated by the Sikhs. In the 1760s, however, Sardar Gujjar Singh seized the city and began to repopulate it, giving encouragement and satisfaction to 'people from all places'. Ganesh Das goes on to describe the city at some length, with a subdued feeling of pride, mentioning by name over a score of its administrators under Sikh rule.[18] The case of Sialkot was even more interesting. The Khalsa sacked the city in the time of Ahmad Shah Abdali and razed its tall mansions to the ground. 'Its houses were deserted and its population was dispersed.' After sometime, four leaders of the Khalsa jointly occupied Sialkot and partitioned it among themselves, covering each locality, lane and shop. 'They brought back the dispersed people to rehabilititate the town.' Ranjit Singh seized it in 1808, repaired its old wall and its fort, and reassured the people about his concern for the place. 'But even so the population of Sialkot has not reached its original limits.'[19]

The population of Wazirabad, founded by Hakim Ilmuddin (Alam-ud-din) who was better known by his title Wazir Khan in the reign of Shah Jahan 'dwindled in the beginning of Sikh rule'. Afterwards, however, Sardar Gurbakhsh Singh Waraich and his son Jodh Singh 'repopulated the city' and it became a flourishing place once again. In 1832, Ranjit Singh appointed Avitabile as the *nazim* of Wazirabad and added to its beauty 'after his own heart': he constructed a new locality, known as Ram Katra, on the side of the Lahori Gate, he widened the main bazaar, constructed a *baradari* and erected an octagonal tower in the *sarai* of Wazirabad.[20] Another town described by Ganesh Das at some length is Eminabad which was founded by Muhammad Amin, a *faujdar* of the reign of Akbar.[21]

However, the most obvious example of a Mughal city surviving under Sikh rule was Lahore. It was ravaged by the Khalsa in the early 1760s before being occupied by three Sikh chiefs in 1765. Gujjar Singh specially tried to revive the city, building a new fort in its vicinity. In 1799, Lahore became the capital of Ranjit Singh's expanding kingdom. Ganesh Das devotes several pages to Lahore in his own style. We may quote the following:[22]

> During the invasions of Ahmad Shah and the upsurge of the Khalsa known as the Singhs, the city of Lahore became totally deserted. The twelve localities which were outside the city wall were razed to the ground, and in the nine localities inside the city wall only a few mansions survived. However, when the chiefs of the Khalsa came into possession of Lahore, they paid attention to populating the city and induced people of various places to settle here. When

this capital city fell into the hands of Maharaja Ranjit Singh, new impetus was given to its development. The fort, the towers, the royal mansions, the octagonal tower and the throne were all beautified to a high degree. The city wall which had been built by Akbar was repaired in Sammat 1870. The residents of the city were thus made safe against thieves. Furthermore, a ditch, battlements and many *deodis* adjoining the gates were constructed to add strength to the city.

Ganesh Das does not forget to add that many eminent men, officials and nobles, each according to his status, built beautiful mansions in the city after purchasing *havelis* and plots of land from their original owners. Craftsmen of all kinds came to live in the city of Lahore in large numbers, in addition to the men of learning and the nobles.[23]

The number of new urban centres came up during the late eighteenth century. Qila Sobha Singh, a city according to Ganesh Das, was founded by Sardar Sobha Singh in 1788 on and around a mound where a *darvesh* named Bulaqi Shah used to live.[24] Three years later, another town was founded by Suba Singh, the younger son of Sardar Sobha Singh. It was known as Qila Suba Singh.[25] Gujranwala was 'a small village' before it was adopted by Sardar Charhat Singh as his headquarters in 1766. 'It became a large town'. It served as the capital of Sardar Mahan Singh and his son Ranjit Singh till 1799. When Ranjit Singh appointed Hari Singh as the administrator of Gujranwala, he added to its population and prosperity, laying out a garden, constructing a tank, building new *samadhs* of Mahan Singh and Charhat Singh.[26] Rawalpindi, a *pargana* headquarters in the Mughal times, was merely a village according to Ganesh Das when it was adopted by Sardar Milkha Singh as his headquarters in the late 1760s. 'Since the Sardar was considerate of the well-being of its inhabitants, traders and merchants and other people came from various places and settled here'. Rawalpindi became a large town.[27] The town of Ramdaspur, founded by Guru Ram Das in the reign of Akbar, developed into the city of Amritsar in the late eighteenth century. Three forts and a number of *katras* were built around Ramdaspur by several Sikh chiefs, just as *bungas* were constructed around the sacred tank with the Golden Temple in its midst. In the early nineteenth century, Amritsar frequently served as the residence of Ranjit Singh. Its population was larger than that of Lahore. Ganesh Das was right in asserting that no city in the whole of the Punjab was as large as Amritsar.[28] There is a unique example of a new town which had little to do with administration. This was Dera Baba Nanak, originally founded by Guru Nanak as Kartarpur on the right bank of the Ravi. It became 'a large town' under Sikh rule. People used to come here for pilgrimage and a *langar* remained open all the time for visitors.[29]

It must be added that new towns were not founded by the Sikh chiefs alone. Jalal Khan Bhatti founded Pindi Bhattian near Hafizabad.[30] When the town of Buchcha was depopulated, Chaudhari Ghulam Muhammad Chattha founded Rasulnagar which survived into the early nineteenth century as Ramnagar.[31] Chaudhari Rehmat Khan encouraged people to reside in Jalalpur in the Chaj Doab and they responded to his call, particularly after the devastation of Gujrat by the Sikhs. Jalalpur became 'almost a small city'.[32] The town of Dinga was the result of Chaudhari Wali Dad's initiative in bringing *khatris* and craftsmen to this place.[33] Dinanagar was founded by Adina Beg Khan even before the establishment of Sikh rule.[34]

However, we get the impression that in the area of the strongest political upheaval, quite a few of the old urban centres either disappeared or declined, although, the number which survived throughout the eighteenth century was much larger. A considerable number of towns were founded all afresh in the late eighteenth century. The only new town founded in the reign of Ranjit Singh was Haripur, built by Hari Singh Nalwa in Hazara.[35] The pattern which began to emerge got reinforced in the early nineteenth century. Between the late eighteenth and the early nineteenth century, thus, there was greater continuity than between the early and the late eighteenth century.

If we turn to Appendix 9A where places identified and located by Irfan Habib in the upper parts of the Sindh Sagar, Chanhat, Rachna and Bari Doabs and the Bet Jalandhar Doab are listed,[36] together with places similarly identified and located by Veena Sachdeva in a map of the late eighteenth century,[37] we find that the number of places in the latter case are far larger. This is probably due to the fact that more information is available for the late eighteenth century than for the sixteenth or the seventeenth. This large number nevertheless was also due to the fact that new urban centres had come into existence.

There were at least nine places in the upper Sindh Sagar Doab which served as the headquarters of the new rulers, both Sikh and Muslim: Ahmedabad, Kot, Kusak, Makhad, Malot, Pind Dadan Khan, Pindi Gheb, Rawalpindi and Talagang. Out of these, Malot, Pind Dadan Khan, Pindi Gheb and Rawalpindi were old places. Their adoption by the new rulers as their headquarters increased their importance. The other five places were new and they enjoyed at least a short spell of importance. It is equally significant that the two most important places of the upper Sindh Sagar Doab during the Mughal period, namely Attock and Rohtas, were no longer urban centres. It is remarkable, however, that a number of other important places: Garjakh, Hasan Abdal, Hazro, Jhelam, Jogi Tilla (Tilla Balnath), Kallar Kahar, Khewra, Makhiala, Pharwala, Reshan, and Sarai Kala survived the political change.

This broad pattern can be seen in the upper Chaj, upper Rachna and upper Bari Doabs also. There was only one place in the upper Chaj Doab which served as the headquarters of the new rulers, the old city of Gujrat. It appears to have become important in the late eighteenth century. Among the new places to acquire some importance were Dinga, Kunjah and Qadirabad. Though the old places like Bahlolpur, Daulatanagar, Helan, Jokali, Kariala and Kharian survived, but none of these appear to have been of any importance. The new places which served as capitals of the new rulers in the upper Rachna Doab were Alipur (Akalgarh), Daska, Doda, Ferozke, Gujranwala, Miraliwala, Naushehra, Pindi Bhattian, and Rasulpur (Ramnagar). Several old places were also adopted as capitals by the new rulers: Pasrur, Sheikhupura, Sialkot, Wazirabad and Zafarwal. A few other places also emerged as urban centres, like Qila Didar Singh, Qila Sobha Singh, Qila Suba Singh, and Sambrial. Of the old places, Aurangabad and Sodhra went down, but Eminabad survived. The number of capitals in the upper Bari Doab was pretty large: Adina Nagar, Amritsar, Batala, Chunian, Durangala, Fatehabad, Fatehgarh Churian, Jandiala, Kanganpur, Kathu Nangal, Lahore, Pathankot, Qadian, Qasur (Kasur), Saurian and Sri Hargobindpur. Batala, Fatehabad, Kasur and Lahore were, however, old centres which survived the political change alongwith Chamiari, Goindwal, Kalanaur and Narot. The upper Bari Doab on the whole appears to have witnessed a greater degree of change than the upper Rachna, upper Chaj or the upper Sindh Sagar Doab.

The position in the Bist Jalandhar Doab appears to have ranged between the upper Bari and the other Doabs. In all, ten places served as capitals: Banga, Hariana, Jalandhar, Kapurthala, Kathgarh, Nakodar, Phagwara, Phillaur, Rahon, and Talwan. Four of these were new, namely Banga, Kapurthala, Kathgarh, and Phagwara. Some of the old places which survived were Bajwara, Balachaur, Bhunga, Dasuya, Garhdiwal, Hajipur, Nawanshahr, Nur Mahal, Sham Chaurasi and Sultanpur but appear to have lost some of their old importance. Among the new places to arise, were Adampur, Begowal, Bhogpur, Garh Shankar, Hoshiarpur, Kartarpur, Mukerian and Tanda-Urmar. Hadiabad disappeared, and Balot became village Bholath. The most important new urban centre was Kapurthala and the most important among the old centres now were Jalandhar and Nakodar. It may be added that the place of Hadiabad was taken by the neighbouring Phagwara, indicating the symbiotic relationship in general between the country and the town.

III

The lower Doabs of the Punjab were affected by the political changes of the eighteenth century but somewhat less than the upper Doabs. Appendix 9B shows the comparative position of places in the early eighteenth and the early nineteenth century.[38] Once again we notice a far larger number of places in the second-category over seventy against about a score in the first and for the same reasons.

The difference of degree in the character of change in urbanization between the lower and upper Doabs is partly explicable in terms of the political process itself. The bulk of the territory in the upper Doabs was conquered and partitioned by a large number of Sikh chiefs. Each of them functioned as an autonomous ruler in his little kingdom with its own headquarters. A large number of Sikh rulers needed new places for this purpose. Furthermore, the bulk of the Sikh rulers had little to do with the framework of the Mughal empire: they were neither *jagirdars* nor intermediaries, nor grantees. They had to raise new administration as well as to raise new places. Their activity came to have a direct bearing on the existing pattern of urbanization. Not only the headquarters of new rulers, whether old or new places, but also the other urban centres had to undergo readjustment in the new political situation. In the lower Doabs, on the other hand, the majority of the new rulers were former *jagirdars, zamindars* and large grantees. Most of them had places for headquarters and a rudimentary form of administration. Only a few of them needed new places as their capitals. On the whole, thus, the pattern of urbanization in the lower Doabs was affected much less than in the upper Doabs.

The pattern of urbanization was least affected in the hills which were attached to the Mughal province of Lahore. These territories were under more or less autonomous administration of vassal chiefs.

With the decline of Mughal power they had only to withhold tribute and contigents to become independent rulers. Even when they became subordinate to some new power, it did not change their basic position and administrative machinery. There was no need to change their capitals. If we compare the early eighteenth century places with the early nineteenth century places in the hills we can find only a few changes (Appendix 9C).[39] Even this change was partly due to change in the names. Raja Sansar Chand of Kangra developed a new capital at Tira (Sujanpur Tira) and Jammu gained considerably due to change in the trade route between Delhi and Kashmir which now passed through Bilaspur, Kangra and Jammu. Thus the change in the pattern of urbanization was the minimum in the hills from the seventeenth to the early nineteenth century. With the doubtful exception of Jammu and Kangra, there was no large urban centre in the hills.

IV

So far we have discussed the number of urban centres irrespective of their population. No figures are available for the period of Mughal and Sikh rule in the Punjab. There are qualitative or comparative statements of contemporary writers about the size of urban centers. Ganesh Das, for instance, talks of 'almost a town', a small town, an average town, a large town, a small city, a city, a large city and a *baldah.* This categorization of towns (*qasbas*) and cities (*shahrs*) is quite impressive in terms of their range and also systematic. But his categories do not provide safe evidence on comparative demography. The population figures given in the census of 1855, within a decade of the completion of the *Char Bagh* by Ganesh Das, show that all his statements about the relative size of the towns and cities cannot be taken as accurate. Quite often, he used the terms city and town as synonyms for urban centres. His 'city' of Sialkot had less than 11,000 people whereas his 'large town' of Gujranwala had a population of over 17.500. His 'city' of Sahiwal had less than 10,000 people and his 'small city' of Jalandhar had more than 28,000. None of the 'towns' of Ganesh Das had a population of less than 5,000. But we know that there were such urban centres.[40]

The census of 1855 provides figures of population for a score of urban centres in the Punjab: three in the Jalandhar Doab, five in the Chaj Doab, and four each in the upper Sindh Sagar, Rachna, and the upper Bari Doabs. As shown in Appendix 9D, the largest city of the Punjab, that is Amritsar, had a population of over 1,20,000. Lahore had a little less than 95,000. Next to Lahore was Jalandhar, with only about 28,500 people. The largest city of the Rachna Doab was Sialkot, with a population of over 19,000. But it was smaller than Batala, the third city of the upper Bari Doab with a population of over 26,000. The largest urban centre of the Sindh Sagar Doab was Rawalpindi, with nearly 16,000 people. It was larger than Gujrat which was the largest urban centre of the Chaj Doab with a population of over 14,500.

If we look at the average population of these urban centres, we find that the upper Bari Doab had by far the largest average: over 64,000 people for an urban centre. It was followed at a great distance by the Bist Jalandhar Doab, with the average of less than 16,500. The Rachna and Chaj Doab had the average, respectively, of less than 14,500 and less than 11,500. The upper Sindh Sagar Doab had the average of over 12,000. Compared with the Mughal times, it is quite certain that the capital city of Lahore went down rather drastically. It is equally certain that Amritsar came up in a big way. There were two other places which gained considerably in population: Gujranwala in the Rachna, and Rawalpindi in the upper Sindh Sagar Doab.

In retrospect, we can see that the sixteenth and seventeenth centuries witnessed a spurt of urbanization in the Mughal Punjab. Urban centres began to decline in the second quarter of the eighteenth century. The process of decline in urbanization was accentuated by the political upheaval of the third quarter when a considerable number of urban centres went down. However, many of them were revived before the end of the third quarter itself. A large number of new towns were founded in the second half of the eighteenth century. The pattern that emerged in the late eighteenth century continued, by and large, to develop in the early nineteenth. The maximum change in the old pattern of urbanization took place in the upper Doabs. The change was moderate in the lower Doabs and minimal in the hills. The most conspicuous change was the emergence of Amritsar as the largest city of the region. Two other new towns to survive conspicuously after the end of Sikh rule were Gujranwala and Rawalpindi. In the process of de-urbanization and re-urbanization between 1725 and 1850, it is difficult to say that the share of urban population became larger. But it is equally difficult to maintain that it became smaller.

NOTES

1. The province of Lahore was enlarged by Akbar so as to contain all the five *doabs*. It was equated with the Punjab (*panj-doab*) because it was the only province in the Mughal empire to have five interfluves. Even the neighbouring province of Multan did not have five *doabs*. The Persian historians of the seventeenth and eighteenth centuries used the term Punjab invariably for the Mughal province of Lahore. Ganesh Das, in his formal description of the Punjab in the mid-nineteenth century, also equates it with the former Mughal province of Lahore.
2. For some detail on the political process in the Punjab during the eighteenth and the early nineteenth century, Indu Banga, *Agrarian System of the Sikhs*, New Delhi: Manohar, 1978, pp. 11–38.
3. For detail on the new rulers of the Punjab, Veena Sachdeva, *Polity and Economy of the Punjab During the Late Eighteenth Century*, New Delhi: Manohar, 1993, pp. 1–63 and 160–93.
4. It is possible to make a distinction between the hills and the plains first in terms of the nature of political change and its effects and then between the upper parts of the *doabs* (including the whole of the Bist Jalandhar Doab) and the lower portions.
5. Chetan Singh, *Region and Empire: Panjab in the Seventeenth Century*, New Delhi: OUP, 1991, pp. 173–91.
6. Ibid., pp. 204–35.
7. Muzaffar Alam, *The Crisis of Empire in Mughal North India: Awadh and the Punjab, 1707–48*, New Delhi: OUP, 1986, pp. 142, 143, 304, 316 and 317.
8. Ganesh Das, *Char Bagh-i Punjab*, ed. Kirpal Singh, Amritsar: Khalsa College, 1965, p. 39.
9. Ibid., p. 45.
10. Ibid., p. 92.
11. Ibid., p. 78.
12. Ibid., p. 109.
13. Sachdeva, p. 103.
14. Ibid., pp. 140–1.
15. Ibid., pp. 141–3.
16. Ibid., pp. 130–4.
17. Veena Sachdeva has identified a large number of capitals and located them on the map appended to her work.
18. Ganesh Das, pp. 56–66.
19. Ibid., pp. 79–80.
20. Ibid., pp. 91 and 93–4.
21. Ibid., pp. 97–9.
22. Ibid., pp. 115–16.

23. Ibid., 114–24.
24. Ibid., p. 76.
25. Loc. cit.
26. Ibid., pp. 105–6.
27. Ibid., p. 42.
28. Ibid., pp. 132–4.
29. Ibid., p. 135.
30. Ibid., pp. 108–9.
31. Ibid., pp. 106–7.
32. Ibid., pp. 68–9.
33. Ibid., pp. 53 and 67.
34. Ibid., p. 134.
35. Ibid., p. 41.
36. Irfan Habib has located about 150 places in the Punjab. He was not able to locate all the *pargana* headquarters for lack of information. In the Bist Jalandhar, Bari and the Rachna Doab he was able to identifiy less than half of over 170 *parganas.* His information is incomplete. But it is unlikely that any important urban centre was missed. It may be pointed out that there were no *sarkar* headquarters in the Punjab. Therefore, Irfan Habib has shown the *dastur* headquarters: Jalandhar in the Bist Jalandhar Doab; Batala and Patti in the Bari Doab; Sialkot, and Pasrur in the Rachna Doab; and Rohtas in the Sindh Sagar Doab. *An Atlas of the Mughal Empire,* New Delhi: OUP, 1982, Sheets 4AB.
37. Veena Sachdeva has located nearly 350 places in the former Mughal province of Lahore. It is safe to assume that no important places has been left out.
38. Irfan Habib has indicated in his Atlas the places which are found mentioned in the seventeenth and eighteenth century sources. These places are included in our alphabetical lists. Therefore, it is not inappropriate to say that these places were there in the 'early eighteenth century'. Similarly, Veena Sachdeva's 'places' largely cover the 'early nineteenth century' as much as the late eighteenth.
39. As in Appendix B, the places listed in Appendix C come from the maps of Irfan Habib and Veena Sachdeva.
40. Besides Amritsar and Batala in the districts of Amritsar and Gurdaspur, there were four places with population ranging between 5,000 and 8,000. At the same time there were eight places with population ranging from 3,000 to 4,000; there were thirty-six places with 2,000 to 3,000 inhabitants. All these were listed as 'towns'. Bachan Singh Hira, *Social Change in the Upper Bari Doab (1849–1947),* Amritsar: GNDU, 1996, p. 34.

APPENDIX 9A

1. Places in the upper Sindh Sagar Doab

Early 18th Century	Early 19th Century	
Attock	Ahmadabad	Nurpur
Dangri (Dhangrol)	Chakwal	Pachhand
Dhangot	Dangli	Pharwala
Dharab	Fatehjang	Pind Dadan Khan
Fatehpur	Girjakh	Pind Sultani
Girjakh	Gujjar Khan	Pind Gheb
Hasan Abdal	Haranpur	Rawalpindi
Hazara Gujran (Hazro)	Hasan Abdal	Reshan
Jhelum	Hazro	Rohtas
Kheora	Jalalpur	Sagar
Khoora	Jhelam	Saiyidan
Khor Darwaza (Kallar Kahar)	Jogi Tilla	Sarai Kala
Makhiala	Kahun	Shadheri
Malot	Kahuta	Shamsabad
Maral	Kallar	Tara Garh
Margala	Kallar Kahar	Wah
Nandanpura (Nandana)	Khewra	
Nilab	Khunda	
Pharhala	Kot	
Rawalpindi	Kot Fateh Khan	
Reshan	Kot Sarang	
Ribat	Kusak	
Rohtas	Makhad	
Shamsabad (Pind Dadan Khan)	Makhiala	
Tilla Balnath	Malot	

2. Places in the upper Chaj Doab

Early 18th Century	Early 19th Century	
Bahlolpur	Bahlolpur	Kuthala
Daulatabad (Daulatnagar)	Bhagwal	Lala Musa
Gujrat	Daultnagar	Maghowal
Hario (Haria)	Dinga	Malakwal
Helan	Fakirian	Mamdana

(contd.)

APPENDIX 9A.2 (contd.)

Early 18th Century	Early 19th Century	
Jokali (Jokalian)	Gangwal	Mianwal
Karyali (Kariala)	Gujrat	Nagarianwala
Khari (Kharian)	Helan	Pakhowal
Rasulpur	Jalalpur	Phalia
	Jokali	Qadirabad
	Kalianwala	Sadullapur
	Kharian	Sherowal
	Kotla	Sohawa
	Kunjah	

3. Places in the upper Rachna Doab

Early 18th Century	Early 19th Century		
Chima Chatta	Alipur (Akalgarh)	Gojra	Miraliwal
Daulatabad	Aurangabad	Gondal	Muradpur
Eminabad	Bodana	Gondalanwala	Narowal
Fazlabad	Badoke	Gujranwala	Naushehra
Hafizabad	Bajra	Hafizabad	Pindi Bhattian
Hemnagar	Bhagowal	Harseh Sheikh	Pirkot
Jamia Ghakkar	Bhikhi	Ikhlaspur	Ram Nagar
Kala Pind	Bhopalwala	Jalalpur	Ramba Chattha
Parasrur (Pasrur)	Chak Bhatti	Jamki	Rangrur
	Chaklala	Jandiala	Rasulpur (Ramnagar)
Ramgarh	Chawinda	Jassar	Sambrial
Shahdara	Chaprar	Kalianwala	Sankhtara
Sialkot	Chitti Sheikhan	Karyal	Shahdara
Sodhra	Chuhar Kana	Dila Didar Singh	Shahkot
Talwandi	Daska	Kila Sobha Singh	Sharqpur
Wazirabad	Dhamoki	Kila Suba Singh	Sheikhupura
Zafarwal	Dham Thal	Kot Nikka	Sialkot
	Doda	Kotli Bajwa	Wadala Sandhuan
	Eminabad	Kotli Loharan	Wazirabad
	Fazlabad	Maharajke	Zafarwal
	Ferozke	Mahmudpur	
	Galotian Kalan	Maral	

4. Places in the upper Bari Doab

Early 18th Century	Early 19th Century	
Andaura	Adinanagar	Lahore
Batala	Amritsar	Lopoke
Bhirowal	Attari	Majitha
Buh	Bahrampur	Mananwala
Chamiari	Batala	Narot
Fatehabad	Bhasin	Pathankot
Govindwal	Chamiari	Patti
Jalalabad	Dera Baba Nanak	Qadian
Kahunwan	Dhariwal	Raiwind
Kalanaur	Fatehabad	Raja Sansi
Kasur (Qasur)	Fatehgarh Churian	Rayya
Khokharwal	Fazilpur	Sathiala
Lahore	Ghumman	Saurian
Narot	Goindwal	Sohian
Naurangabad	Harike	Sri Hargobindpur
Nuruddin	Jandiala	Sujanpur
Paithan (Pathankot)	Kalanaur	Taragarh
Paniyal	Kasur	Taran Taran
Patti Haibatpur	Kathu Nangal	Verka
Sarai Amanat Khan	Khalra	
Shahpur	Khem Karan	
Sindhuan	Kot Lakhpat	

5. Places in the Bist Jalandhar Doab

Early 18th Century	Early 19th Century	
Balachaur	Adampur	Nawan Shahr
Bajwara	Bajwara	Nur Mahal
Balot (Bholath)	Balachaur	Phagwara
Bhunga	Banga	Phillaur
Dadial	Begowal	Rahon
Dasuya	Bhogpur	Sham Chaurasi
Garhdibala	Bhunga	Shahkot
Hadiabad	Dasuya	Sultanpur
Hajipur	Garhdiwal	Talwan
Harhana (Hariana)	Garh Shankar	Talwara

(contd.)

APPENDIX 9A.5 (contd.)

Early 18th Century	Early 19th Century	
Jalandhar	Hajipur	Tanda
Kothi	Hamira	Urmar
Nakodar	Hariana	
Naunangal (Narunangal)	Hoshiarpur	
Nawanshahr	Jalandhar	
Nur Mahal	Kapurthala	
Phillaur	Kartarpur	
Rahon	Kathgarh	
Salimabad	Mahatpur	
Shaikhupur	Malsian	
Sham Chaurasi	Miani	
Sultanpur	Mukerian	
Talwan	Nakodar	

Hunter, G.R., *The Script of Harappa and Mohenjo-daro*, London, 1934.
Indian Archaeology—A Review (*1953–4*) for Ropar and Bara.
Lal, B.B., *Indian Archaeology Since independence*, Delhi, 1964.
Lal, B.B., and B.K. Thapar, 'Excavations at Kalibangan, New Light on Indus Civilization', *Cultural Forum*, 1967.
Lal, B.B., and S.P. Gupta, *Frontiers of the Indus Civilization*, New Delhi, 1984.
Piggot, S., *Prehistoric India*, Penguin Books, 1950.
Possehl, G.L., *Ancient Cities of the Indus*, New Delhi, 1979.
Sankalia, H.D. *Prehistory and Protohistory in India and Pakistan*, Poona, 1974, 2nd edn.
Spate, O.H.K. *India and Pakistan—A Regional Geography*, London, 1957.
Subbarao, B., *The Personality of India*, Baroda, 1958, 2nd edn.
Suraj Bhan, *Excavations at Mitathal and Other Explorations in the Sutlej-Yamuna Divide*, Kurukshetra: Kurukshetra University Press, 1975.
Vats, M.S., *Excavations at Harappa*, 2 vols., New Delhi, 1938.
Wheeler, Sir R.E.M., *Civilization of Indus Valley and Beyond*, London: Thames and Hudson, 1966.

APPENDIX 9B
Places in the Lower Doabs

Sind Sagar		Chaj		Rachna	
Early 18th Century	Early 19th Century	Early 18th Century	Early 19th Century	Early 18th Century	Early 19th Century
Behal	Bhakkar	Bhera	Ahmadnagar	Chandiot	Adilwala
Bel (Patti)	Dallewal	Hazara (Midh Ranjh)	Bhagtanwala	(Chiniot)	Bharwana
Ghazi Khan	Darya Khan		Bhalwal	Jhang Sialan	Chiniot
Bilot	Daud Khel	Lolor	Bhera	Mangtanwala	Haveli Bahadar Shah
Chinna	Dhak	Shakarpur	Faruka	(Mihirabad)	Jhang
Chopara (Chotara)	Fatehgarh	Shorpur	Jhawarian	Shor (Shorkot)	Khiwa
Darya Khan	Garh Maharaja		Kot Ise Khan		Kot Ahmad Yar
Karor	Girot		Kot Sultani		Kot Khuda Yar
Khushab	Haidarabad		Massan		Kot Lakhnana
	Inayat Shah		Miani		Kot Wasawa
	Jandanwala		Midh		Madu Ki Pindi
	Kallar Kot		Nurewal		Maghiana
	Karor		Nurpur		Mukiana
	Khola		Phularwan		Muradwala
	Kiran Kot		Pirkot		Rajoa
	Khushab		Sahiwal		Roranwali
	Kot Maldeo		Shadipur		Shorkot
	Kot Shakir		Shahpur		

APPENDIX 9B (contd.)

Sind Sagar		Chaj		Rachna	
Early 18th Century	Early 19th Century	Early 18th Century	Early 19th Century	Early 18th Century	Early 19th Century
	Kundian		Shah Jiwana		
	Leiah				
	Machhiwal				
	Mankera				
	Mari				
	Mari Shah Sakhira				
	Mianwali				
	Mittha Tiwana				
	Naushehra				
	Nawankot				
	Nurpur (Tiwana)				
	Piplan				
	Rajbana				
	Rashidpur				
	Sakesar				
	Shergarh				

APPENDIX 9C
Places in the Hills

Early 18th Century		Early 19th Century	
Akhnandur (Akhnur)	Mankot (Ramkot)	Akhnur	Lakhanpur
Basohli	Masrur	Bahu	Maha Morian
Bhotiyal	Mihil Mori (Kahun)	Baijnath	Mandi
Bhimbar	Mihirpur (Mirpur)	Bangahal	Mangla
Bilaura (Bilaur)	Malot	Basohli	Mankot (Ramkot)
Dada	Nadaun	Bhadu	Mari
Darband	Palam (Palampur)	Bhimbar	Mirpur
Dhameri (Nurpur)	Paoni	Chineni	Mulot
Gwalior (Guler)	Purmandal	Darband	Nadaun
Hiantal	Ramgarh	Datarpur	Nara
Indarhal (Hel)	Samba	Guler	Nurpur
Jammu	Shahpur	Jammu	Palampur
Jasrota	Sherpur	Jasrota	Ramgarh
Jwalamukhi	Siba	Jaswan	Riasi
Kangra	Sujan	Jwalamukhi	Samba
Kathua	Sultanpur	Kangra	Sarai Niamat Khan
Khari (Mangla)		Khari	Shahpur
Kotkehr (Kotlehr)		Khariyali	Suket
Kotla		Kirmchi (Bhoti)	Sultanpur
Lakhanpur (Sujanpur)		Kotla	Tira
Mandi		Kutlehr	Tirikot
Mangli			

APPENDIX 9D
Census Figures of 1855 in Descending Order

Amritsar	:	1,22,184	Pind Dadan Khan	:	13,583
Lahore	:	94,143	Pindi Gheb	:	13,264
Jalandhar	:	28,422	Jalalpur	:	12,349
Batala	:	26,208	Kartarpur	:	11,539
Sialkot	:	19,249	Maghiana	:	10,768
Gujranwala	:	17,650	Chiniot	:	10,028
Rawalpindi	:	15,813	Sahiwal	:	9,437
Gujrat	:	14,724	Nur Mahal	:	8,891
Bhera	:	13,913	Jhelam	:	6,060
Kasur	:	13,905	Miani	:	6,005

10

Urban-Rural Interaction: The Upper Bari Doab (*c.* 1550–1900)

INDU BANGA

Only during the past few decades have the historians, geographers, sociologists, economists and planners given some attention to interaction between the town and the country. There is a growing realization among the social scientists that the study of these interactive aspects is essential for understanding socio-economic transformation. Both the town and the countryside are parts of the same 'structure of space', sharing land, soil, water, climate and communication linkages. The system of relations persists despite political and technological changes, though these might result in extension in the sphere of influence of some urban centres, rise of some new ones, and the relapse of some others to villages. From this perspective, we propose to examine the changing fortunes of small urban centres in the upper portion of the Bari Doab under the Mughal, Sikh and British rule from about 1550 to about 1900.

The interfluve between the Beas and the Ravi was an urban region *par excellence* in the pre-colonial period. It had all the three cities of the Punjab: Lahore, Amritsar and Multan and several large towns like Pakpatan, Dipalpur, Qasur and Batala. The upper or the north-eastern portion of the Doab was also dotted by several small towns and one large urban centre. Demarcated by the Shivaliks in the north-east and the isohyet of 20" in the south-west, it can be regarded as a geographical subregion. With the rainfall ranging from about 20" to 45", it came to have somewhat distinct vegetation and a rather large proportion of the livestock. This region was mostly an upland plain with mainly alluvial soil, a high water table, and ample facilities for irrigation by wells and canals. The seasonal rhythm allowed at least two harvests, making

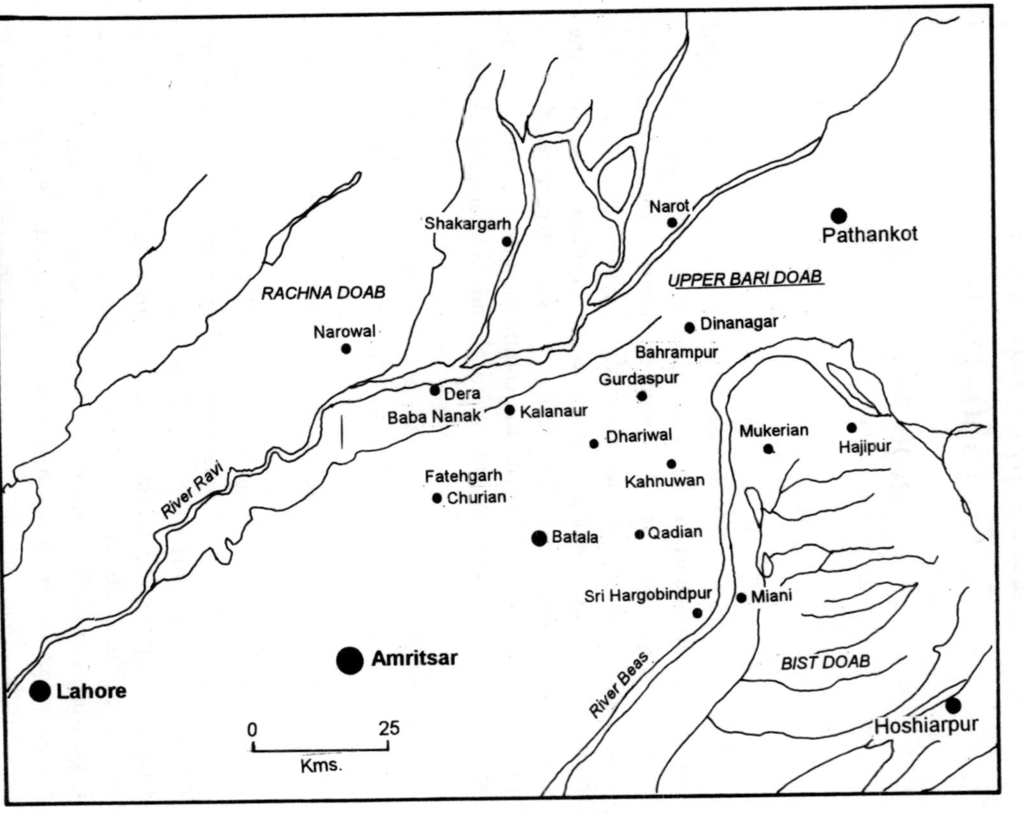

Fig. 10.1: Upper Bari Doab

the region eminently suitable for expansion and improvements in agriculture. Rehabilitated in the fifteenth century, after a great flood and mainly cultivated by peasant proprietors who were quick to take to the Persian wheel, the upper Bari Doab was able to produce sufficient agricultural surplus to facilitiate the emergence of a large number of human settlements.

The earliest available statistical information on this region comes from the first decade of colonial rule. In the 1850s it had over 1,500 rural settlements of varying sizes, with an average population of 280. Its large villages or small *qasbas,* with population between 1,000 and 2,000, exceeded sixty and the chief towns, with population ranging from 2,000 to 6,000 numbered seventeen. One urban centre, Dera Baba Nanak, had a population of over 7,500 and one large town, Batala, had a population of over 24,000. About a dozen of these towns functioned as administrative headquarters under the Mughal, Sikh and British regimes.

Our discussion is mainly centred on Batala, Pathankot, Kalanaur, Kahnuwan, Adina Nagar, Dera Baba Nanak, Sri Hargobindpur, Sujanpur, Fatehgarh Churian, Narot Jaimal Singh, Behrampur, Qadian, Gurdaspur, and Dhariwal. Located in a well-populated countryside, or on the highway or ferries, or at cross roads on the edges of two geographically and economically different regions, these towns essentially had local nodality and grew as local centres of trade. The market remained their *raison d'être,* enlivening their generally placid existence in moments of intense interaction through fairs and harvesting seasons. Their fortunes, albeit in a less substantial way, were also affected by their administrative status.

I

In the administrative organization of the state, the small towns under study served at various levels in the changing political contexts. In the *Ain-i-Akbari* four towns figure as *pargana* headquarters: Kalanaur, Pathankot, Kahnuwan and Batala. Two *jagirdars* founded Behrampur and Qadian in fertile tracts, but both remained small towns. After the extension of cultivation around Batala by the seventeenth century, Kalanaur ceased to function as a *pargana* headquarters, yielding its position of prominence to Batala. Kahnuwan, which had been patronized by the Mughal emperors as a *shikargah,* was virtually in ruins by the beginning of the eighteenth century. Pathankot retained its position largely due to its location at the foot of the hills. In the 1740s, Adina Beg Khan founded the township of Adina Nagar. Out of the old *pargana* headquarters, Batala alone continued to flourish, serving even as the provincial capital under the short-lived governership of Adina Beg Khan in the 1750s.

The decline of the Mughal empire by the middle of the eighteenth century led to the piecemeal occupation of the region by the Sikh sardars. Till the rise of Ranjit Singh half a century later, nearly a dozen Sikh chiefs ruled in different towns of the region. The multiplicity of rulers resulted in the multiplication of administrative headquarters. Some old towns like Sujanpur, Behrampur and Qadian were revived. Three new towns were founded to serve as capitals: Sri Hargobindpur by Jassa Singh Ramgarhia, Fatehgarh by Haqiqat Singh Kanhiya and Narot by Jaimal Singh Kanhiya. Through repairs and revenue grants and other incentives, collectively several rulers and *jagirdars* contributed towards the revival of Dera Baba Nanak, a township founded originally by Guru Nanak.

After the establishment of a relatively centralized kingdom by Ranjit Singh in the early decades of the nineteenth century, the status of the erstwhile capitals changed to that of ordinary towns. Pathankot and Sri Hargobindpur became the headquarters of a *pargana*. Adina Nagar and occasionally Sujanpur, was chosen by the Maharaja for a short stay. Dera Baba Nanak continued to flourish through additional charitable grants from Ranjit Singh and his *jagirdars*. Most of the other towns were included in the *jagirs* of different sardars and princes. Prince Sher Singh alone chose to reside in his *jagir* of Batala. His fondness for hunting revived Kahnuwan for a while.

The annexation of the region by the British in 1849, turned Pathankot and Batala into tahsil headquarters. The village of Gurdaspur was chosen for founding the district headquarters. Sujanpur was given the status of a sub-collectorate. In the hierarchy of municipal administration, Sujanpur, like Sri Hargobindpur, came to have a class II municipal committee. Kalanaur, Dera Baba Nanak, Fatehgarh, Narot Jaimal Singh, and Behrampur came to have class III municipalities. In 1886 the last three were placed in the lowest rung as 'notified areas', and placed under small committees for municipal purposes. Dina Nagar (except for a very short time after annexation), Qadian, Kahnuwan and Behrampur did not acquire any administrative or municipal status.

As centres of administration, the small towns in the upper Bari Doab had a broadly similar kind of interaction with the countryside. The *amil* under the Mughals, the *diwan* or the *kardar* under the Sikhs and the tahsildar or the naib tahsildar under the British continued to assess and collect land revenue from the countryside. The *qanungo's* office was retained by all the regimes and he functioned as the registrar of land records, ensuring a certain degree of continuity in revenue practices. The *qazi's* court continued to function at several places till the advent of British rule. People from within the towns and the countryside resorted to it for the execution of deeds concerning sales, purchases, mortgages and bequests. The Sikh rulers and *jagirdars* too functioned as the source of justice, occasionally helped by touring justices called *adaltis* under Ranjit Singh. The administrative headquarters continued to have garrisons or a police force for the maintenance of law and order in the countryside. However, when we consider the quality and intensity of interaction between the administrative centres and the countryside, the apparent similarity between the structure and functions of the successive regimes begins to disappear.

It may be assumed that had it not been for the special encouragement of the Afghan and Mughal administration and their *ijaradars* and the *madad-i ma'ash* grantees, the upper Bari Doab would not have been rehabilitated so extensively within a century. However, the phase of the closest interaction between the rulers and the ruled appears to have been the late eighteenth century when this subregion was ruled by a number of small chiefs. This period has been interpreted differently as a phase of decline and political disintegration or as a phase of political decentralization. What is reasonably certain is that under the rulers belonging to the area, there was greater participation of the local people in the army and administration as soldiers, *jagirdars*, and revenue functionaries. There was greater patronage to religious personages and establishments, and greater encouragement to local fairs in which people from both rural and urban areas participated. While the walls and fortresses of the capital towns offered security to the countryside, the rulers vied with one another to give incentives to traders and craftsmen to reside and work in their headquarters. In all probability, in the much larger regional state of Ranjit Singh, reasons for this kind of interaction were relatively less. During his rule, the importance and administrative status of the small towns in the upper Bari Doab was reduced considerably. They were held mostly by absentee *jagirdars*, and visited occasionally by the ruler.

Backed by better technology and wider communication linkages, there was much tighter administrative control of the region under the British. The administration was not well disposed towards religious grants and other *muafis* which were generally curtailed or even resumed. The recording of landed rights froze a fluid situation. Combined with the access of the region to the global market, this measure facilitated the creation of market in land. The price of land began to rise steadily. The rising costs of cultivation and living encouraged indebtedness in rural areas, while the complexity of the new legal system enabled the largely urban-based money-lenders to have the land transfers effected in their favour. After the codification of the customary law for disputes concerning property and succession, rural people increasingly resorted to the law courts. Within a few years of annexation, the courts at the district and tahsil headquarters came to be thronged by litigants of several kinds. The new class of judicial officers, pleaders, and petition writers of several grades mediated between the legal system and the people, largely to the disadvantage of the rural population.

II

The measures of the state, however, could not altogether alter the economic balance in the region. The location of many of these towns on or close to the trade routes from Jammu, Kangra, Nurpur and Chamba to the cities of Amritsar and Lahore sustained their economic viability. Sujanpur and Pathankot were the centres of exchange of goods between the hills and the plains. Pathankot specialized in the procurement of timber and its thriving timber market was the result also of its proximity to the hills. Sujanpur obtained wool, turmeric, rice and other mountainous produce, including hemp. Narot Jaimal Singh was the principal collecting centre for produce from the Jammu region and from the sub-mountainous area that abounded in rice cultivation. Understandably, octroi became the principal source of income for the municipalities of these towns in the late nineteenth century.

All urban centres functioned as centres of collection and distribution for the villages in the immediate neighbourhood. All of these, with the exception of Kahnuwan which derived its importance from game, had bazaars with numerous retail and wholesale shops. Every town had a grain *mandi.* The *arhtia* in the *mandi* had regular links with the keepers of two or three shops (*hattis*) in most villages, who functioned as his agents for the procurement of grains, pulses, and oilseeds. The agricultural produce was marketed within the upper Bari Doab or taken to Amritsar. Jaggery from Batala had a wider market in the province. Vegetables and fruits grown in the neighbourhood of the town were sold locally through green grocers, or even directly. Milk was mostly sold directly; the supply of ghi had to be supplemented from outside the region. The Chamars in the countryside abounding in cattle specialized in processing raw hides which were used for making leather goods in nearly all large villages and towns. In addition, nearly fifty annual fairs in the region which had continued into the 1850s, stimulated the exchange of commodities and livestock between villages and towns. Villagers came to towns for fine cloth, fine tools and implements, and gold and silver ornaments. Even the necessities like salt, spices, paper and iron and copper came from outside. The other items like scales, *bahis,* ink, soap, rosewater, dry fruits, muslin, Gujrati *khes* (thickly woven figured sheet), Multani *lungi,* double *loi* (coarse woollen blanket) of Khemkaran and such other specialized products largely had an urban market in the region.

Most of the towns were linked with one another by unmetalled roads, while villages and towns were linked by cartable stretches. After annexation, the British retained the old lines of communication which remained usable by carts, tongas and boats on the ferries. The only metalled road constructed by the British was between Amritsar and Pathankot which ran parallel to the Amritsar-Pathankot railway line opened in 1884. Though, there was some improvement in the conditions of road transport after the introduction of motor vehicles in the 1920s, the road links in the upper Bari Doab remained more or less unchanged.

Yet, within a few decades of annexation, there was a qualitative change in the largely localized trade of the region. The zone of trade in both agricultural produce and manufactured goods was extended not only to the rest of the subcontinent, but also to Europe and other parts of the world. In 1865, Lahore and Amritsar became linked by rail with Karachi which became the port nearest to Europe after the opening of the Suez Canal in 1869. In 1870, the region became linked with the ports of

Calcutta and Bombay by rail via Amritsar and Delhi. Wheat from the upper Bari Doab began to be exported, which affected the cultivation of other grains like gram and barley and almost put an end to the cultivation of inferior grains which were the staple food of the poor in the countryside. Wheat cultivation was aggressively promoted, and virtually every wheat producing village became linked with the global market through the mediacy of the *arhtias* and brokers at the nearby grain *mandis.* They dealt with the village trader-cum-moneylender on the one hand and the agents of the exporting firms based in cities on the other. The *arhtias* and brokers often advanced loans to the producers and traders to ensure that the bulk of the produce was lifted by their cartmen from the village itself in return for the credit advanced by the village moneylender. In anticipation of good prices, the exporting firms used their agency even for making forward purchase of wheat from the ensuing harvest. After the fall in the prices of wheat by the mid-1920s, the agents of the exporting firms encouraged the production of cotton which became the 'principal export' of Karachi in the 1930s. On the whole, the bulk of the export trade in the upper Bari Doab, as elsewhere in the Punjab, was much larger than that of the imports. The imports mostly consisted of cotton piece-goods, both European and Indian, iron and steel, sugar, wool manufactures, gunny bags and cloth, dyes, tans, and liquors to which petroleum products were added later on. These goods were distributed chiefly through Amritsar, Lahore and Batala, while every small town was mainly the local collection centre for exports.

III

Manufactures complemented trade as the economic backbone of the towns in the upper Bari Doab and as the means of greater economic integration between them and the countryside. In the pre-colonial times, in all towns and villages some sort of manufacturing related to the local needs was done on hereditary basis. The services of carpenters, blacksmiths, leather workers, potters, weavers, oil-pressers, hide-jar makers, tanners, tailors, metal-burnishers, turners, masons, lime-burners, metal-vessel makers, and goldsmiths were available in towns as well as the countryside. Villages often shared the services not directly related to agricultural operations. The small urban centres and large villages were probably not much different in the degree of refinement and specialization in these basic kinds of manufactures. In view of the shared hereditary and caste bases and the relatively small area of operations, it may be assumed that the rural and urban artisans in the upper Bari Doab did not necessarily belong to two closed circuits and that they often shared manpower and skills.

However, refined craft production, based on a specialized division of labour, was carried on in the larger towns. There were several kinds of weavers of woollens, carpets, cottons, silks and tapes; dyers specialized in the dying of different textile products and leather; metal workers specialized as blacksmiths, coppersmiths, brass-vessel makers, and gold and silversmiths; the wood-workers included the carvers of wood and the makers of household furniture, cabinets, door and window frames and implements. Then there were embroiderers, calico-printers, glass-workers, and toymakers. With the exception of the workers in wool who happened to be Kashmiri migrants, the craftsmen probably belonged to the region. Because their products had a wider market, many of them tended to work in shops and manufactories financed by capitalist traders who were mostly Banias, Mahajans and Khatris. It is also possible that while working for the urban market the craftsmen were actually residing in villages. The traders advanced money, raw materials and often even implements to the craftsmen. The craftsmen generally were not able to extricate themselves from the advances known as the *baqi* which virtually obliged them to work at low wages or for low profits. It is not certain, however, whether the artisans working for the landed classes under the *sepi* or the so called *jajmani* system had access to some of these specialized circuits of production.

Different towns in the region came to specialize in various products largely made of the locally available raw materials. Thus, Batala, Pathankot, Kalanaur, Adina Nagar, Sujanpur, Fatehgarh and Dera Baba Nanak manufactured coarse blankets, shawls and *lois*, using the wool from the hills. Cotton textiles – plain, printed, embroidered and dyed – were manufactured at Batala, Sujanpur and Fatehgarh. These places also produced some silk cloth. Saddlery and leather work was well-established at Batala and Adina Nagar. Refined sugar was produced at Batala, Qadian, Dera Baba Nanak, Sujanpur, and Sri Hargobindpur. The last mentioned town was also known for its wooden combs. The largest of the urban centres of the region, that is Batala, also specialized in carpet-weaving, metal vessel-making, ornament-making, embroidery, inlay work, and wood-carving.

Within two or three decades of the establishment of colonial rule in the Punjab, however, the manufacturing activity in the region was substantially reduced or reoriented. Among other things, the inflow of factory made goods, whether from Great Britain or the other parts of India, significantly curtailed the market for local goods. Consequently, the quality and volume of the specialized products of the region, particularly cotton and woollen textiles, leather goods and agricultural manufactures, were adversely affected. In due course, the traditional manufactures were crippled.

In the absence of other opportunities, urban artisans clung to their profession, but producing mainly for the local market and the countryside. The rural artisans too were losing the security of the traditional system of mutual support because of the agriculturists turning to the factory made implements and accessories. Yet, the factory products were slow to reach the small towns and the adjoining villages. Only a small proportion of artisans felt encouraged to explore new opportunities and occupations; others sought the expertise of the town based middlemen to find new avenues for the sale of their products, losing in the process, the possibility of obtaining a fair price for their labour.

The modern industrial ventures that the British introduced in the upper Bari Doab were based on the locally available raw materials which made a further dent in the traditional manufactures of the area. Sujanpur came to have a sugar refinery, a rum-distillery and silk filatures. Gurdaspur had a brewery and a distillery, making use of the locally grown barley and sugar cane. The most important British controlled venture was the Egerton Woollen Mills established at Dhariwal in 1882 to tap the supply of wool from the hills and to use canal water for power for the first time. Situated on the Amritsar-Pathankot railway, Dhariwal continued to grow steadily but slowly.

By the beginning of the twentieth century, over 50,000 agriculturists and artisans from the upper Bari Doab had migrated to the newly developed canal colony areas in the south-western Punjab. There was a decline in population also due to the epidemics of the plague, smallpox, influenza and malaria. Till the early 1920s, the rate of population growth in the towns of the region was equal to the rate only of natural increase. In the 1920s and the 1930s, there was 30 to 40 per cent increase in the population of Pathankot, Adina Nagar, Gurdaspur, Dhariwal and Batala. The other towns, however, remained in a state of protracted decline.

IV

Batala proved to be the most resilient of the urban centres of the region. By 1931, its population increased to over 33,000, registering around 37 per cent increase over the first census taken in 1855. By 1940, it came to be recognized as the 'premier centre' of the iron foundry industry in north India. Its twenty-six foundries were manufacturing agricultural machinery of various sorts: cane-crushers, chaff-cutters, rice-hullers, flour-mills, cotton-carding machines, oil-presses, and ploughs, besides other miscellaneous machines and implements. The initiative had come in the 1880s from a local Khatri, Rai Sahib Ganda Mal, who brought one hundred sugarcane-crushers from Delhi to let them out on hire at one rupee a day. The eager demand for cane-crushers encouraged him to add a foundry to his small workshop for fitting the machinery and executing repairs. Soon the local artisans took over the industry and in 1940 twenty-two of the twenty-six units in Batala came to be owned by Lohars. By 1940, one-third of the 700 or so workers in the foundries came from villages within the radius of ten kilometers and belonged to the Lohar and Arain castes. Several blacksmiths in the neighbouring villages were making accessories for foundries. In addition to the local initiative and skills, a particular kind of sand available locally was regarded as peculiarly suitable for moulding.

The industrial growth of Batala would not have been possible without another set of advantages. Batala was located at the centre of a fertile tract known for the production of sugarcane, wheat and oilseeds. By the second decade of the twentieth century, nearly 80 per cent of the tahsil was under cultivation. The area under irrigation was 56 per cent and, compared to Gurdaspur, the use of the Persian wheel was four times. Cultivation was done mainly by Jat and Arain peasant-proprietors who were well known for their industriousness and initiative. Moreover, Batala had road linkages with Amritsar which was only about forty kilometres away, and with small urban centres in five other directions. Finally, the town had prosperous and enterprising business communities of Khatris and Khojas. At least thirty Khatri sub-castes were living in Batala when the British annexed the Punjab. At this time, the town had over a dozen bazaars, two grain *mandis*, many *mohallas*, in addition to a large number of *sahukars*, petty shopkeepers, artisans and labourers. In fact, much before the onset of colonial rule, Batala had gathered sufficient skills and capital to adjust to the changing circumstances of the later centuries.

The survival and growth of Batala illustrates the strength of organic relationship between the town and the countryside which provided it with economic viability to withstand politico-administrative changes and adverse economic circumstances. It appears that the rural-urban networks before the colonial intervention were of a kind that allowed the small towns a more autonomous existence; they served the countryside administratively, culturally and economically, sharing in its prosperity and without squeezing it too hard. After the replacement of their easy going 'parasitism' (to borrow an expression from Braudel) by the determined, almost relentess exploitation of the land and the market by the colonial rulers, in alliance with the trading and professional classes, there was a marked decline in the quality of life for many sections of the population in the region. The bulk of the peasantry and artisanal and labouring classes, besides the men of piety and traditional learning, in both rural and urban areas, were dislodged from their positions of relative economic security.

V

A few observations may now be made on the over all nature of rural-urban interaction. It is generally maintained that through its administrative functions, market mechanisms, preservation of cultural values and generation of new ideas, the town sustained and enlivened the countryside. Whether small or large, the town survived and prospered by maintaining a tenuous balance between what it received and what it returned. It had to perpetually adjust this balance according to the changing socio-economic forces and political regimes. Yet, mutuality did not necessarily mean parity, as the town and the countryside did not have an equal relationship. The rural areas suffered a multiple squeeze in terms of food and raw materials and drain of labour and skills. The unfavourable place, time and rates at which the producer was obliged to sell his produce, or labour worked to the advantage of the urban traders and consumers.

However, it is not enough to say that the town as a whole dominated the countryside. Different people and groups in urban and rural areas were affected differently by different modes of urban-rural interaction. While the urban poor can be equated with the underprivileged in the rural areas, the rural rich had more in common with the privileged sections in the towns. There was an unconscious alliance between the urban elite and the rural landlords who generally managed to get the maximum of accommodation from the state functionaries in the assessment and collection of land revenue, and the administration of justice and police. The privileged sections in the countryside also cornered much of the available credit and other inputs. Furthermore, the bearing of the political order on urban-rural interaction varied with the nature of the state. In the pre-colonial times the town siphoned off a large share of the rural resources, but since the range of communication linkages was small and technology was less developed, the influence of dominant economic and political interests remained relatively limited. Unless aggravated by natural calamities, the societal dislocations were also limited in scale and impact. The proliferation of small towns in a region like the upper Bari Doab in fact contributed towards comparatively greater urban-rural integration.

Under colonial rule, on the other hand, greater administrative centralization was accompanied by the administrative units becoming much larger. This obliged the rural people and the residents of small towns to cover longer distances and spend more time, effort and money in order to have access to the administrative, judical and other services available at the district and tahsil headquarters. The new revenue system and trade policies ensured a much larger extraction of rural surplus. The state used the available technology, largely through the railway and the irrigation schemes, mainly for the purpose of mobilization of natural and human resources to meet the requirements of the metropolitan economy.

Moreover, the railways altered the existing balance among different urban centres. While new towns came up and the old ones expanded, the small towns away from the railway line lost their markets and virtually became villages. There was no deliberate policy for the rehabilitation of the displaced artisans from the small towns of the upper Bari Doab or elsewhere. The pressure on the nearby cities of Amritsar and Lahore was allowed to increase without necessarily providing for employment opportunities to the artisans and labourers, let alone any urban amenities for the increased population. Nor were the avowedly 'pro-rural' policies of the 'elected' government of the Unionist Party (1923–47) necessarily beneficial for all sections of the rural society in the Punjab. The Unionist policies and measures were determined as much by the self-interest of the rich landlords as by the colonial imperatives. The small peasant proprietors and tenant cultivators who constituted the bulk of the agriculturists in the region became increasingly impoverished in the early decades of the twentieth century. On the whole, the heightened urban-rural interaction under colonialism accentuated the relative disadvantages not only of the countryside but also of the small towns *vis-à-vis* the cities.

REFERENCES

Anand, Roshan Lal, *Tanning Industry in the Punjab*, The Board of Economic Enquiry, Punjab, Publication no. 61, 1939.

Bal, Rupinder, 'Wheat Production and Structure of Marketing in the Punjab under Colonial Rule (1901–47)', Ph.D thesis, Panjab University, Chandigarh, 1997.

Banerjee, Himadri, *Agrarian Society of the Punjab 1849–1901*, New Delhi: Manohar, 1982.

Banga, Indu, *The Agrarian System of the Sikhs: Late Eighteenth and Early Nineteenth Century*, New Delhi: Manohar, 1978.

———, 'Polity, Economy and Urbanisation in the Upper Bari Doab', in J.S. Grewal and Indu Banga (eds.), *Studies in Urban History*, Amritsar: Guru Nanak Dev University, 1981.

———, ed., *The City in Indian History*, New Delhi: Manohar, 1994.

———, 'Karachi and its Hinterland Under Colonial Rule', in Indu Banga (ed.), *Ports and Their Hinterlands in India*, New Delhi: Manohar, 1992, pp. 337–58.

——— 'Formation of the Sikh State, 1765–1845', in Indu Banga (ed.), *Five Punjabi Centuries: Polity, Economy, Society and Culture, c. 1500–1900*, New Delhi: Manohar, 2000, pp. 84–111.

Census of India 1931, vol. XVII: Punjab, pts. I & II, comp. Ahmad Hasan Khan, Lahore, 1933.

Chandra, Satish, *Fernand Braudel on Towns*, Occasional Papers, Chandigarh: Urban History Association of India, 1992.

Cust, R.N., *Statistical Report of the Amritsar Division*, Lahore, 1861.

Das, Dial, *Vital Statistics of the Punjab, 1901 to 1940*, The Board of Economic Enquiry, Punjab, Publication No. 80, 1943.

Davies, R.H., *Report on the Revised Settlement of the Greater Part of the District of Gurdaspur* (formerly known as Batala), Lahore, 1859.

Dawar, L.R., *Iron Foundry Industry at Batala*, The Board of Economic Enquiry, Punjab, No. 71, 1941.

Dickinson, Robert E., *City and Region: A Geographical Interpretation*, London: Routledge and Kegan Paul, 1972 (5th imp.).

Fox, Richard G., *Lions of the Punjab: Culture in the Making*, Berkeley: University of California Press, 1985.

Gosal, G.S., 'Agricultural Development and Urbanization, 1921–81', in Indu Banga (ed.), *Five Punjabi Centuries*, New Delhi: Manohar, 2000, pp. 358–74.

Gosal, G.S. and Gopal Krishan, 'Upper Bari Doab', in *R.L. Singh* (ed.), *India: Regional Studies*, New Delhi: 21st International Geographical Congress, 1968, pp. 1–30.

Grewal, J.S., 'Medieval Batala', in *Historian's Punjab: Miscellaneous Articles*, Amritsar: GNDU, 1974, pp. 123–31.

———, '*In the By-Lanes of History: Some Persian Documents from a Punjab Town*, Shimla: Indian Institute of Advanced Study, 1975.

Grewal, J.S. and Indu Banga tr. & ed., *Early Nineteenth Century Punjab: From Ganesh Das's Char Bagh-i Panjab*, Amritsar: GNDU, 1975.

Grewal, Reeta, 'Polity, Economy and Urbanization: Early 19th Century Punjab', *Journal of Regional History*, vol. IV, 1983, pp. 56–72.

———, 'Urban Revolution Under Colonial Rule', in Indu Banga (ed.), *Five Punjabi Centuries*, New Delhi: Manohar, 2000, pp. 438–54.

Hira, Bachan Singh, *Social Change in the Upper Bari Doab (1849–1947)*, Amritsar: GNDU, 1996.

Imperial Gazetteer of India: Provincial Series: Punjab, vol. I, Calcutta, 1908.

Kaur, Harpal, 'Marketing of Agriculutral Produce in the Punjab, 1849–1947', M.Phil dissertation, GNDU, Amritsar, 1988.

Kennaway, E.W., *Final Report of the Revision of the Settlement of the Gurdaspur District, 1912*, Lahore, 1912.

Kessinger, Tom G., *Vilyatpur, 1848–1968: Social and Economic Change in a North Indian Village*, New Delhi: Young Asia, 1979.

Kumar, Ravinder, 'The Changing Structure of Urban Society in Colonial India', *The Indian Historical Review*, vol. V, nos. 1–2, July 1978–Jan. 1979. pp. 200–15.

Mayer, Harold M. and Claude F. Kohn, eds., *Readings in Urban Geography*, Allahabad: Central Book Depot, 1967.

Mukerji, Karunamoy, 'Land Prices in Punjab', in M.K. Chaudhary (ed.), *Trends of Socio-Economic Change in India 1871–1961*, Simla: IIAS, 1969, pp. 529–46.

Narain, Brij, *Eighty Years of Punjab Food Prices, 1841–1920*, The Board of Economic Enquiry, Punjab, No. 8, 1926.

Potter, Robert B. and Tim Unwin, eds., *The Geography of Urban-Rural Interaction in Developing Countries: Essays for Alan B. Mountjoy*, London: Routledge, 1980.

Punjab District Gazetteers, vol. XXI A: *Gurdaspur District*, Lahore, 1915.

Ramchandran, R., *Urbanization and Urban Systems in India*, New Delhi: OUP, 1997 (6th imp.)

Report on the Census, taken on the 1st January 1855, of the Population of the Punjab Territories. Selections from the Records of Government of India (Foreign Dept.), Calcutta, 1856.

Sachdeva, Veena, *Polity and Economy of the Punjab During the Late Eighteenth Century*, New Delhi: Manohar, 1993.

Sharma, Harish Chandra, *Artisans of the Punjab: A Study of Socio-Economic Change in Historical Perspective, 1849–1947*, New Delhi: Manohar, 1996.

Sharma, Radha, *Peasantry and the State: Early Nineteenth Century Punjab*, New Delhi: K.K. Publishers, 2000.

Singh, Chetan, *Region and Empire: Panjab in the Seventeenth Century*, New Delhi: OUP, 1991.

Singh, Harminder, 'Industrial Development in the Punjab (1901–47)', M. Phil. dissertation, GNDU, Amritsar, 1981.

Sohal, Sukhdev Singh, 'British Policies and Money-lenders in the Agrarian Economy of the Punjab', *Journal of Regional History*, vol. IV, 1983, pp. 115–27.

Talbot, Ian, *Punjab and the Raj, 1849–1947*, New Delhi: Manohar, 1988.

Tanwar, Raghuvendra, *Politics of Sharing Power: The Punjab Unionist Party 1923–47*, New Delhi: Manohar, 1999.

11

Urbanization in Colonial Punjab

REETA GREWAL AND J.S. GREWAL

This paper relates essentially to change in the pattern of urban centres in the Punjab during the period of British rule, and to the nature of the links between the town and the countryside. In the first section we outline the pre-colonial perspective on urban centres with evidence from a contemporary writer in order to bring the colonial perspective into high relief. In the second section we outline change in the pattern of urban centres in terms of definition and classification introduced by the British, and take up the development in four sub-regions of the Punjab in detail. Three basic factors are postulated to account for the change: politico-administrative measures, economic and cultural policies, and the new means of communication and transportation. The issue of links between the country and town with reference to the Chenab Colony is taken up in the third section. The next section elaborates this theme with reference to the town of Lyallpur. The fifth section sums up the basic findings.

I

At the beginning of colonial rule in the Punjab, Ganesh Das wrote *Char Bagh-i Panjab* which contains ample information on its towns during the early nineteenth century.[1] He makes a clear distinction between the village (*mauza*) and the town (*qasba* or *shahr*). His awareness of this distinction is paradoxically evident also from his reference to places as 'a large village, like a town'.[2] The size of population was not the basic criterion for Ganesh Das. Most of the urban centres he mentions were centres of administration. But not all and the exception is more important than the rule. Indeed, Ganesh Das is explicit on the point: what imparts urban character to a settlement is the activity of traders and craftsmen, that is, commerce and manufacture.[3] There is an uncanny similarity between Ganesh Das and Braudel about what constituted a town.[4]

Ganesh Das identifies about ninety urban centres in the Punjab which can be equated with the former Mughal province of Lahore.[5] The terms he uses for his urban centres are *qasba, shahr* and *baldah.* It is generally assumed that the term *qasba* was used for a small town and the term *shahr* was used for a large urban centre. Ganesh Das uses the term *qasba* consistently for thirty places and the term *shahr* for fifteen others.[6] But he also uses both the terms for Gujrat and Sialkot, which were well known to him.[7] Hence, it is quite clear that at times Ganesh Das uses the two terms somewhat loosely also.

Nevertheless, Ganesh Das indicates the relative size of his urban centres by using the phrases small (*khurd*) and large (*kalan*) for both the *qasba* and *shahr.* For most of the urban centres, however, adjectives are not used. These, therefore, could be taken as his average category. Indeed, the word *miana* or *mutawassit* is occasionally used to indicate the average or the 'middling' size of an urban centre. Thus we have three classes of towns in the text of Ganesh Das: small, middling and large. To these classes should be added the places for which he reserves the term *baldah.* Since this term is used only for Lahore and Amritsar, it may be taken to stand for an exceptionally large city.[8]

Not even rough figures of population are given by Ganesh Das for his towns and cities. It is possible, however, to form some idea of their size on the basis of figures available in the census of 1855, taken within five or six years of Ganesh Das's qualitative statements. This comparison reinforces our earlier suggestion that he was rather impressionistic in his estimation of the relative size of his towns and cities. It became equally clear that his urban centres belonged to several classes, since the population ranged from 6,000 to over 100,000. If no town with less than 5,000 persons figures in our comparison, it is only because the census of 1855 does not include such a place in the list.[9]

The colonial rulers were more mechanical and more methodical in defining the urban centres. In the census of 1901, for instance, the town is defined to include municipalities, civil lines and cantonments and any place with no less than 5,000 inhabitants which has 'urban characteristics'.[10] In the census of 1931, it is further clarified that a 'town' according to the census included every municipality; all civil lines not included within municipal limits; every cantonment; every other continuous collection of houses inhabited by not less than 5,000 persons, which the provincial superintendent of census may decide to treat as a town for census purposes; and the capital of every Indian state except the minor states in the Simla Hills. 'The essential difference between a rural and an urban population is that the former is mainly engaged in agriculture and the latter in commerce, manufactures and other occupations.'[11] If a place with a population of 5,000 or more did not possess 'urban characteristics' it was treated as a village. On the other hand, a cantonment with a few hundred persons and the capital of a princely state with a few thousand, was treated as a town. In 1921 and 1931, a number of places with less than 5,000 persons, but having 'urban characteristics', were included in the list of urban centres. In any case, all the towns in the census of 1881, did not have a population of 5,000 or more. In terms of the size of population, the range of urban centres in the census of 1881 was broadly similar to the range in Ganesh Das's conception of urban centres.

For an easy comparison with the European situation, the urban centres during the period of colonial rule were classified on the criterion of population alone. The centres with a population of 100,000 and more were placed in class I. These were considered cities. All other urban centres were regarded as 'towns'. In class II were placed those towns which had a population of 50,000 to 99,999. The range of population for the centres in class III was from 20,000 to 49,999. In class IV were places with population ranging from 10,000 to 19,999. The range of population for the towns of class V was 5,000 to 9,999. At the lowest rung were towns with less than 5,000 persons. Such towns were placed in class VI. In some of the census reports, all urban centres are placed in three categories: cities or class I urban centres, large towns of class II, middling towns of class III, and small towns of classes IV, V and VI. The middling category was sometimes divided into 'large' and 'small'. These categories are broadly similar to but do not exactly correspond with the categories emerging from the *Char Bagh-i Panjab*. The *qasba-i-khurd* of Ganesh Das has now become 'the small town' which can have even 19,999 inhabitants, a number which is larger than the number of people living in some of the '*shahrs*' and '*qasba-i-kalan*' of the *Char Bagh*.

In the census of 1881, the number of small towns was over 220 out a total of about 240. By 1941, however, the proportion had changed. Out of a total of about 300 urban centres, about 50 were in the top three classes.[12] The number of cities rose from two in 1881 to seven in 1941, of class II towns from zero to six and of class III towns from fourteen to thirty-four. Furthermore, the population of the 'middling' and 'large' towns as well as of the 'cities' increased so much that the gap between them and the small towns became really wide. The percentage of urban population in cities rose from one in 1881 to about four in 1941; in class II towns, it rose from less than two to over two; and in class III towns, it rose from less than six to over fourteen. For all these urban centres put together, the percentage of urban population rose from eight in 1881 to twenty in 1941.[13] Speaking relatively in this context, the small and middling towns of Ganesh Das and some of his large towns also, became the 'small towns' of the colonial period. This was what happened in Europe much earlier.[14]

During the colonial period, the number of small towns increased only by about a dozen, from 222 in 1881 to 233 in 1941. These figures conceal a significant change that was taking place in relation to small towns as much as in relation to urban centres in general. The number of towns in class IV was 35 in 1881 and 54 in 1941. The towns in class V numbered 83 in 1881 and 117 in 1941. There was thus, an appreciable increase in the number of urban centres with population ranging from 5,000 to 20,000. In class VI, however, the number of towns decreased from 104 in 1881 to 62 in 1941. The majority of the towns in this class consisted of cantonments, capitals of small princely states, and new market towns with a future. We can see, therefore, that the size as well as the number of towns in class IV and class V was very much on the increase.

We can appreciate the development of urbanization in the Punjab under colonial rule better if we turn to the sub-regions or zones within the province, called 'natural divisions' in the census reports.[15] In some of them, the province is divided into four such divisions, including princely states but excluding the North-West Frontier Province. One of these four was the 'Himalayan' zone, covering the British districts of Simla and Kangra; the princely states of Sirmur, Bilaspur, Mandi, Suket, Chamba and the Simla Hill states. The second 'division' was the 'sub-Himalayan' zone, covering the districts of Ambala, Hoshiarpur, Gurdaspur, Sialkot, Gujrat, Jhelam, Rawalpindi and Attock, and the princely state of Kalsia. The third 'division' was referred to as the Indo-Gangetic Plain West, covering the districts of Gurgaon, Rohtak, Karnal, Hissar, Ferozepur, Ludhiana, Jalandhar, Amritsar, Lahore, Sheikhupura and Gujranwala, and the states of Loharu, Dujana, Pataudi, Jind, Patiala, Nabha, Malerkotla, Faridkot and Kapurthala. For our purpose, it may be better to refer to this 'division' as the eastern plain. The fourth 'division' was referred to as the North-West Dry Area which for our purpose is better termed as the western plain. It covered the districts of Montgomery, Multan, Jhang, Lyallpur, Shahpur, Mianwali, Muzaffargarh and Dera Ghazi Khan, and the state of Bahawalpur. Not exactly a 'natural division', each one of these four zones did possess some common natural economic and demographic characteristics.

In the Himalayan zone, there was no city and no town in class II or class III in 1881. Therefore, all the urban centres of this zone were small towns. The most important town was Simla which served as the summer capital of the British empire, besides being a hill resort. It was placed in class IV. There were four towns in class V: all these were capitals of princely states. Some of the state capitals had a population of less than 5,000 and they were therefore placed in class VI. The only old town in class VI which was not serving as a capital was Sujanpur (Tira).[16] The other towns in class VI were created by the British, like Sanawar, Dalhousie and Murree. Unlike the older towns, these new townships had no linkages with the villages around.[17]

Sixty years later, in 1941, the number of urban centres in the Himalayan zone had risen to more than a score. But this increase was not an indication of the real character of urbanization. Simla was still a class IV town. In class V, there were still only four towns, in fact Dharamsala had come up and Nalagarh had gone down. Two of the towns of 1881, Nagar Bhojpur and Sujanpur had actually become mere villages. Obviously, the increase in the total number of towns was due to increase in the number of towns in class VI. By far the majority of the new towns were meant to serve as cantonments for European troops: Bakloh, Balun, Dagshai, Jutog, Kasauli, Kasumpti, Sabathu and Solan. In imitation of the British, the chief of Nahan established a small cantonment at Shamsherpur. Only two other new towns came up. One of these was Joginder Nagar, the product of a hydro-electric project; the other was Sunder Nagar, the product of another similar project.

The sub-Himalayan zone was much richer in urban centres in the pre-colonial days. This was reflected in the census of 1881 when the total number of urban centres in their zone was more than fifty. There was no 'city' and no town in class II, but there were five towns in class III: Ambala, Hoshiarpur, Batala, Sialkot and Rawalpindi. In class IV there were six towns: Sadhaura, Jagadhri, Ropar, Gujrat, Jhelam and Pind Dadan Khan. In class V, there were fifteen towns: three between the Jamuna and the Satlej, three in the Bist Jalandhar Doab, two each in the Bari and Rachna, one in the Chaj, and four in the Sindh Sagar Doab. There were twenty-five towns in class VI. Only one of these was a cantonment. All the rest were old urban centres which were in existence during the late eighteenth and early nineteenth centuries, with a certain degree of concentration in the districts of Gurdaspur and Sialkot.[18]

In 1941, the number of urban centres in the sub-Himalayan zone was a little less than in 1881. About a score of the towns of 1881 had lost this status by 1941. Most of the places which lost this status were in the districts of Gurdaspur and Sialkot. More than a dozen places also acquired urban status by 1941. These new towns were rather evenly spread over the zone. There were five towns in class III in 1881. In 1941, there were four, but only because three others had become cities. The number of towns in class IV rose from six in 1881 to twenty-two in 1941. There was a drastic decrease in the number of towns in class VI from twenty five in 1881 to three in 1941. Thus, whereas more than half of the small towns of the zone were in class VI in 1881, nearly all the small towns in 1941 were in class IV and V. The towns had become larger and they were more evenly spread and spaced.

In the eastern plain, there were more than a hundred urban centres in 1881. Two of these were 'cities': Lahore and Amritsar. In class II, there were two towns: Jalandhar and Patiala. There were nine towns in class III: Karnal, Panipat, Rewari, Bhiwani, Narnaul, Malerkotla, Ludhiana, Ferozepur and Kasur. There were ninety-four small towns, eighteen in class IV, forty in class V and thirty-six in class VI. Of the class IV towns, only five were between the Sutlej and the Jamuna. Similarly, twenty eight of the forty towns in class VI were in this tract. Of the thirty-six towns in class VI, however, only sixteen were in the *doabs* between the Sutlej and the Ravi. In terms of the total number of urban centres, the eastern plain was the most important in 1881. It contained some of the old settled districts and the districts which had begun to receive canal irrigation in the nineteenth century.[19]

In 1941, the total number of urban centres in the eastern plain was a little larger than in 1881. This, however, was the least significant aspect of the change in sixty years. More significant was the increase in the number of cities, large towns and middling towns, shooting up from thirteen to thirty-one. There were four cities now, Jalandhar and Ludhiana were added to Lahore and Amritsar.. There were four towns in class II: Patiala, Ferozepur, Kasur and Gujranwala. The number of towns in class III rose from nine to twenty-three. With the exception of Wazirabad and Sheikhupura, all these towns were in the tract between the Sutlej and the Jamuna. In class IV the number rose from forty to forty-eight. Of the small towns, there were now only six in class VI, in place of thirty-six in 1881. On the whole, the number of small towns in the zone decreased by eight and the number of towns in class VI decreased by thirty. The upward movement at all levels is clearly demonstrated by these figures.

It is not without significance that over two dozen towns of 1881 in the eastern plain were towns no more in 1941. These towns had been situated in nearly all the districts of the zone. In their place, however, nearly a score of new places had become urban centres. Their location was more interesting. Most of these were in the lower parts of the Sutlej-Jamuna Divide, like Faridabad, Hodal, Farrukh Nagar, Jhajjar, Meham, Abohar, Mansa, Jaito, Bhatinda, Gidderbaha, Dabwali, Narwana and Sanaur. In the *doabs*, the new centres were Nankana Sahib, Sangla, Chuharkana, Kamonki and Akalgarh. Nearly all these new towns were in areas where irrigational facilities had been made available.[20]

In the western plan, there was no 'city' in 1881. The only large town of the zone was Multan, placed obviously in class II. There were forty-six small towns, exactly half of which were in class VI. In class V there were seventeen and in class IV there were only six towns. Neither in terms of the number of centres nor in terms of their size, thus, was the zone urbanized to any appreciable degree. By 1941, Multan had become a city. There were at least two towns in class II: Jhang Maghiana and Lyallur. The former in a sense was old but the latter was totally new. There were seven towns now in class III: Bhera, Chiniot, Dera Ghazi Khan, Mianwali, Bahawalpur, Montgomery and Sargodha. The first five were old towns but the last two were new. The number of small towns rose from forty-six in 1881 to eight-two in 1941. The majority of these were new centres. In the zone as a whole, the total number of urban centres rose from less than fifty in 1881 to more than ninety in 1941. Nearly two-thirds of the urban centres in 1941 were new.

The staggering proportion of new towns in the western plain needs a little more attention for a better appreciation of the development that was taking place. Though about thirty of the old towns retained their urban status, or rose up in scale, about a dozen of the old towns were no longer enjoying that status in 1941. A considerable number of places in the state of Bahawalpur were treated as urban centres though their population was rather small, in fact much below 5,000. The number of towns in class VI was pretty large even in 1941, being thirty-five. Some of the new towns actually represented a revival of pre-colonial urban centres which had gone down in the early decades of colonial rule and become larger during the colonial period. Nevertheless the number of new urban centres in the scale above class VI was quite remarkable. It was more than thirty. Out of the ten urban centres in classes I, II and III, four were new. In class IV there were four new centres and in class V there were more than twenty. Thus, the western plain was marked by the emergence of new towns at nearly all levels, but predominantly at the level of small towns, Nearly half of the new small towns were in class IV and V, with a population ranging from 5,000 to 20,000.

In the Punjab, as a whole, the increase in the number of new urban centres under colonial rule was much larger than the total increase in the number of urban centres. This was because a large number of old centres lost urban status by 1941. There were others which did not increase appreciably in size, or actually became smaller. Nevertheless, there was an upward movement in the size of population in urban centres from class VI to class I, with the exception of the Himalayan zone. The upward movement on the one hand and the emergence of new towns on the other, was the dominant phenomenon of the colonial period. The majority of the new urban centres belonged to the category of small towns. In the Himalayan zone and the western plain, most of the new centres were in class VI. But in the sub-Himalayan zone and the eastern plain, the majority of the new towns were in class V and IV. In the Himalayas, most of the new towns were certainly meant to serve as cantonments and health resorts; in the western plain they were meant primarily to serve as markets.

The overall process of urbanization in the Punjab can be understood in terms of the politico-administrative measures of the colonial rulers, their economic and cultural polices and the new means of communication and transportation developed by them. A large number of troops were stationed not only in the North-West Frontier Province but also at Rawalpindi, Sialkot, Lahore, Jalandhar, Ferozepur, and Ambala in addition to the troops stationed in the hill cantonments. The number of departments for civil administration, law and order, revenue and development proliferated. Coupled with the large size of administrative units, this proliferation resulted in a certain degree of 'centralization' of administrative machinery in the provincial capital and in the divisional and district headquarters. Educational facilities were also concentrated in these centres of administration. The number of tahsil headquarters was much smaller than the number of *parganas* in the pre-colonial Punjab.[21] Nearly all administrative centres were initially located in towns. The upward mobility of some of these towns was due partly to their administrative status and this status remained important for the small towns as well.

However, more important for the process of urbanization under colonial rule were the economic policies of the rulers and the new means of communication and transportation. The two things were actually linked together. The primary objective of the new rulers of the Punjab was to exploit its resources. The best prospect appeared to be offered by agrarian production. To increase agrarian production was the primary objective. In the early decades, record of rights in land and periodic settlement of revenue were regarded as the basic instruments of increasing production from land. Before the end of the nineteenth century, canal irrigation became the most important means of adding to the agrarian production of the province. However, increased production was of little use if it could not be syphoned off through a suitable mechanism of marketing and adequate means of transportation. It was not an accident, therefore, that the majority of the new urban centres sprang up in the areas brought under canal irrigation. Like the rest of the province, these areas were served by a network of railways which linked the urban centres with Karachi as well as with Bombay and Calcutta, the ports which linked the province with the world market.

III

To underline the inevitable link between the towns and the countryside, Braudel remarked that 'there is no town, no townlet without the villages'.[22] The close connection of urban centres with the countryside was demonstrated most obtrusively in the canal colonies in the western plain where towns and villages sprang up at the same time, both needed one another. Braudel observed elsewhere that every urban settlement is bound 'to live by maintaining a balance between what it receives (or takes) and what it gives (or returns). The balance has perpetually to be adjusted, the point of equilibrium is never fixed'.[23] In this dynamic process, the rural-urban interaction is generally the outcome of 'a series of underlying economic, social, political and ideological processes'.[24] We propose to turn to the question of urban-rural linkages in the canal colonies, not because there was something unique in those linkages, but because of a unique opportunity for studying those linkage in as area in which villages and towns sprang up together.[25]

Of all the canal colonies, the Lower Chenab Canal Colony came to be looked upon as the most important. The project was completed by 1896. In 1902–3, the canal was irrigating not much less than a million and a half acres of Rabi crop—far in excess of the most sanguine expectations.[26] By 1914–15, the Lower Chenab Canal was irrigating more than 2,300,000 acres which was nearly one and a half times the area covered by all the innundation canals put together, or by the next largest canal.[27] James Douie, who looked upon 'the magnificent system of irrigation canals' as among 'the greatest achievements of British rule in the Punjab', felt gratified to observe that the Lower Chenab Canal was 'one of the greatest irrigation works in the world'.[28]

The twofold purpose of colonization in the lower Rachna Doab was stated officially in the following words:

1. To relieve the pressure of population upon the land in those districts of the province where the agricultural population has already reached, or is fast approaching, the limit which the land available for agriculture can support.
2. To colonize the area in question with well-to-do yeoman of the best class of agriculturists, who will cultivate their own holdings with the aid of their own families and of the usual menials, but as much as possible without the aid of tenants and will constitute healthy agricultural communities of the best Punjab type.

This euphemistically declared purpose of colonization embodies the colonial philosophy of maximizing agricultural production. It is not surprising, therefore, that from the very beginning, arrangements were made to syphon off surplus produce. The railway from Wazirabad, which was on the trunk line from Lahore to Peshawar, was taken to Lyallpur in 1896 and through Gojra, to Khanewal in 1900. Khanewal was already linked with Karachi. Another line linked Lahore with Khanewal through Jaranwala and Toba Tek Singh. Jaranwala was linked with Lyallpur. Already, in the Gazetteer of the Chenab Colony it was recorded: 'The canal made the colony possible, but it was the railway which made it a success'.[30]

In 1903, over a score of commodities were being exported from the Chenab Colony through its railway stations: Sangla, Chiniot Road, Lyallpur, Gojra and Toba Tek Singh among others. Important in the commodities exported were wheat (over 1,500,000 maunds), cotton (over 225,000 maunds), cotton seeds (over 175,000 maunds), oil-seeds (over 150,000 maunds), *jawar* and *bajra* (over 80,000 maunds), sugar (over 22,000 maunds), pulses (over 9,000 maunds), *ghee* (nearly 5,000 maunds) and raw wool (over 1,100 maunds). Ahead of all other railway stations was Lyallpur, with its 2,358,190 maunds of total exports.

Wheat and flour constituted two-thirds of the total exports from the colony. The other main items were cotton and cotton seed, oil-seeds, *jawar*, *bajra* and unrefined sugar. And these were the commodities produced by the colonists largely for export. The great bulk of the wheat went to Karachi to be exported to England and the continent. Three-fourths of cotton went to Karachi and Bombay for export to Europe and Japan. Well could the gazetteer record that the 'rise or fall of prices in the colony depended in an ordinary year on the state of foreign trade'.[31] Thus, the amount of rent from land depended not only on the quality of the soil and the nature of the water-supply but also on the distance of a village from the railway. Consequently, the colonists gained from famine conditions in the country. However, it was not a one-way traffic. The ten most important items of import to the colony were Indian piece goods, wrought iron and steel, unwrought timber, salt, rice, gram, refined sugar, raw tobacco, fruits and gunny bags. These items indicate the needs of the colony, including the countryside.[32]

The railway alone could not solve the difficulty in disposing of the produce from land. Roads had to be built to link the villages with railway stations and with market towns. The whole colony was covered by a network of inter-village roads which were wide enough to allow two bullock carts to pass each other. The advantage of metalled roads was well appreciated. The stretch of about 8 miles from Lyallpur to Khanuana, when metalled, reduced the freight of agricultural produce by half anna per maund. Soon this road was extended to Satiana.

Metalled roads linked Sangla with Shahkot, Chiniot Road with Pauliana, and Lyallpur with Rodukaru—a total length of 52 miles. From this modest beginning, metalled roads were to be built between all the large and small towns of the colony. As the headquarters of a district, Lyallpur was linked by metalled roads with Lahore, Multan, Jhang and Chiniot.[34]

'Say roads and you say towns'.[35] This was how Braudel underlined the importance of the means of transportation for urbanization. Roads, however, were equally important for villages, How otherwise was the produce to be taken to the railway station or the market? Once the crop was harvested it had to be sold. Very little grain or produce was retained by the cultivator beyond what was necessary to supply his basic needs. The majority of the cultivators had their own carts to carry the produce to the nearest market. The large cultivators usually took their produce to the *mandi* and sold it to merchants through brokers (*arhtias*), paying 0.50 to 0.75 per cent on the value of the commodity sold. Not all the cultivators however, could or did carry their produce to the market. There were shopkeepers in the villages to serve as middlemen, or who represented a branch connected with a large firm to purchase the produce. The agents of merchants and firms sometimes visited the villages to make quick or adequate purchases. The majority of these middlemen were Aroras from Jhang, followed by Khatris, with Khojas and Banias far behind.[36]

There was no mention of towns or cities in the scheme of colonization for the lower Rachna Doab, but a number of new towns came into existence due primarily to colonization, demonstrating the inevitable link between urban centers and the countryside. If there could be no towns without the villages, there could be no prosperous countryside without the towns. Before colonization, there were only five towns in the lower Rachna Doab, all in the category of small towns: Maghiana in class IV, Jhang and Kamalia in class V, and Sharakpur and Sheikhupura in class VI. By 1941, all these towns had improved their class: Jhang and Maghiana, together as class II; Sheikhupura to class III; Kamalia to class IV; and Sharakpur to class V. What is more significant, a much larger number of new towns came up: Jhumra in class VI; Shorkot, Sangla, Jaranwala, Toba Tek Singh, Chuharkana, and Tandalianwala in class V; Gojra and Nankana Sahib in class IV; and Lyallpur in class II. If the Chenab Colony was the most important of all the canal colonies, Lyallpur was its most important town. Founded in 1896 as the headquarters of a tahsil of the Jhang district, it was still a second class municipality in 1899. Within five years then, it became the headquaters of a district and a class IV town. Ten years later, it was no more a 'small town'.[37]

Lyallpur was designed in the form of a square with eight bazaars radiating from a central circular *chauk* with a clock tower at its centre. A 'circular' bazaar intersected the blocks created by the eight bazaars. This designed town covered only a little more than hundred acres. In its north and north-east were offices and residences of officers, the municipal garden and the police lines. On the north-west was an experimental agricultural farm (which developed into a college and is now the Punjab Agricultural University of Pakistan). In the south-west, there was a lot of vacant land for residential colonies and educational institutions. It was in this part that the Government College eventually came up. In the east of the designed town was the railway area, with the passenger railway station about half a mile from the down-town. The goods station, however, was closer to the town. There were numerous mills, mostly for cotton cleaning and ginning, in the south-east of the town. There were two grain markets inside, and on its west there was a large vacant space for the annual cattle fair, horse fair and agricultural show. Eventually it came to be used also for tournaments in various sports for school students. Apart from the buildings of the district courts, the treasury, the tahsil and the police station, there were telegraph and post offices, hospitals, the jail, the Dak Bunglow and the PWD Resthouse. There were three slaughter-houses and four bathing tanks. The quarters for the sweepers, the *gawalas*, and the tenants of the town farm were on the outskirts of the designed town. At the beginning of the twentieth century, the area of the municipality covered more than 3,000 acres. The PWD looked after the drainage and water supply schemes, in addition to buildings and roads.[38]

More relevant than the morphology of the town are its officials for us for the present. Foremost among them was the colonization officer who held the rank of a deputy commissioner. The assistant colonization officer too was a deputy commissioner. As revenue collector, the deputy commissioner was assisted by tahsildars and naib tahsildars. The assessment on cultivation was made by the irrigation department which was represented by a superintending engineer at Lyallpur. A district superintendent of police was posted at Lyallpur after the creation of the district in 1904. For the administration of justice, there were district magistrates and munsifs. The town had numerous barristers, pleaders and petition writers. The civil surgeon was suprintendent of the district jail as well. There were no non-official sub-registrars because the deputy commissioner and the tahsildar acted as registrar and sub-registrar for the registration of wills, deeds of sale, and powers of attorney.[39]

These officials resided in Lyallpur but their authority covered the whole district, the villages as well as the towns. Through the executive engineer, the deputy commissioner and the zaildar, the superintending engineer of irrigation was represented in the villages by the canal patwari, who was in charge of three or four villages for the assessment of revenue on account of irrigation. Through the tahsildar, the naib tahsildar and the *qanungo*, the deputy commissioner was represented in the villages by the zaildar, the lambarder and the patwari. On an average there was one zaildar for twenty villages; there were two lambardars in a village and a patwari for three or four villages. The revenue demand and cesses were collected through the lambardar who was entitled to five per cent of the collection. The zaildar was paid his inam from the patwar fund. Through the inspector and the deputy inspector of police, the district superintendent of police was represented in the village by a rural constable, generally known as the chaukidar. However, the lambardar and the zaildar were also an integral part of the police network for dealing with crime. In fact, the lambardar was more important than the chaukidar or the zaildar for the police too, because he was much superior to the chaukidar and he was available on the spot while the zaildar was present only in one village out of nearly twenty. Above all, the lambardar was the representative of the village cultivators as much as of the administration.[40]

The countryside was linked with Lyallpur in some other ways too. The Department of Irrigation not only planted trees along the canal but also encouraged land holders to plant trees, particularly *shisham*, along their fields. Many a land-owner of the district got additional land as '*inam* for planting *shisham* trees. In order to increase and improve cattle breeding the Civil Veterinary Department had not only a veterinary hospital at Lyallpur but also itinerating veterinary assistants who were expected to visit the villages as an essential part of their duty. For postal arrangements, the concerned department established one post office for a small group of villages. The only telegraph office was still at Lyallpur. The telegraphic facilities of the canal offices were confined to official use and not extended to the public. The cattle and horse fair and the agricultural show at Lyallpur attracted a large number of people from the villages for transacting business, for learning something about improved seeds and implements, for drawing inspiration to breed better cattle and horses and for entertainment. There were only a few schools but all their students were not drawn from the town. Furthermore, the District Board and some 'private' organizations were founding schools, nearly all for boys, in the countryside. The District Board, especially, was an institution that linked the villages with Lyallpur in ways more than one.

IV

According to Braudel, the agricultural zone just outside the city, which produced fruit and vegetables, was the first circle, 'an inner belt representing the modest beginnings of what was a sort of colonial empire'. A city was bound to draw on 'several successive supply areas and zones of influence'. These zones were concentric, but only in theory. Nevertheless, there were zones for dairy and kitchen gardens, cereals, wine, livestock, forest, and longdistance trade. 'Within these successive zones were markets, and even towns, which acted as intermediaries'.[42] In this context, it may be suggested that, when Lyallpur became a middling and a large town, its links with villages depended upon whether or not there was an 'intermediary' town between them. In other words, the villages which remained linked with Lyallpur directly, without the immediacy of a market or a town, experienced a certain degree of intensification in interaction.

In order to elaborate this point, we may draw upon information available for a particular village during the 1930s and 1940s when Lyallpur was fast becoming a large town.[43] This village was Chak No. 46 J.B. on the Jhang Branch of the lower Chenab Canal. It was almost equidistant from three towns: Jhumra, Chiniot and Lyallpur. The metalled road between Lyallpur and Chiniot was about 2 km. from Chak No. 46 J.B. but there was no metalled road towards Jhumra. *A priori* we may expect no close links with Jhumra. A few persons in a year could make use of the Jhumra railway station for travelling towards Lahore, because Jhumra was closer to Lahore than Lyallpur. Before the construction of the metalled road between Lyallpur and Chiniot, a few carts could also go to the grain market at Jhumra for the sale of wheat or some other produce from land. The people of Chak No. 46 J.B. went to Chiniot even more rarely. Therefore, this village had nearly all its links with Lyallpur.

The preference of the people of Chak No. 46 for Lyallpur was determined essentially by the fact that the village, being in Lyallpur tahsil, had all its administrative links with Lyallpur. To the linkages already mentioned may be added the constituencies for election to the District Board and the provincial legislative council. The District Board extended its educational activity to an increasing number of villages. Chak No. 46 came to have a lower primary school on an experimental basis in the early 1930s. But the experiment failed due largely to the presence of an anglo-vernacular middle school in the neighbouring, Chak No. 2 J.B. which attracted students from No. 46. The Punjab Agricultural College at Lyallpur and the Department of Agriculture became active enough to reach the villages, including Chak No. 46, with acceptable suggestions on improved varieties of wheat, cotton and sugarcane and on improved agricultural implements and processes of sowing and harvesting. They encouraged horticulture too and Chak No. 46 began to grow mangoes, oranges, lemons, bananas, pomegrenates and grapes in addition to the *ber* and mulberry of the earlier decades. Some vegetables were also introduced in addition to turnip, raddish, carrot, and melon, Perhaps the most interesting addition was that of tomato. None of the fruits and vegetables was meant for the market. Kitchen-gardening for the market remained confined to villages around the town.

The agricultural produce meant for the market in Chak No. 46 consisted almost entirely of wheat, cotton, *toria*, unrefined sugar, gram and pulses. Only a small portion of this produce was carried directly to Lyallpur for sale. Much of it was sold locally to the agents of merchants and firms based in Lyallpur. One of the village shopkeepers, a Kapur Khatri, was actively participating in these transactions as a middle man. By 1947, he had become more affluent than an average landholder of the village. There were three other shopkeepers in the village, all Aroras, known as Jhangis. One of these three was doing better than the other two but not so well as our middle man. He was the only one to bring machine-made cloth, refined sugar and almonds to the village. However, most of the land-holders bought cloth and shoes directly from Lyallpur. About half a dozen persons visited the town almost every day. In fact, there was a *tonga* service from the village to the town, and buses were available for travel from the neighbouring Chak No. 2 on the metalled road. The list of articles brought from the town to the village was long, ranging from medicinal herbs to luxury goods and ornaments of gold.

In the first decade of the twentieth century, the cultural and political links between Chak No. 46 and Lyallpur were quite negligible. There were only two schools in the town: one was an anglo-vernacular middle school of the Municial Board, and the other was a normal school for training school teachers. In the 1940s, there were three colleges in Lyallpur: one was the Punjab Agricultural College, another was a Government College for Arts and Sciences and the third a Khalsa College. There were half a dozen high schools, including an Islamia, an Arya and a Khalsa school. Some of the young boys of Chak No. 46 went to Lyallpur for matriculation after completing the middle stage upto the eighth standard at Chak No. 2 J.B. One of them graduated from the Punjab Agricultural College to become an agricultural inspector. Another graduated from Forman Christian College at Lahore, having passed the matriculation and the 'intermediate' examinations from Lyallpur. With some increase in literacy in the village, it became common to see a newspaper or a monthly brought from the town to be read by all who could. Folk literature became available in print. The increasing linkage of the village with the town was reflected in the influence which the Singh Sabha Movement came to have in Chak No. 46. In the 1940s, the voters of the village were being wooed by the Indian National Congress and the Shiromani Akali Dal, with greater success by the latter because of kinship ties with other villages which had come under Akali influence. Indeed, the linkages of Chak No. 46 with Lyallpur did not exhaust its connections and interaction with the 'outside world', both rural and urban.

V

In retrospect, we can see that urbanization was fairly well developed in the pre-colonial Punjab and a contemporary writer had a fairly clear perspective on urbanism in terms of what essentially constituted an urban centre, the varying sizes and features of urban centres, and their grades and hierarchy. But he remained impressionistic, not giving the exact figures of population even for the town in which he lived. Population figures became the basic criterion for classifying urban centres during the period of colonial rule. The percentage of urban population in the colonial Punjab improved between 1881 and 1941, but it does not follow that the percentage of urban population in the 1940s was necessarily higher than that in the 1840s according to the contemporary definition or perception of 'urban'. It is clear, however, that the size of urban centres and, consequently, the number of large urban centres, began to increase in the colonial period, with an increasing proportion of urban population coming to live in large urban centres.

In the Himalyan zone, all the new towns were meant to serve as cantonments for European troops, with the exception of Simla which served as the summer capital of the empire. A few of the older hill towns were reduced to the status of villages. In the sub-Himalayan zone, about a score of towns lost their 'urban' status but a dozen new places became 'urban'. On the whole, these centres also became larger and more evenly spread and spaced. Continuity of many old urban places was accompanied by a certain degree of change in the overall pattern. In the eastern plain, the most significant change was in terms of increase in the size and number of the large urban units. Over a score of towns went out and nearly a score of new towns came into existence in areas with new irrigational facilities. In the western plain, the total number of urban places nearly doubled, with a high proportion of new towns in the category of small centres. Even in the top urban centres in this area, four were new. In the Punjab as a whole, a large number of old towns went out of existence or shrank in size. At the same time, a considerable number of new towns came into existence and many of the old centres became much larger in size.

The close connection between the urban centres with the countryside was best demonstrated by the simultaneous rise of villages and towns in the canal colonies in the western plain. Export of surplus produce from the countryside required roads and railways. Understandably, the new markets and towns were close to the railway stations. That the nexus between the countryside and the towns was not solely economic is amply demonstrated by the relationship of Lyallpur with a particular village at a distance of about twenty kilometers. Not only administrative and political but also cultural linkages were in witness before the end of colonial rule in 1947.

NOTES

1. The text of the *Char Bagh-i Panjab* was edited by Kirpal Singh and published by the Sikh History Research Department, Khalsa College, Amritsar, in 1965. The long portion in which the author gives a description of the Punjab has been translated into English by J.S. Grewal and Indu Banga and published by Guru Nanak Dev University, Amritsar in 1975. For a general analysis of the work J.S. Grawal, 'Ganesh Das's *Char Bagh-i-Panjab*', *The Historian's Punjab*, Amritsar: Guru Nanak Dev University, 1947, pp. 134–45. All references in this paper are to the Persian text edited by Kirpal Singh.
2. About Sambrial, for instance, it is said that it was a 'large village' (*mauza-i-kalan*), or 'like a town' (*misl-i qasba*): *Char Bagh-i Panjab*, p. 246.
3. Apart from mentioning the presence of traders and craftsmen in many of the urban centres, Ganesh Das makes a specific statement in some cases that these became towns because of their presence. About Dinga for example, he says that its muqaddam, Chaudhari Wali Dad, brought '*khatris*' and craftsmen from many other places to reside there; it was 'because of this' (*azin mujib*) that Dinga became a well-known town: *Char Bagh-i Panjab*, p. 205.
4. 'Without a market, a town is inconceivable', says Braudel, quoted by Satish Chandra, *Fernand Braudel and Towns*, Ocasional Papers Series, Chandigarh: Urban History Association of India, 1992, p. 11.
5. The towns mentioned by Ganesh Das are given in Reeta Grewal, *Urbanization in Colonial India: The Punjab Region*, New Delhi: Manohar (forthcoming), Chapter 2.
6. The places for which Ganesh Das uses only the term *qasba* include Rahon and Nawanshahr in the Bist Jalandhar Doab; Batala and Chamiari in the Bari Doab; Shahdara and Hafizabad in the Rachna Doab; Dinga and Bhera in the Chaj Doab; and Mianwali and Musakhel in the Sindh Sagar Doab. Among the places for which he uses only the term *shahr* were Haripur, Hazro, Makhad, Chakwal, Haranpur, Khushab, Kila Sobha Singh, Kalanaur, Goindwal, Dipalpur and Jalandhar.
7. Ganesh Das had lived in Gujrat virtually as its hereditary *qanungo* and knew the town thoroughly well. His collaterals had lived in Sialkot for several generations and he would certainly have seen the place. There are many other places for which he uses both the terms *shahr* and *qasba*, as for Rawalpindi, Sahiwal, Eminabad, Pakpattan, and Khiva Sial.
8. *Char Bagh-i Panjab*, pp. 206, 220 and 250.
9. Some of the places mentioned by Ganesh Das and included also in the census of 1855 are: Amritsar (122,184), Lahore (94,143), Jalandhar (28,422), Batala (26,208), Sialkot (19,249), Gujranwala (17,650), Dera Ghazi

Khan (15,899), Rawalpindi (15,813), Gujrat (14,724), Bhera (13,913), Kasur (13,905), Pind Dadan Khan (13,588), Pindigheb (13,364), Jalalpur (12,639), Kartarpur (11,539), Maghiana (10,768), Chiniot (10,028), Sahiwal (9,437), Nurmahal (8,891), Jhelem (6,060), and Miani (6,005).

10. *Census of India, 1901*, vol. XVII: *The Punjab*, part I, Simla, 1902, p. 14.
11. *Census of India, 1931*, vol. XVII: *The Punjab*, part I, Lahore, 1933, pp. 88 and 89.
12. All classes of urban centres in 1881 and 1941 are listed in Reeta Grewal, *Urbanization in Colonial India: The Punjab Region*, New Delhi: Manohar (forthcoming), Chapter 3.
13. These percentages have been worked out by Reeta Grewal for her forthcoming book.
14. 'Would it not be true to say', observes Braudel, 'that the market is still the essential attribute of the French bourg, even today, although the minimum population level to qualify as such has risen . . . to 10,000 to 20,000 inhabitants'. He goes on to add that in the Middle Ages 'that would be the size of a large town'. *The Identity of France*, vol. 1, *History and Environment*, tr. Sian Reynolds, London: Collins, 1988, p. 165.
15. As in the *Census of India, 1931*, for instance.
16. Even Sujanpur Tira had served as the capital of Raja Sansar Chand in the early decades of the nineteenth century.
17. The perceived need of a health resort and new technology induced the new rulers to build towns on a much greater height than that of the precolonial towns which were in close proximity to hamlets in the valleys. The temperate climate then came to be seen as optimal for work.

    A.D. King looks upon the 'hill station' as a unique illustration of urban development in India under colonial rule in which the 'modern-industrial' element was provided by technology; its related socio-economic dimension, the 'Western' elements, was provided by the contemporary 'British culuture'; and the specifically 'colonial' element was provided by 'Power relationship'. The variable of culture was crucial in this situation:

    > It accounts for the particular set of environmental preferences explaining settlement in 'the hills'; it explains the distinctive 'residential models' available for the colonial community in the earlier decades of the nineteenth century when the hill stations were established, such models being based on the state of urban development in the metropolitan society; and thirdly, it explains the particular ethnomedical theories supporting the view that 'hill stations' were 'healthier' than residence on 'the plains'. The variable of technology is important in that levels of economic, scientific and technological development attained in the metropolitan society

were utilised so that substantial urban settlement could be located on previously uninhabited mountain areas at heights between 6,000 to 8,000 feet. And perhaps of most importance, the power-relationship of colonialism both enabled the settlements to take place and the resources to be organised to maintain the hill stations once they were established.

'Colonialism and the Development of the Modern South Asian City: Some Theoretical Considerations', Kenneth Ballhatchet and John Harrison (ed.), *The City in South Asia*, London: Curzon Press, 1980, pp. 8–9.

18. The total number of towns in these two districts in 1881 was over a score; in 1941, it was about a dozen.
19. The first canal dug by the British for irrigation in the Punjab was the old West Jamuna Canal; it started irrigating the fields in the first quarter of the nineteenth century; it was modernized and enlarged in the last decade of the century. The Sirhind Canal was completed before the end of the third quarter. These two canals supplied water to the districts of Hissar, Karnal, Ludhiana and Ferozepore, and some of the princely states between the Satlej and the Jamuna.
20. By the early 1930s, all irrigational projects had been completed and with the exception of Sialkot, all the districts in the Rachna Doab were receiving canal water for irrigation, some more than others but surely all.
21. In the whole of the British Punjab in the first decade of the twentieth century there were about eighty places which served as the headquarters only of a tahsil, whereas the number of *parganas* in the Mughal province of Lahore alone was over two hundred. The number of *parganas* or *ta'alluqas* in the former Mughal province of Lahore in 1849 was not much different, though the old boundaries changed in many a case, making the new units smaller in some cases and larger in others. The administrative arrangements in a British tahsil were similar to the arrangements at the district headquarters, but on a smaller scale.
22. Fernand Braudel, quoted by Satish Chandra, *Fernand Braudel on Towns,* p. 4.
23. Fernand Braudel, *The Identity of France,* p. 189.
24. Tim Unwin, 'Urban-Rural Interaction in Developing Countries: A Theoretical Perspective', *The Geograhy of Urban-Rural Interaction in Developing Countries: Essays for Alan B. Mountjoy,* London: Routledge, pp. 189–230.
25. The close connection between the founding of new villages and new towns in the colony was reflected in a poem on Lyallpur, written as early as 1889 by a Punjabi bard who, among others things, refers to the 'wheat-market' of the town and its flourishing trade: *Gazetteer of the Chenab Colony,* Lahore, 1905, pp. 34–5.
26. *The Punjab Colony Manual,* Lahore, 1934 (rev. edn.), pp. 6–9.

27. James Douie, *The Punjab, North-West Frontier Province and Kashmir*, Lahore, 1916, p. 133.
28. Ibid., p. 132.
29. *Gazetteer of the Chenab Colony*, p. 29.
30. Ibid., p. 188.
31. Ibid., p. 107.
32. Ibid., pp. 115–17.
33. Ibid., pp. 73 and 119
34. *Census of India, 1931*, pt. I, p. 50.
35. Braudel, *The Identity of France*, p. 209.
36. *Gazetteer of the Chenab Colony*, p. 56. Whereas the Aroras were more than 24,000 in the colony as a whole, the Khatris were only about 7,000, and the Khojas were a little over 1,300.
37. Already in 1911, the population of Lyallpur was 19,578, and in 1921 it was more than 28,000.
38. *Gazetteer of the Chenab Colony*, pp. 122–6, 150–1 and 158–9.
39. Ibid., pp. 126.
40. Ibid., pp. 107 and 129.
41. Ibid., pp. 160–3.
42. Braudel, *The Identity of France*, pp. 182–3.
43. This information is based on recollections of J.S. Grewal and his visit in 1991 to Lyallpur (Faisalabad) and his village, Chak No. 46 J.B.

12

Socio-Cultural Change in Amritsar as Reflected in Punjabi Fiction

J.S. RAHI

Amritsar, the hub of socio-political activity in the Punjab, has been the locale in many Punjabi novels. The portrayals, however, do not always bring out the flavour and character of Amritsar, throbbing with its own drives, tensions and conflicts. It remains a mere amorphous space concerning issues which do not have much to do with the tangibility of Amritsar.

There is one novelist, however, who depicts the tangible Amritsar in four of his novels related to the period from the end of the nineteenth century to the early 1940s. This novelist is Surinder Singh Narula, the first important novelist of the realistic tradition. Born and brought up in Amritsar, his perceptions of the city are intimate and extensive. He supplemented these perceptions by combining the tedious and tangled municipal records to know its physical features and the varied occupations of its inhabitants prior to his experience.

In his portrayals of Amritsar, Narula's favourite themes are its physical features, the dynamics of their transformation, the composition and character of the middle class, the socio-political movements, the dynamics of local administration and the underworld. His documentary details of the city and its life are fascinating and significant. Since they are based upon actual observation and researched facts.

Narula's four novels about the city are: *Peo Puttar* (Father and the Son), 1946; *Rang Mahal* (The Luxury Palace), 1950; *Sil Aluni* (The Saline Rock), 1965; and *Ratan Hoian Vaddian* (Longer Became the Nights), 1983. These novels portray Amritsar of different but specific periods.

We propose to look at Amritsar as portrayed in *Peo Puttar* and *Sil Aluni.* The latter is a sequel to the first. Though the two novels are based on actual historical events and characters their explication is superfluous. But the Amritsar that emerges from fictional details may not be accessible in historical works.

In *Peo Puttar*, the economic, social, cultural and historical aspects of the life in Amritsar are juxtaposed with the religious movement like the Gurdwara Reform, and with the political episodes of the Kamagata Maru and the Jallianwala Bagh.

The narrative in the novel revolves round the childhood and youth of Hira Singh, a prototype of Narula's own father. His life is a tale of voyage from poverty to prosperity. It reflects the changes that came about in the lifestyle of the new generation during the first two decades of the twentieth century. In this process, members of the emerging middle class are found pre-occupied with personal prosperity rather than the issues of public interest. The new generation although wants to discard the old tradition, but the old *sanskaras* prove to be a hurdle.

New *pucca* houses start coming up in place of the single-storeyed shabby *kutcha* houses in the Hall Bazaar. Prominant in the Hall Bazaar were two Muslim *tandoors*, two or three sweet shops and Chacha Harnama's fruit shop. The bazaar that linked Hall Bazaar with Katra Baggian had only four or five *dohattas* with wide doors fixed at level with the drain outside. A *dharamshala*, standing at the Chowk where the low-roofed single storeyed row of shops in the Hall Bazaar ended, looked like a big *haveli*.

The scene starts changing when the Nauhriyas of Bikaner, battered by a famine, shift to Amritsar and enter the trade. They brought with them gold and silver in huge quantities. Initially they were goldsmiths, but they soon captured the textile market which earlier was under the control of the Banias. The Banias were short in capital then. They could not afford to do business on credit and wanted cash payment for all transactions with the customers from outside. The Nauhriyas on the other hand, were an affluent community and readily gave credit, giving them an edge over the Banias. They soon also started purchasing houses and shops. Katra Ahluwalia, a centre of prostitutes, also known as Mughal Bazaar then, was occupied by the Nauhriyas after pushing out the prostitutes. Even the Banias sold off their houses there and shifted to petty business in other areas of the city. There was a butcher, Ghulam Nabi and a *safanwala pathan* who could not shift to any other business. With the opening of a new, big butchery, Ghulam Nabi loses his occupation and consequently goes mad. The *safanwala pathan* becomes a beggar.

Thus, economic spurt was the source of unemployment too. Though in a small way, capitalism had reached Amritsar.

The way in which the Nauhriyas lived, affected the lifestyle of the emerging middle class. Hira Singh's maternal grandmother (*nani*) and other women like her had always worn an ash-coloured *chaddar* as head-gear. But the Nauhriya women wore richly embroidered, heavy *ghagaras* and costly jewellery, besides a conspicuous use of cosmetics.

The ethos of Amritsar was changing from that of a 'village' to that of a 'town'. In imitation of the Nauhriyas, the local *shahs* began to put up curtains in their drawing rooms (*baithaks*). Hira Singh's wife, Satwant, too started saving money for interior decoration which was never dreamt of by her husband's *nana* and *nani* who believed in *rukkhi-missi* and never tried for anything more. The interior of rooms during their time was always black with smoke. The wooden ceiling once broken would remain broken. Hira's Singh's *nana* was a small-time old-fashioned *vaid*, with bottles of medicine haphazardly placed in his shop. His jerky *takhtposh* was supported by some bricks. The absence of initiative of any kind provided sufficient spare time to men and women which they spent in petty occupations or in sleep, in gossip or gambling in *dharamshalas* and gurdwaras.

The initiative of the Nauhriyas broke a new ground. The new generation signified by Hira Singh and his wife Satwant removed the cobwebs in the house and improved the quality of living through small savings. His ambition was to be a *patwanta*, i.e. an elite of the town. From *khaddar* he shifted to silken attire but his *sanskaras* did not change much. Despite his revulsion against the ritual of 'marriage' of *tulsi* plant, which in folk psyche was equated with the merit of *kanyadan* by the pundits, he could not persuade himself to try to stop it. He lacked the will to displace a redundant ritual.

Superstitions reigned in the cultural life of the people and were a strange amalgam of different faiths. The *purohit* enjoyed a pre-eminent position in the performance of rituals concerning marriage and death, both among Hindus and Sikhs.

Paradoxically, the political situation in Amritsar was marked by upheavels during the period. This was because of the impact of the Namdhari and the Singh Sabha movement of the second half of the nineteenth century. If material development generated jealousy among individuals, sectarian aspirations resulted in communal tension. The Singh Sabha movement which was launched for emancipation from

Brahmanism and the Purohits was caught up in internal conflicts. The Namdharis who were against cow slaughter murdered some Muslim butchers in Amritsar, which became a source of Hindu-Muslim tension in the city. The government was also after the Namdharis, but they slipped away. Yet the tension become grimmer nonetheless. Stray incidents of tension were common. The opposing groups indulged in scuffles that led to bloodshed. The shopkeepers shifted their business to the localities of their respective communities. Communal chauvinism was quite visible.

Political consciousness appeared to dawn with the Kamagata Maru episode. Its failure was an index of the power of the British rulers. The property of the protagonists of this movement was confiscated by the government. They were prosecuted on various grounds. Some of them even lost their mental balance. The tragic fate that overtook them is signified in the miserable plight of Thakur Singh's family, a protagonist of the movement.

Another dimension of the political attitude is revealed by peoples' attitude towards *vadda hasptal* (now known as Guru Tegh Bahadur Hospital). Doctors were not available there in adequate number. The *angrez* doctors there preached Christianity along with the treatment of patients. Their purpose was to create goodwill and popular support for the *angrezi sarkar*. The people who had been awakened to the idea for freedom did not like it. They chose to depend on *hakims, vaids, maulvis* and *sadhus* for the treatment of their ailments. People would not like to go there even for cases related to epidemics like the plague. They felt more satisfied with dubious treatment by *hakims* and *vaids*. The death rate in the city was quite high because of the peoples' preference for the personal touch of the traditional practitioners based though on conjecture rather than proper diagnosis.

For similar reasons, quite a good number of students were sent to *pandhas* and *granthis*. The learning of 'tables' was considered to be an achievement. The protagonists of the Kamagata Maru movement, however, were spreading a new kind of educational awareness, including the necessity of educating girls.

Child marriage was a common practice. Hira Singh's sister, Shiv Kaur, was married to an aged *hatwania*. The typical middle-class self-centredness does not allow Hira Singh to make any effort to stop this unequal match. He avoids any kind of tension and conflict for the sake of his personal prosperity, a typical trait of the middle class of that time.

This class identified itself with the idea of freedom and struggle only when the national bourgeoisie saw the possibility of becoming more prosperous through it. *Peo Puttar* is a portrayal of the middle class in Amritsar when the freedom movement had not yet gained momentum.

To sum up we may say that the Kamagata Maru episode, the Namdhari and the Singh Sabha movements provide historical backdrop to the political environment in Amritsar. Magical charms, untouchability and indigenous system of medicine throw light on the cultural scene. In popular psyche, the British rulers were keen to propagate Christianity, especially through *angrez* doctors. The Khatris and the Nauhriyas were the major beneficiaries of economic development. The middle class remains preoccupied with personal prosperity.

Sil Aluni shows Amritsar divided into two zones of the underworld lords, recognized and accepted by the district administration. The lords of the two zones keep on shifting their affiliation from the Gurdwara movement to the district administration and vice versa, with fluctuations in their equation with the authorities. If one group is with the district authorities, the other group seeks to dislodge it by seeking identification with the movement for the freedom of gurdwaras. The issues concerning untouchability and institutionalized prostitution are also found linked to this tussle.

The common man undergoes a sea-change in his socio-political attitude under the influence of the Akalis against the misdeeds of the *mahants*, the traditional managers of the sacred Sikh shrines.

The British government had already wrested political power from the Sikhs. Now it wanted to have control over their religious shrines too in order to perpetuate their rule over the country as a whole. The keys of the *toshakhana* of the Darbar Sahib were handed over to a *sarbarah* appointed by the government. The Akalis took it as a challenge and launched *Kunjian da Morcha.*

It began from rural areas and later reached Amritsar. The wounded in the *morcha* were brought to *vadda hasptal* in Amritsar. The scene radically changes the attitude of many women towards religion and the *mahants* who can get anybody arrested anytime.

Women arrange a mock mourning session (*siapa*) outside the house of a person who collaborates with the authorities for political arrests.

The Akali movement could not be suppressed despite the cruelest possible actions. The government ultimately yields to the Akalis for the management of gurdwaras by the Sikhs themselves.

Thus, Amritsar becomes a centre of struggle for national freedom through the Akali movement, having its base in the Darbar Sahib and the surrounding areas. It shows how urban localities function as centres for secular struggle through religion. The Akali movement centered in Amritsar brings people, who are circumscribed in thinking and interest, into a broader field of action.

There is an entertainment dancer Anwaree Bai. She too is influenced by *Kunjian da Morcha.* The underworld lords compete for her favours. But she makes no compromise when the issues boil down to her political preferences. Hira Singh's sister Shiv Kaur and his maternal uncle Satti Pehlwan, support the Akali Morcha, the latter simply because he is opposed to Nihale Shah, the government man.

Vadda hasptal was called *vadda* because it had an operation theatre, a dispensary and *angrez* doctors. Otherwise in high summer noon, the attendants of the patients had only the shade of walls to take rest. People preferred *jogis, bairagis* and *sadhus* for the alleviation of their ailments. People's revulsion against the propagation of Christianity by *angrez* doctors, as portayed in *Peo Puttar*, figures in this novel too.

Untouchability, discarded in the Akali movement, remains in practice by proxy, not only against the low-castes but also against Muslims and Christians. People keep *Ganga-jal* at their homes and use it to purify themselves after passing through motley crowds. But those who strove for the emancipation of gurdwaras and the country abhorred this practice.

The social environment in the town suffers frequent violence between bad characters. The gentle citizens feel tormented as their sons (not daughters yet) are often beguiled into the gambling dens of the town mafia who provide liquor and prostitutes too. The police is in collusion with the mafia as it is afraid of them. The underworld lords have direct links with the corridors of power.

An atmosphere of insecurty prevails in the city. The mafia consider themselves more powerful than the police. Every new SHO calls upon them. Their writ overrules the law. Fights between the opposing mafia often result in grievous and deadly injuries.

Hira Singh of *Peo Puttar* is found striving for a better living. But within a period of about six years his prosperity, as depicted in *Sil Aluni*, makes him a stooge of the government. He starts working as a conduit for investing money, embezzled from the Darbar Sahib, at higher rate of interest. This engulfs him in various kinds of conspiracies which include manipulated arrests. His wife Satwant, who was earlier a beloved companion, now starts hating him on this count.

There is another paradoxical character, Narinder Singh, a compounder in the *vadda hasptal* and brother-in-law of Hira Singh. He is more popular among the patients than the *angrez* doctors. He writes medical reports and attends to patients after he has been adequately bribed. The police too depend upon him. But when the injured from the *morcha* come to the hospital, he cares for them without any bribe. His wife distributes fruit among the patients. As camouflage, he gets reports published against himself in the *Khalsa Sewadar* to the effect that he maltreats the Akalis. Thus he cheats the government to help the Akalis.

In the fictional depiction of Narula, Amritsar appears to be a world of paradoxes under the British regime during the first quarter of the twentieth century. Increasing prosperity and poverty existed side by side as the two facets of capitalistic economy. A certain degree of improvement in material culture did not change the intellectual and moral life of the people. Reactionary attitudes existed side by side with the liberal, and subservience to the British existed alongwith sympathy for the protagonists of anti-British movements. Communitarian consciousness, involving mutual tensions, was accentuated alongwith the sentiment of nationalism. Political awareness brought women out of their homes to protest, and prostitution was no bar for support to political agitation. The agencies of law and order and the underworld mafia existed side and side, and even met; the mafia aligned itself with political agitators when its interests so dictated. Most of these contradictions appear to have persisted in the psyche of the average urbanite in the Punjab till the present times.

13

Urbanization Process in the Undivided Punjab

KUSUM CHOPRA, ATIYA HABEEB KIDWAI
AND SUBHASH MARCUS

The 'urban' variable in a region can be studied either in terms of individual urban communities or broader historical processes. The first approach falls in the realm of 'urban history' and the second in the 'history of urbanization'. This paper is conceptualized within the parameters of the latter. The history of urbanization is generally written in the context of an accepted periodization and in relation to the politico-economic, social and technological environment, specific to a historical epoch. The main analytical concern here is the settlement response to this environment. The following are the components of this analysis:

(a) delineration of the contours of urban growth from a temporal benchmark;
(b) identification of periods of stability and discontinuity in the urban phenomenon;
(c) identification of city systems and city regions; and,
(d) mapping the spatial pattern.

In this paper an attempt is made to seek entry points into the analyses of the urbanization process in the Punjab. Since the focus is on deciphering long term trends, the approach is statistical-demographic because comparable time series data are available only for the urban population in the region. All quantitative analyses are done with a specific purpose: to indicate the 'what' and 'where' of the urban variable in the region. The crucial question of 'why' is answered only partly, at times through a quantitative analysis of explanatory variables and at times through conjectures which need further verification. The study concludes by posing questions for future interdisciplinary research.

I

The period of analysis covers one hundred and twenty years from 1871 to 1991. This necessitates that our heuristic framework takes into consideration the political economy of colonialism as well as that of an independent mixed economy. The region under consideration approximates in extent the *suba* of Lahore of the Mughal period, major part of the kingdom of Ranjit Singh, the Punjab province of the British period and the contemporary Punjabs in India and Pakistan.

The characteristic features of the province before the British annexation were reported thus by Hamilton:

> . . . its fertility has been too much extolled: for except in the immediate vicinity of rivers, no portion can be compared with the British provinces of Upper Hindostan, and still less with Bengal, which it has been said to resemble.[1]

Hamilton further stated that 'no open trade exists' in the region, and though there are 'many fine villages and some large towns' the latter 'are mostly tending to decay'. Hamilton attributed this decay simply to the fact that the British 'possess no territory or influence' in Punjab. After its annexation, the British are said to have begun its 'planned development' with emphasis on canalization and opening up of vast tracts for agricultural development. Already in 1868–9, Dadabhai Naoroji estimated that the Punjab stood next only to Bombay Presidency in terms of per capita agricultural output and was way above Bengal, Bihar and Orissa.[2] Estimates of 1881 put the Punjab in the fourth position after Bomaby, Madras and Central Provinces. This, however, could not be the result only of the British rule of thirty years or so.

The present Punjab is one of the smallest states of the Republic of India. With an area of 50,362 sq. km. it represents 1.6 per cent of the country's area and 2.39 per cent of its population, according to the census of 1991. Demographically and geographically, it is not so significant as it is in economic terms. It has been the harbinger of the Green Revolution and is now one of the more prosperous states.

An interesting, though contentious entry-point into the history of colonial India is through the oft debated and monolithic hypothesis of de-urbanization and for the post-Independence period through the framework of 'dependent urbanization'. In an earlier study of the hinterland of Calcutta comprising of undivided Bengal, Bihar, Orissa, the northern part of Central Provinces and the eastern half of the United Provinces, Kidwai tested the first hypothesis and came to the conclusion that it does hold true for that region.[3] However, her subsequent analyses in certain other regions in India revealed that it is important to make cross regional comparisons in this regard because several macro-regions in the country may not have replicated the urbanization trends of eastern India. This paper is an attempt in that direction.

The *Atlas of Mughal India* prepared by Irfan Habib marks about 320 settlements in the *suba* of Lahore which were perhaps urban in character. In Hamilton's *Gazetteer* of 1828 we find description of 208 'towns' in the Punjab and Kohistan which made up the Sikh kingdom. Thornton's *Gazetteer* of 1854, on the other hand, describes 462 urban places in the province of the Punjab.[4] In the first proper census of the province undertaken in 1868, only 128 urban places were identified. This significant reduction in the number of urban places in this census was due to the fact that, according to the census definition, only those places were recognized as urban which satisfied the criterion of the minimum population of 5,000. The next census, however, was more realistic as it recognized all settlements as urban which were known as 'towns' in the local context and listed 263 such places.

This great variation in the number of urban settlements was primarily due to various definitions or perceptions of such places in the minds of those who were writing about them. In the pre-census times, in the absence of systematic population counts, 'urbanity' was taken as the determining criterion. In most historical studies one has to evolve a definition or criteria specific to the purpose in hand. In this study, when dealing with pre-census sources, we have taken into consideration all settlements which a particular source recognizes as urban. For the period for which census counts are available, we accept these counts and do not subject the definition of a town in a specific census to scrutiny because we assume that census commissioners were aware of the local perception in that context. It is not appropriate to have a uniform definition of a phenomenon which is time and region specific. What was called a 'town' in 1900, may not be considered so today.

For the pre-census period we have taken the information given in

Irfan Habib's *Atlas* as the benchmark and have constructed the directory of towns from *c.* 1700 onwards.[5] The two sources we depend on for the subsequent period are the *Gazetteers* of Hamilton and Thornton. These *Gazetteers* give more or less complete information about the number of urban places in existence during the time when they were compiled. Since there is a wide variation in the number of places listed in these sources, we tried to make these lists comparable in order to establish the stability and continuity in the urban network. We listed the towns in the Census of 1881 and then compared this list with that based on Irfan Habib's *Atlas.* We find that seventy-five towns of the Punjab were common to both these lists, i.e. they have been in more or less continuous existence since 1700. We then identified their status in the Census of 1931 and 1991. By 1931 only fifty-nine of these towns existed. In 1991 all these towns emerged again in the Indian Punjab (Appendix). We do not have information for West Punjab after 1947.

II

These 75 towns which have continued to exist throughout the last three centuries can be considered as the permanent nodes in the urban system of the Punjab. Some interesting facts emerge from these lists:

1. Towns of all classes existed on a continuous basis for several centuries. Twenty-two (30 per cent) of the seventy-five towns forming the backbone of the regional urban system in the Punjab were very small and had a population of less than 5,000 in 1881. They were smaller than the threshold size stipulated by the census. Only thirty-one towns (41 per cent) in the province had a population of more than 10,000.
2. An urban hierarchy once established, maintains itself over extended periods and proves relevant in diverse politico-economic situations. If we take the largest twenty-five urban places of the Punjab as in 1881 from the above mentioned 75 urban places and rank them according to population size in 1931 and 1991, we find that very few of them experienced a marked variation in their ranks over the last century (Table 13.1). Lahore, Delhi, Rawalpindi, Jalandhar, Sialkot, Ludhiana and Ferozepur remained in the first tier of the hierarchy throughout the colonial period. Six urban places experienced a gain or loss of only one rank and ten places of two to five

Table 13.1: Variability of Ranks of the Cities (1881–1991)

City	1881	1931	1991	Range of rank	Gain + Loss-	Popu. 1881 (a)	Popu. 1991 (b)	Ratio b/a
Lahore	1	1	–	0	0	149,369	–	–
Delhi	2	2	1	1	+1	173,393	8,375,188	48.30
Ambala	3	6	9	6	-6	67,463	119,338	1.76
Rawalpindi	4	3	–	1	+1	52,975	–	–
Jalandhar	5	5	4	1	+1	52,119	216,096	4.07
Sialkot	6	4	–	2	+2	45,762	–	–
Ludhiana	7	7	2	5	+5	44,163	1,042,740	23.61
Firozepur	8	8	15	7	-7	39,570	78,738	1.98
Panipat	9	13	6	3	+3	25,022	191,212	7.64
Batala	10	12	11	1	-1	24,281	103,367	4.26
Rewari	11	17	16	5	-5	23,972	75,342	3.14
Karnal	12	15	3	9	+9	23,133	885,797	38.29
Dera Ghazi	13	14	–	1	-1	22,309	–	–
Jhelum	14	21	–	7	-7	21,107	–	–
Malerkotla	15	19	12	3	+3	20,621	88,600	4.29
Narnaul	16	22	21	5	-5	20,052	51,976	2.59
Gujrat	17	16	–	1	+1	18,743	–	–
Kasur	18	9	–	9	+9	17,336	–	–
Rohtak	19	11	5	14	+14	15,699	216,096	7.64
Bhera	20	23	–	3	-3	15,165	–	–
Kaithal	21	24	18	3	+3	14,754	71,142	7.28
Hissar	22	20	7	15	+15	14,167	181,255	12.79
Jalalpur	23	28	–	5	-5	12,839	–	–
Hansi	24	26	19	5	+5	12,656	59,653	2.24
Makhiala	25	66	–	41	-41	12,574	–	–

ranks. In East Punjab only Ambala (-6), Ferozepur (-7), Karnal (+9), Rohtak (+14), and Hissar (+15) experienced a marked change in their ranks between 1881 and 1991. In West Punjab, for which this change has been calculated for the period between 1881 and 1931 only two places, Kasur (+9) and Makhiala (-41), experienced a marked shift in their ranks.

3. The gain or loss in the rank of an urban centre is irrespective of the rate of growth of its population. Places which experienced substantial growth in their population sometimes went down in their relative rank (Ambala, Ferozepur, Batala, Rewari, and Narnaul).
4. Stability of rank is a characteristic common to both large and small urban settlements.

There has been continuity as well as gradual change in the urban system in the Punjab. The urban network which was established during the medieval period, based on a feudal economy and hinged to 'parasitic cities', served as the base on which an expanding colonial economy rested and a flourishing modern agricultural economy was created. The questions hence to be answered are:

(a) What gave the medieval urban network this resilience and adaptability?
(b) Is a mature urban system a pre-modern achievement in India as it was in the West?

III

We have identified the nodes in the urban system of the Punjab. It is now important to find out regional urban base on which this system emerged. The next step in our analysis, therefore, is to consider the volume and growth of the total urban population. We find that until 1891, the growth rate of urban population was lower than the total population, increased marginally until 1921 and went on increasing until 1971. It is important to note here that in the decades in which total population registered a decline the urban population also did so. Rural population growth followed more or less the same pattern as total population growth.

Urban growth in the Punjab has taken place in the context of low levels of urbanization. The mean (average) level of urbanization for undivided Punjab during the colonial period was 11.99 per cent, which was very close to the national mean. This was comparable to the levels in England and Wales and the Mediterranean region around 1700 and was higher than that of Germany, central and eastern Europe of the same period.[6]

This comparability in the levels of urbanization, however, should not prompt us to think that the processes of urbanization in Europe and the Punjab were qualitatively the same. There were two important differences.

(a) European urbanization was taking place in a situation where rural population was declining in absolute terms. In the Punjab on the other hand, rural population growth kept pace with total population growth and the rural-urban ratio remained very low throughout the region.
(b) The levels indicated above for Europe are based on data in which only towns with a population of more than 10,000 are considered. In the Punjab however, more than half of the urban places considered, had a population lower than that threshold.

The urbaniztion pattern in the Punjab was a collage of several localized patterns. The levels of urbanization ranged from 1 per cent in some districts to about 20 per cent in others in 1872–1931 and from 10 per cent to 50 per cent in 1951–91.

IV

The characteristics of the regional pattern of urbanization in the Punjab could be highlighted by finding answers to the following questions:

(a) What was the pattern of urbanization in the region?
(b) Was it characterized by de-urbanization?
(c) Was the process of urbanization gradual and broad based? or,
(d) Was it rapid and sporadic?

In order to investigate this pattern, we have deviated from the usual norm of analyzing the levels of urbanization as the percentage share of urban to total population. Instead, we have considered the 'mean city size' at the district and princely state level. This is a measure of the level of urbanization which attempts to take into account not only the urban population as a share of the total population but also the size of urban concentrations. It has the advantage of being a product of the urban proportion and the average of the city size of residence of the urban population.

The results obtained from an analysis of the district-wise mean city size indicate that unlike the trend in eastern India, the percentage share of districts with a mean city size of less than 5,000 increased over time. However, between 1872 and 1931 only 2 to 5 per cent of the districts had cities with a mean size of more than 25,000. But this share gradually increased over the decades. There was a dramatic increase in this share after 1951 when it was 24 per cent. The percentage share remained the same in 1991. In the Punjab, therefore, we find no evidence of de-urbanization in the colonial period as a whole though the mean city size remained small in most of its sub-regions. In the post-Independence period, the percentage share of districts with a mean city size between 10,001–25,000 experienced the greatest increase. The Punjab has been a region of medium sized towns. This is specifically true for the Green Revolution period.

The urbanization process in the Punjab has been broad based. When we measure the district-wise level of urban concentration on a scale ranging from 0–1000, we find that during the colonial period only 3 to 9 per cent of the districts had a concentration index above 501. During the post-Independence period, however, the process of concentration quickened and by 1991 a quarter of the districts reached this mark. This process of concentration has again been a post-Green Revolution phenomenon.

It is interesting to note that there have been three distinct phases of city growth in the Punjab. During the colonial period more than 50 per cent of the towns were in the category of 5,001–10,000. Immediately after Independence most of this growth took place in the size class of 10,001–20,000. In the post-Green Revolution period the higher size categories (50,000+) gained importance. Part of this trend was due to the movement of towns to higher categories through a natural process of growth because after 1951 only 11 new towns came up. Part of this growth could be attributed to the growth of the regional economy. It is therefore important to isolate and assess the impact of the Green Revolution on urban growth.

V

What then would explain the trend and pattern of urbanization and urban growth in the Punjab over the nineteenth century? The explanatory variables rooted in the history of the region could be long distance

Table 13.2: Mean City Size (1872–1991)
Number and Percentage (% in parenthesis) of Districts

Mean city size		1872	1891	1911	1931	1951	1971	1991
Above 25,001	No	0	1	2	2	4	3	4
	%	(0.00)	(2.33)	(5.00)	(4.44)	(23.53)	(16.67)	(23.53)
10,001–25,000	No	2	1	2	4	1	6	6
	%	(7.69)	(2.33)	(5.00)	(8.89)	(5.88)	(33.33)	(33.33)
5,001–10,000	No	0	5	4	5	4	5	5
	%	(00.00)	(11.63)	(10.00)	(11.11)	(23.53)	(27.78)	(27.78)
2,001–5,000	No	5	8	5	8	7	3	3
	%	(19.23)	(18.60)	(12.50)	(15.56)	(41.18)	(16.67)	(16.67)
1,001–2,000	No	7	9	12	10	0	0	1
	%	(26.92)	(20.93)	(30.00)	(22.22)	(0.00)	(0.00)	(5.56)
0–1,000	No	12	19	15	16	1	1	0
	%	(46.15)	(44.19)	(37.50)	(35.56)	(5.88)	(5.56)	(0.00)
Total	No	26	43	40	45	17	18	18
	%	(100)	(100)	(100)	(100)	(100)	(100)	(100)

Table 13.3: Concentration of Urban Population (1872–1991)
Number and Percentage (% in parenthesis) of Districts

Concentration Index (0–1000)		1872	1891	1911	1931	1951	1971	1991
Above 501	No	1	2	2	4	2	3	2
	%	(3.85)	(4.65)	(4.76)	(8.89)	(11.79)	(16.66)	(16.66)
401–500	No	0	2	1	0	1	1	1
	%	(0.00)	(4.65)	(2.38)	(0.00)	(5.88)	(5.55)	(5.55)
301–400	No	0	0	1	2	1	2	2
	%	(00.00)	(0.00)	(2.38)	(4.44)	(5.88)	(11.11)	(11.11)
201–300	No	1	2	1	1	1	1	2
	%	(3.85)	(4.65)	(2.38)	(2.22)	(5.88)	(5.55)	(11.11)
101–200	No	1	3	5	7	3	3	3
	%	(3.85)	(6.98)	(11.90)	(15.56)	(17.64)	(16.66)	(16.66)
51–100	No	4	8	4	4	3	3	3
	%	(15.38)	(18.60)	(9.52)	(8.89)	(17.64)	(16.66)	(16.66)
0–50	No	19	26	26	27	6	5	4
	%	(73.08)	(60.47)	(66.67)	(60.00)	(35.29)	(27.77)	(22.25)
Total	No	26	43	40	45	17	18	18
	%	(100)	(100)	(100)	(100)	(100)	(100)	(100)

trade, agricultural development, railway and road networks, small scale and rural industrialization and inter-regional migration. In this paper we have looked at only one of these variables, i.e. agricultural development. This does not imply that we consider the other variables any less important.

The strength of the rural-urban relationship depends on the key economic activities a region performs. Traditionally the growth of these activities and their distribution depended on the demand created by local communities or by regions and communities outside it. According to Schultz, economic development occurs in a specific location matrix; there may be one or more such matrices in a particular economy. This means that the process of economic growth does not necessarily occur in the same way, at the same time, or at the same rate in different locations.[7] While Schultz attributes development to industrial-urban locational matrices and posits that agricultural development takes place best in those parts which are situated favourably in relation to such centres, evidence from western economic history indicates that the existence of a substantial agricultural surplus is a pre-condition for industrial development and hence of urban growth.

The Punjab is an interesting case to analyse because here we have a region which did not have a strong industrial base, survived on the basis of a trading web by serving as a main channel of trade with Europe and Middle East via Kabul and gradually developed a network of commercial centres and a well-entrenched urban hierarchy, in the evolution of which, marketing of agricultural commodities played an important role. During the early part of the British rule, since agriculture was less developed the role of agricultural surplus in promoting urban growth was negligible. Even until the beginning of the twentieth century, the Punjab was marked by severe droughts and famines mostly affecting tracts in the dry region of present day Haryana and in the sub-montane north-western Punjab. As a result of these calamities, the prices of food grains escalated not only in these areas but also in the neighbouring ones which exported their produce to meet the demand from the affected regions. Increase in production during the colonial period was possible by extending acreage and to do so, marginal lands had to be brought under cultivation. The obvious policy in such a situation was to concentrate on extending irrigation in such areas, a policy the British pursued with single-mindedness. Several canal projects like the Upper Bari Doab, Western Jamuna, Sirhind, Lower Chenab, Lower

Jhelum, and Triple Canal were undertaken during the last quarter of the nineteenth century and in the beginning of the twentieth century. Another measure introduced to give a boost to agriculture was the advancing of *taccavi* loans to the farmers to dig wells. Consequently, the share of irrigated cultivation according to the *Gazetteers* doubled from 22 per cent in 1900–1 to 44 per cent in 1937–8. The development of canal colonies reduced the population pressure in the districts of central Punjab, and resulted also in out-migration of both labour and capital from the region, affecting its output growth.[8]

Agricultural technology in the Punjab remained unchanged until the beginning of the twentieth century despite the significant development of irrigation. Farmers had little knowledge of new agriculutral practices. The British administration did make efforts at developing wastelands but 'neglected the institutional arrangements necessary to bring about overall agricultural and regional growth. The increase in agricultural output was negligible. It was only in the first decade of the twentieth century that with an increase in the demand for finer cotton and with the introduction of newer varieties of cotton and of wheat, agricultural development received a boost. Further incentive was provided by the rise in prices of all agricultural commodities. 'The rise in the price of food grains which became particularly marked during the first decade of the twentieth century helped the land owning classes a great deal. The spread of transport facilities and of improved methods of cultivation, however slow, placed the actual cultivator in a more favourable position'.[9]

The onset of the First World War led to an increase in the export demand for foodgrains and raw material and provided an impetus to agricultural production in the Punjab. The base created in the province during the post-war decades helped this region to gradually become one of the agriculturally more developed regions of the country. These early developments, however, received a setback in 1947 when the country was partitioned. East Punjab on the Indian side received only a minor share of the created canal irrigation potential. But the awareness of the irrigation technology and later developments, both in bringing canal and tubewell water to the cultivated fields and in the use of chemical and biological innovations, made it possible for the Punjab to become the cradle of the Green Revolution in the subcontinent. This prosperity, however, did not favour all parts of the province during the different phases of its development.

An attempt hence is made to formulate an index of the levels of agricultural development in the province. This analysis has been done at the district or princely state level for three structurally distinct periods:

(a) colonial (1929–30).
(b) pre-Green Revolution (1962–3), and
(c) post-Green Revolution (1992–3).

In order to even out the impact of weather fluctuations three year averages have been used. For inter-district comparisons during the colonial period, output of ten major crops was taken in 'equivalent units of wheat output'. For the two post-partition periods, output of nineteen major crops was aggregated in value terms.[10]

Only three variables have been selected to represent agriculutral development:

(a) total crop output per hectare;
(b) share of irrigated area; and
(c) intensity of cropping.

The results of this analysis are given in Table 13.4 and are represented in Maps 13.1 and 13.2. By superimposing the maps of the levels of agricultural development on the maps of levels of urbanization in the Punjab, some interesting observations are given in Table 13.5. It is clear that, over time, there seems to have been no distinct pattern or consistency in the relative position of the districts of the Punjab in terms of the levels of urbanization and agricultural development. The relationship between these variables has also been inconsistent in many districts. For instance in 1929–32, Lyallpur, Montgomery and Sheikhupura had the highest levels of agricultural development but the lowest levels of urbanization. This is because these were the newly settled towns following establishment of canal colonies. Amritsar, which had the highest rank in terms of both these variables in 1929–32 shifted to the second position in 1962–5. Its position droped down to the third in terms of levels of urbanization in 1992–5 but remained second in terms of levels of agricultural development. Moreover, in the pre-Green Revolution period, very few districts have shown a direct relationship between the levels of urbanization and the levels of agricultural development, i.e. they have had the same position in terms

Table 13.4: Punjab Districts ranked according to Levels of Agricultural Development

	West+East Punjab (Excl. Simla)	East Punjab Excl. Simla+Kangra	
	1929–32	1962–5	1992–5
1	Lyallpur	Ludhiana	Sangrur
2	Montgomery	Jalandhar	Ludhiana
3	Sheikhupura	Kapurthala	Ferozepur
4	Multan	Ferozepur	Patiala
5	Amritsar	Patiala, Bhatinda	Jalandhar
6	Lahore	Sangrur	Bhatinda
7	Jhang	Amritsar	Amritsar
8	Gujranwala	Ropar	Kapurthala
9	Jalandhar	Gurdaspur	Karnal
10	Shahpur	Hoshiarpur	Jind
11	Muzaffargarh	Jind	Gurdaspur
12	Ludhiana	Karnal	Ropar
13	Sialkot	Rohtak	Ambala
14	Gujrat	Hissar	Hissar
15	Ferozepur	Ambala	Hoshiarpur
16	Gurdaspur	Gurgaon	Rohtak
17	Karnal	Mahendragarh	Gurgaon
18	Kangra		Mahendragarh
19	Hoshiarpur		
20	Dera Ghazi Khan		
21	Rohtak		
22	Ambala		
23	Gurgaon		
24	Jhelum		
25	Rawalpindi		
26	Hissar		
27	Mianwali		
28	Attock		

of both these variables. However, data for the post-Green Revolution period (1992–5) shows that the relationship between agricultural development and urbanization is becoming more defined over time as there are many more districts which have the same position, though at lower levels, in terms of both these variables (II and III in Table 13.5).

Table 13.5 (I): Levels of Agricultural Development and Urbanization (1929–32)

Agr. Dev. Levels	Urban Dev Levels	I (High)	II	III	IV (Low)
I (High)		Lahore, Amritsar	Gujranwala Jalandhar	Multan, Jhang	Lyallpur, Montgomery Sheikhupura
II		–	Shahpur, Sialkot, Ludhiana	Ferozepur	Muzaffargarh
III		Rawalpindi	–	Gurdaspur Karnal	Gujrat
IV (Low)		Ambla	Dera Gazi Khan, Hissar	Attock, Mianwali, Jhelum, Gurgaon. Rohtak	Hoshiarpur, Kangra

Table 13.5 (II): Levels of Agricultural Development and Urbanization (1962–5)

Agr. Dev. Levels	Urban Dev. Levels	I (High)	II	III	IV (Low)
I (High)		–	Jalandhar, Ludhiana	–	–
II		Ambala (*Yamuna Nagar)	Patiala, Amritsar	Ropar, Kapurthala Sangrur, Ferozepur (*Faridkot) Gurdaspur, Jind	Bhatinda, Hoshiarpur
III		–	Gurgaon (*Faridabad) (Rewari)	Karnal (*Kuru-kshetra Kaithal) Hissar (Sirsa *Bhiwani)	Rohtak (*Sonepat) (Panipat in old Karnal)
IV (Low)				Mahendragarh	

Table 13.5 (III): Levels of Agricultural Development and Urbanization (1992–5)

Agr. Dev. Levels	Urban Dev. Levels	I (High)	II	III	IV (Low)
I (High)		Ludhiana, Sangrur	–	–	–
II		Jalandhar	Patiala, Karnal, (*Kuru-kshetra) (*Panipat) Kapurthala (Faridkot)	Rohtak, Bhatinda, Ferozepur, Amritsar	Kaithal in old Karnal
III		Ambala	Ropar (Yamuna Nagar)	Hoshiarpur Gurdaspur, Jind, Hissar (*Sirsa *Bhiwani)	–
IV	(Low)	(Faridabad)			

Notes:

1. The Urban data is for the census years 1931, 1961 and 1991.
2. Districts in parentheses with a * sign are a part of the main accompanying district while those in parentheses without * are treated separately for levels of urbanization but are considered at the same level as the parent district for levels of agricultural development. For agricultural development the parent districts are considered as follows:

Punjab	Haryana
1. Amritsar	1. Ambala (includes major part of Yamuna Nagar)
2. Bhatinda (include some part of Faridkot)	2. Gurgaon (includes Faridkot and some parts of Mahendragarh, Rewari, Bhiwani)
3. Ferozepur (includes major part of Faridkot)	3. Hissar (includes Sirsa and major parts of Bhiwani)
4. Gurdaspur	4. Jind (includes major part of Panipat, Kurukshetra)

(contd.)

Punjab	Haryana
5. Hoshiarpur	5. Karnal (includes major part of Panipat, Kurukshetra, Kaithal, and minor parts of Yamuna Nagar, Ambala and Jind)
6. Jalandhar	6. Mahendragarh (includes major part of Rewari and some parts of Bhiwani)
7. Kapurthala	
8. Ludhiana	
9. Patiala	
10. Ropar	
11. Sangrur	

VI

A further analysis is necessary to answer three crucial questions about the relationship between urbanization and the process of development in the Punjab, an agriculturally prosperous region:

(a) Why was there no de-urbanization during the colonial period?
(b) Why did not a metropolitian city develop despite its continued prosperity?
(c) How does a low average level of urbanization sustain itself?

In a growing economy like the Punjab, agricultural development would have positively affected urban growth provided such developments were nurtured under long-term political stability. During the pre-partition days, the quantum of agricultural surplus which flowed out of the canal colonies did generate allied activities both in their hinterland and in the colony towns. But these towns had not reached their potential growth levels when this region underwent serious turmoil culminating in the partition of the country. East Punjab was relatively, agriculturally less developed and it was only with the development of infrastructure like tube-wells, canal irrigation and transport network that new technology inputs in agriculture were experimented with, leading to an output boom known as the Green Revolution. Its impact on the Punjab's urbanization during 1961–71 is carefully studied by D'Souza who observes that artisan towns which comprised one-fifth of total towns in 1961 were wiped out; service and manufacturing towns declined while

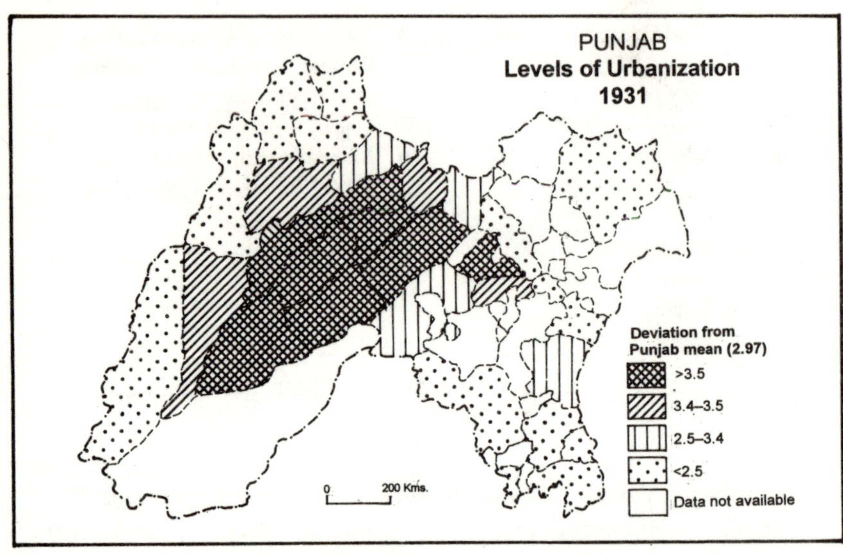

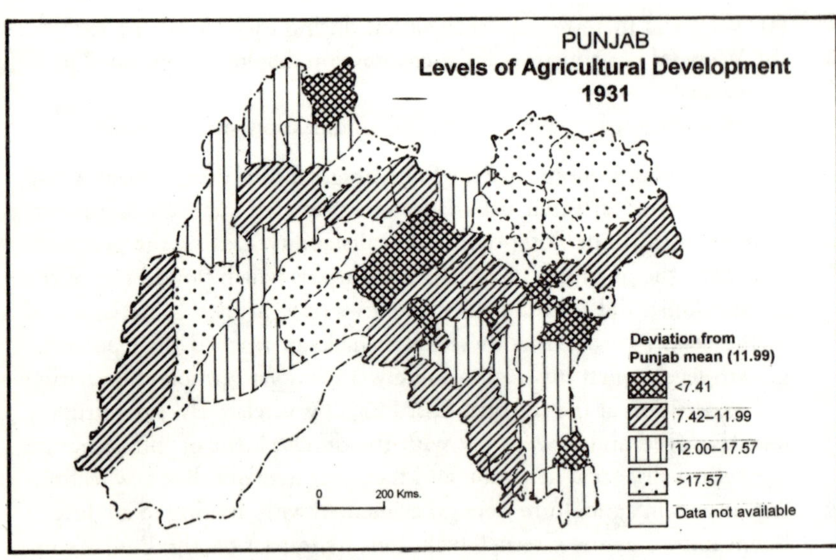

Map. 13.1: The Punjab: Levels of Urbanization and Agricultural Development 1931

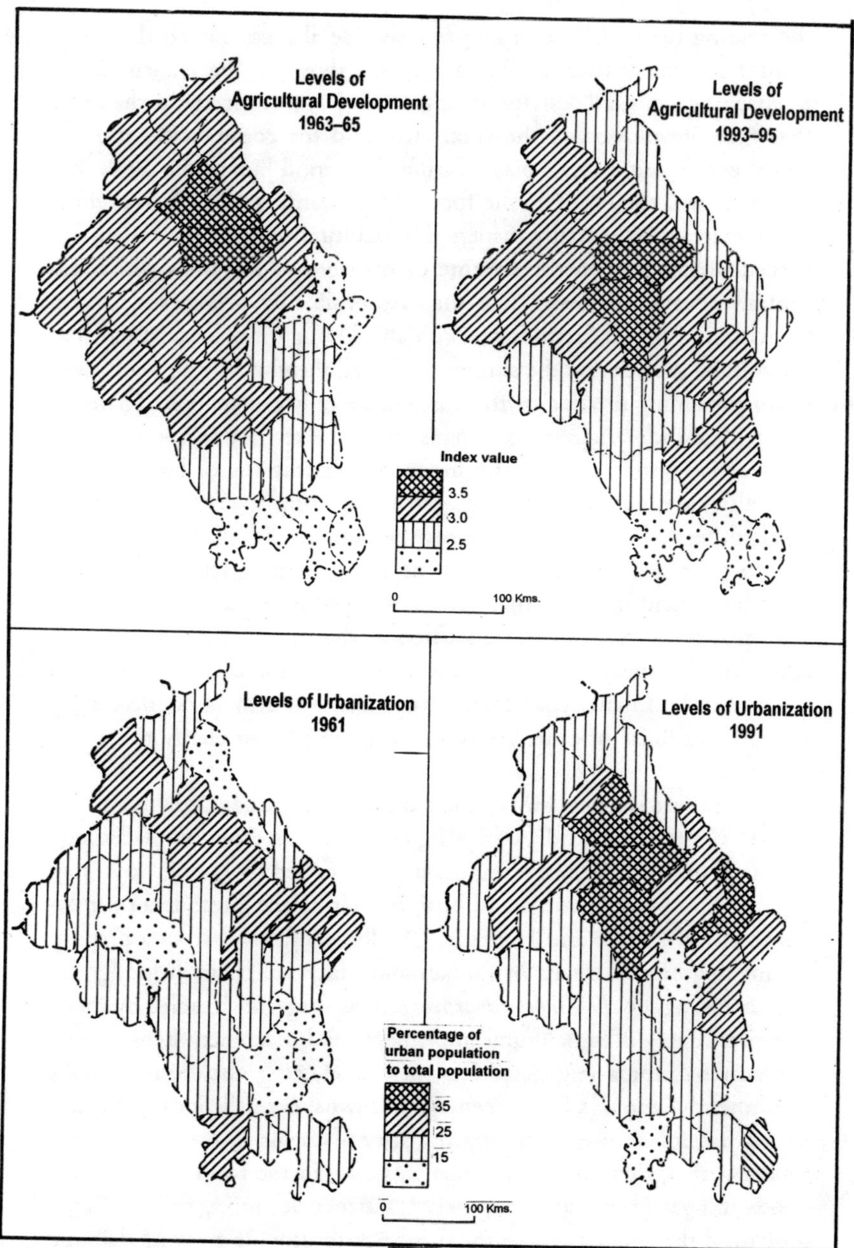

Map 13.2: Punjab-Haryana Region—Levels of Agricultural Development; and Levels of Urbanization 1963–5, 1993–5

the trading towns increased enormously. He also concluded that, 'this feature of urbanization in Punjab can be shown to be related to the intensive agricultural activity during 1961–71, not merely in the sense that green revolution in the rural areas and the commercialization of urban communities took place during the period but in the sense that the latter was the result of the former'.[11] According to D'Souza, enormous increase in spatially dispersed agricultural output led to 'an unprecedented boom in the volume of distributive activities which are centrally located in towns. It is thus responsible for a large-scale transformation of urban functions in Punjab'. Though it is understood that agricultural growth and the surplus generated thereby may be a sufficient factor explaining urban growth, it is not the only explanation. There are others, like industrialization, expansion of the tertiary sector and consequent job generation, establishment of institutions of learning and of health-care, extent of trading activity and similar expansions which need to be studied for a comprehensive understanding. However, it is safe to surmise that towns within the orbit of an agriculturally developed hinterland in the Punjab have developed faster, as was the case in the canal colonies, than those located in the midst of a slow growing agricultural activity. Under the current set-up, a comparison between towns like Ludhiana, Jalandhar, Patiala and Kapurthala of the central Punjab and those of other regions of the Punjab can clarify this statement.

In fact there is a two-way relationship between urban growth and the growth of the hinterland. A growing agricultural sector also places high demands on several types of inputs being supplied by towns, encouraging growth of employment and business. Using the latest data on market towns of Punjab and Haryana, Chadha confirms that 'to a preponderant majority of towns in Punjab and Haryana, trade in foodgrains figures among the *three most important commodity groups* handled by them; likewise, supply of agricultural implements and machinery items as also the current inputs (e.g. fertilizers, pesticides, etc.) also figure equally prominently among a big percentage of towns; even the local manufacturing base of an overwhelming majority of towns in the two states is linked with agricultural requirements, partly in the form of producers' goods and partly as consumer goods'.[12] Further, according to Raj: 'Rapid growth of the agricultural sector also helps to provide growing demand for the products of industry and thus stimulates a high growth in this sector as well. In Panjab, growth of small scale industries appears to draw more sustenance from local demand than in most other regions'.[13]

This, along with the commercial activity based on marketed agricultural surplus which swarms local town *mandis,* manufacture and trading or products to suit different requirements and lifestyles of a progressive economy, construction of bridges and development of rail-road network may well be some of the important reasons for the sustenance of towns. Besides this, towns also serve as investment centres for the hinterland. The Punjab is a unique example of a number of mushrooming small and medium sized towns, not much far apart from each other, with each village being under the orbit of one town or the other, furthering mutual dependence. This is in contrast to a pattern of urban growth focused on one primate city. Perhaps this is the success story of the Punjab. The path of growth would have been different if one large metropolitan city had developed in the state. This may have left several villages untouched by the growth process. Lahore had a strong case for becoming a metropolitan city if its economy had not been hit by the partition. Even some less developed hinterland towns like Ambala, Faridabad, Panipat, Sonepat (currently in Haryana) have grown mainly because of the locational advantage that they enjoy as important transport junctions or as industrial and handloom centres in proximity to a mega-city. While it is true that commercial activity in an agriculturally predominant region is given a 'big push' by a prosperous hinterland, other socio-political processes may hinder its development. For example, political instability during the eighties did stunt the growth process in many towns including those close to the international border. However, the Punjab's urban economy survived because it has strong linkages with a rich agricultural hinterland and regional and national markets. This economic activity has been fairly dispersed over space in the Punjab, where historically the *kacha* and the *pucca arhtiyas* in rural and in urban areas developed permanent links with the regional and national markets. They provided the base for a strong market network which played a significant role in the regional economy. In addition, the Punjab and Haryana towns also have a unique feature: by and large, they specialize in only one type of economic activity or in the manufacture of one type of commodity. For example, Amritsar is known for textiles, Batala for manufacture of sanitary fittings/pipes, Jalandhar for bus-body-building, Kapurthala for the coach factory, Ludhiana for hosiery products, Ambala for scientific instruments, Panipat for handlooms, Sonepat for the bicycle industry and so on. These towns, therefore have created a niche and an identity for themselves in the regional and national economy. It is therefore, not easy for the Punjab to deurbanize, as Bengal did during the British rule, or even under the political upheavals experienced during recent times.

NOTES

1. Walter Hamilton, *East India Gazetteer*, 2 vols., London, 1828, p. 114.
2. A. Heston, 'National Income', in Dharma Kumar (ed.), *The Cambridge History of India*, vol. II, New Delhi: Orient Longman, 1982, pp. 376–462.
3. Atiya Habeeb Kidwai, 'Characteristics and Processes of Urbanization in Colonial India', Ph.D. thesis submitted to Jawaharlal Nehru University, New Delhi, 1979.
4. Edward Thornton, *Gazetteer of the East India Co.*, London, 1854.
5. Irfan Habib, *An Atlas of the Mughal Empire*, New Delhi: OUP, 1982.
6. J. De Vries, *European Urbanization 1500–1800*, Massachusetts: Cambridge, 1984, p. 39.
7. T.W. Shultz, 'A framework for land economics: The long view', *Journal of Farm Economics*, 1951, p. 33.
8. For agricultural development in the Punjab region, Chander Prabha, 'Districtwise Rates of Growth of Agricultural Output in East and West Punjab during the Pre-partition and Post-partition Periods', *The Indian Economic and Social History Review*, vol. 6, no. 4, 1969, pp. 333–50. Ajit K. Dasgupta, 'Agricultural Growth Rates in the Punjab, 1906–42', *The Indian Economic and Social History Review*, vol. 18, nos. 3–4, pp. 327–48. Akhtar Husain Siddiqi, 'Nineteenth Century Agricultural Development in Punjab: 1850–1900', *The Indian Economic and Social History Review*, vol. 21, no. 3, 1984.
9. D.R. Gadgil, *The Industrial Evolution of India*, Bombay: Popular Prakashan, 1954.
10. G.S. Bhalla and Gurmail Singh, 'Recent Developments in Indian Agriculture: A District Level Study of India' (Mimeograph), Centre for the Study of Regional Development, Jawaharlal Nehru University, New Delhi, 1998.
11. Victor D'Souza, 'Green Revolution and Urbanization in Punjab during 1961–71', in S. Manzoor Alam and V.V. Poshishevsky (eds.), *Urbanisation in Developing Countries*, New Delhi: Concept Publishers, 1976.
12. G.K. Chadha, 'Growth and Agricultural Linkages of Market Towns in Punjab and Haryana' (Mimeograph), Centre for the Study of Regional Development, Jawaharlal Nehru University, New Delhi, 1994.
13. K.N. Raj, 'Economic Growth in Punjab', in Varinder Grover (ed.), *The Story of Punjab, Yesterday and Today*, New Delhi: Deep and Deep Publications, 1995.

APPENDIX

Towns in the Punjab During Akbar's Reign (Ranked According to Population Size) + B55

Akbar's reign		Population 1881		Population 1931		Population 1991
1.	Lahore	149,369	Lahore	429,748	Delhi	8,375,188
2.	Delhi	173,393	Delhi	304,420	Ludhiana	1,042,740
3.	Ambala	67,463	Rawalpindi	119,284	Karnal	885,797
4.	Rawalpindi	529,275	Sialkot	100,973	Jalandhar	509,510
5.	Jalandhar	52,119	Jalandhar	89,030	Rohtak	216,096
6.	Sialkot	45,762	Ambala	86,592	Panipat	191,212
7.	Ludhiana	44,163	Ludhiana	68,586	Hissar	181,255
8.	Ferozepur	39,570	Ferozepur	64,634	Karkaunda	176,131
9.	Panipat	25,022	Kasur	46,815	Ambala	119,338
10.	Batala	24,281	Jhang	36,035	Sirsa	112,841
11.	Rewari	23,972	Rohtak	35,235	Batala	103,367
12.	Karnal	23,133	Batala	33,204	Malerkotla	88,600
13.	Dera Ghazi	22,309	Panipat	32,915	Jind	85,315
14.	Jhelum	21,107	Dera Ghazi	28,468	Thaneswar	81,255
15.	Malerkota	20,621	Karnal	26,610	Ferozepur	78,738
16.	Narnaul	20,052	Gujrat	26,511	Rewari	75,342
17.	Gujrat	18,753	Rewari	26,269	Khanna	71,990
18.	Kasur	17,336	Chiniot	25,841	Kaithal	71,142
19.	Rohtak	15,699	Malerkotla	25,240	Hansi	59,653
20.	Bhera	15,165	Hissar	25,179	Palwal	59,168
21.	Kaithal	14,754	Jhelam	23,499	Narnaul	51,978
22.	Hissar	14,167	Karnaul	21,905	Fatehabad	45,500
23.	Jalalpur	12,839	Bhera	19,741	Ropar	37,996
24.	Hansi	12,656	Kaithal	19,418	Tohana	34,215
25.	Makhiala	12,574	Sirsa	18,909	Gohana	32,496
26.	Rahon	11,736	Hansi	18,356	Nawanshahr	29,955
27.	Jhajjar	11,650	Hafizabad	14,431	Nakodar	28,478
28.	Sadhaura	10,794	Jalalpur	12,507	Jhajjar	27,693
29.	Chiniot	10,731	Jhajjar	12,232	Mandi	23,204
30.	Palwal	10,635	Jhind	11,699	Nahan	21,867
31.	Ropar	10,326	Palwal	10,807	Philaur	20,956
32.	Bheri	9,695	Nakodar	9,584	Ghannaur	20,952
33.	Jhang	9,055	Ropar	8,764	Safedon	20,056
34.	Nakodar	8,486	Chinna	8,269	Chamba	17,194
35.	Pasroor	8,378	Parsroor	7,905	Sohna	16,348
36.	Noormahal	8,161	Beri	7,877	Pundri	15,534

(contd.)

APPENDIX (contd.)

Akbar's reign		Population 1881		Population 1931		Population 1991
37.	Chinna	8,122	Sadhaura	7,769	Beri	14,508
38.	Dadri	7,837	Mandi	7,538	Machhiwara	13,554
39.	Shahpur	7,752	Tohana	7,519	Hafizabad	13,263
40.	Gohana	7,444	Eminabad	7,329	Dharamkot	11,981
41.	Sohna	7,374	Dadri	7,260	Sadhaura	11,818
42.	Kalanaur	7,371	Nawanshahar	7,153	Pataudi	11,278
43.	Jind	7,136	Noormahal	7,079	Noormahal	11,149
44.	Phillaur	7,107	Nahan	6,859	Rahon	10,771
45.	Hariana	6,472	Shorkot	6,826	Chaprauli	7,330
46.	Dharamkot	6,007	Dharamkot	6,779	Hariana	6,473
47.	Thanesar	6,005	Rahon	6,692	Pinjaur	5,501
48.	Machiwara	5,967	Khanna	6,555	Jawalamukhi	4,047
49.	Eminabad	5,886	Chamba	6,219	Kalanaur	1,865
50.	Chaprauli	5,389	Safedon	6,169	Zaferwal	NA
51.	Nahan	5,252	Hariana	5,971	Sialkot	NA
52.	Chamba	5,218	Sohna	5,667	Shorkot	NA
53.	Mandi	5,030	Phillaur	5,168	Sharakpur	NA
54.	Zaferwal	4,978	Chaprauli	5,124	Shahpur	NA
55.	Pundri	4,977	Gohana	5,045	Rawalpindi	NA
56.	Nawanshahar	4,960	Thanesar	5,032	Parsroor	NA
57.	Kahlur	4,804	Pataudi	3,667	Naushera	NA
58.	Sharakpur	4,595	Shahpur	3,265	Naher	NA
59.	Attock	4,210	Attock	1,826	Makhiala	NA
60.	Safedon	4,160	Zaferwal	0	Lahore	NA
61.	Tohana	4,155	Shakarpur	0	Kasur	NA
62.	Karkaunda	4,144	Pundri	0	Kahlur	NA
63.	Pataudi	4,052	Pinjaur	0	Jhelum	NA
64.	Khanna	3,988	Naushera	0	Jhang	NA
65.	Deepalpur	3,435	Naher	0	Jalalpur	NA
66.	Fatehabad	2,992	Makhiala	0	Hadiabad	NA
67.	Hafizabad	2,453	Machhiwara	0	Gujrat	NA
68.	Jawalamukhi	2,424	Karkaunda	0	Eminabad	NA
69.	Hadiabad	2,347	Kalanaur	0	Duniyapur	NA
70.	Shorkot	2,283	Kahlur	0	Dera Ghazi Khan	NA
71.	Duniyapur	2,041	Jawalamukhi	0	Deepalpur	NA
72.	Naushera	1,961	Hadiabad	0	Chinna	NA
73.	Naher	1,567	Ghannaur	0	Chiniot	NA
74.	Pinjaur	1,223	Fatehabad	0	Bhera	NA
75.	Ghannaur	1,099	Duniyapur	0	Attock	NA

Note: NA Towns are now in Pakistan.

14

Urbanization in Himachal Pradesh: Analysis of Patterns and Trends (1901–2001)

SURYA KANT

Himachal Pradesh, which till recently was a part of the Punjab, makes a distinct physio-cultural unit, different from the Punjab plains. Among others, urbanization here has a number of features that distinguish it from that of the plains. Urbanization in the hill regions like Himachal Pradesh can easily be identified with a low level, moderate growth, highly uneven distribution, small size and wide spacing of urban centres. As a cultural artifact, hill towns make a bold appearance on the dominant physical landscape of the hilly and mountainous regions (Verma and Krishan 1980). Chief determinants of their location include altitude, terrain, micro-climate, scenic beauty, accessibility, political constraints, strategic importance, personal interest of the founders, and reputation of a locality (Mitchell 1973). Religious importance and availability of technology can be listed as additional factors.

The recent political and administrative history of Himachal Pradesh has a significant bearing on the urbanization process in the area covered by the state. The British rulers established a number of hill stations, sanatoria and cantonments to impart administrative, recreational and military functions in the middle of 19th century. The exogenous urbanization induced by them differed widely from the indigenous urbanization in terms of site, situation, cultural setting and socio-political situation. In the post-Independence era, emergence of Himachal territory into a centrally administered state in 1948, in-migration of refugees from across the border due to partition in 1947, merger of Bilaspur with Himachal in 1954, shifting of headquarters of the Punjab state from Shimla to its new capital at Chandigarh in 1956, transfer of Hindi speaking northern areas from Punjab to Himachal Pradesh under the Punjab Reorganisation Act, 1966, and grant of full statehood to Himachal Pradesh in 1971 made profound impact on the process of urbanization in Himachal Pradesh.

In the present paper a comprehensive analysis of the process of urbanization in Himachal Pradesh has been attempted. The main aspects examined are:

(i) A comparison of urbanization process in the pre and post-Independence history of the Himachal area;
(ii) geographical and size distribution of the urban centres;
(iii) site characteristics of urban centres;
(iv) growth behaviour of urban centres and its consequences; and
(v) functional characteristics of towns.

A reliable and continuous data on various demographic attributes in India are available only from 1901 onwards. The present study will cover a period of 100 years (1901–2001). During this period the eleven population censuses have been conducted. For a comparative study of the urbanization process in the state, this period has been divided into two somewhat unequal sub-periods: 1901 to 1941 and 1941 to 2001. For studying other aspects of urbanization in Himachal Pradesh focus will, however, remain on the period spanning from 1951 to 2001.

Himachal Pradesh: The Study Area

Himachal Pradesh is one of the youngest states of the Indian Union. Formed as a centrally administered territory in April 1948, it attained full statehood on 25 January 1971. The state is currently divided into 12 districts for administrative purposes. It covers an area of 55,673 sq. km. and had a population of 6.08 million in 2001, distributed in 20, 118 villages and 57 towns. The biggest urban centre (Shimla) in the state had a population of 142,161 persons.

Physiographically, the territory is part of the Himalayan system. There is a typical longitudinal arrangement of the various landforms: the Trans-Himalayas, the Greater Himalayas, the Dhauladhar-Shimla Hills, and the Siwaliks enclosing the faulted valleys (*duns*) of Pinjor, Jaswan, and Paonta. The relief ranges from 300 metres to more than 6,000 metres.

About one-half of the total area is higher than 3,000 metres. The major means of communications has always been road transport. Difficult terrain and uncomfortable long journey restricted the interaction between the plains and the hills. Major source of interaction was through trade and pilgrimage. Many of the routes were actually parts of the ancient Indo-Central Asian trade routes. Many of the small settlements located on these routes later emerged as towns. The British constructed roads to link the hill resorts and sanatoria established during their rule.

Historically, the region remained almost undisturbed by the political upheaval of the Punjab plains. The region was ruled by several dynasties, the Katoches of Kangra being the most powerful. During the medieval period, several of them passed into the hands of the Turko-Mughal rulers. The break up of the Mughal Empire encouraged the local Rajput chiefs to raise their heads again. Major change in power system came after the Anglo-Sikh War in 1846 when large parts of the Himachal territory came under the direct rule of the British. In 1864, Simla (now Shimla) became the summer capital of the Imperial government in India. Since majority of the towns established during the period, either by the British or the native rulers, emerged in response to administrative and political needs, their economic base as well as interaction with the rural surroundings was weak.

Administratively, Himachal Pradesh was created as a separate territory in April 1948, by the merger of more than 30 former princely states of northern hill areas of the then Punjab. In 1954 Bilaspur, another former princely state and later on a Part C state of the Indian Union, was also merged with it. In November 1966, under Punjab Reorganisation Act, northern Hindi speaking hill areas of Punjab were merged with Himachal Pradesh. Not only this increased the area size of the state to more than twice but also provided with physical compactness and resource base, needed for administrative efficiency and economic viability. Earlier to it, Himachal territory was divided into two mutually exclusive segments separated as it was by the Punjab territory. On 25 January 1971 Himachal Pradesh attained full statehood, providing impetus to a variety of developmental activities with a significant bearing on the process of urbanization. Since then the state has made tremendous progress in the field of literacy, infrastructure development, hydel-power generation, tourism and horticulture.

Urbanization Process

Himachal Pradesh is the least urbanized state in India. Its share of urban population (9.8 per cent in 2001) is the lowest among all the 28 states in the Indian Union and was nearly one-third of the national average (27.8 per cent). Nevertheless, the pace of urbanization has been increasing, particularly in the post-Independence period. The annual compound growth rate of urban population was twice (2.06 per cent) of the total population (1.1 per cent) in the state during 1901–2001. Remaining quite sluggish till 1931–41, urban growth picked up fast since the 1941–51 decade. Of the total urban population of 517,000, added in the state during 1901–2001, 508,000 or more than 98 per cent came during 1941-2001. The number of towns has grown to 57 in 2001 from just 11 in 1911. During the same period, the proportion of urban population has grown to 9.8 per cent from only 3.1 per cent.

Notwithstanding that urbanization is getting more and more spatially pervasive, there are wide regional variations in size and number of urban centres in the state. Kinnaur and Lahul & Spiti are the two districts in the state where any urban centre is yet to emerge. Shimla, located in the district of the same name, has now attained the status of class I urban centre (population 100,000 +), though majority of towns in the state are small in size.

Low degree of urbanization in the state is explained by a variety of factors:

(i) the difficult terrain dictating the large central villages to act as service centres for the surroundings villages and hamlets; (ii) presence of a large number of small to very small rural settlements failing to provide the threshold required for further growth; and (iii) the low level of industrial development acting negatively on the process of urbanization in the state.

Pre-Independence Period (1901–1941)

During this period, the pace of urbanization remained quite slow. In 1901, the urban population of Himachal Pradesh was only 77,332 persons, i.e. 4.2 per cent of the total population in the state. Thus, only one out of every 25 persons in Himachal Pradesh was an urbanite in 1901 as against one in 10 persons in the country as a whole. In all, there were 21 towns in the area in 1901, 15 of them being the class VI towns (having population of less than 5,000 persons). Shimla, the largest town, had a population of 13,960. Shimla, Kasauli, Sabathu, Dagshai, Jutogh, Dalhousie and Bakloh were located at the hilltops and originated during the British period. Shimla established in 1819 was among the first modern hill stations in India. Located on a saddle ridge, it was well connected to Ambala through Kalka. The cantonments of Sabathu, Dagshai and Kasauli also functioned as convalescent depots and hill stations along the Kalka-Shimla highway. On the other hand, Chamba, Kangra, Rampur, Mandi, Nalagarh, Nurpur and Una were pre-British in origin and were situated in river valleys. Kangra had the distinction of being the capital of the oldest native state and enjoyed considerable importance as a political, cultural and religious centre of the region. Rampur, the capital of Bashahr state and located on the old Hindustan-Tibet road, was an important centre of collection and distribution, attracting trade from long distance. It was also an important Hindu and Buddhist religious centre. Nurpur and Nalagarh located in the hill-foot contact zone enjoyed better accessibility and functioned as important supply and market centres. The process of indigenous urbanization was, thus, progressing simultaneously as a result of trade and administrative and religious activities (Sharma 1992: 6).

During the 1901–11 decade, urban population in the state registered an absolute decline. The share of the urban population in the total also declined from 4.2 per cent in 1901 to 3.12 per cent in 1911. As many as nine towns were declassified and Kasumpti, a separate town in 1901, was merged with Shimla. This reduced the number of towns in the state to 11. Towns were distributed in only six districts of Shimla, Chamba, Mandi, Kangra, Sirmaur and Solan, while Una and Bilaspur districts remained without any urban centre. Interestingly, all towns declassified in the census were native in origin and functioned as the headquarters of native states. Mandi and Chamba, the two capital towns of native states, also registered decline but were not declassified. Almost all the declassified towns were in class VI category of towns. The number of such towns was reduced from 15 in 1901 to 6 in 1911.

Moreover, the 1901–11 decade witnessed several natural calamities. In Kangra district alone the earthquake of 1905 killed thousands of people. The epidemics also took their toll. Urban areas being congested registered higher mortality in comparison to rural areas. In fact, this decade is marked with an overall decline of population in Himachal

Pradesh, because rural population also registered a marginal decline (0.20 per cent). The average growth of urban population was 12.14 per cent during 1901–11. Shimla registered the highest decadal growth rate (39.0 per cent). In fact, 85.0 per cent of the total increase in urban population of the state during the decade was in Shimla town.

During 1911–21, urban population increased by 7,325 persons. The proportion of urban population also increased marginally to 3.46 per cent from 3.12 per cent in 1911, against the national average of 11.20 per cent. Towns of Bhojpur and Nagar were merged to form a new town of Suket. This raised the number of towns in the area to 12 in the 1921 census. The spatial pattern of urbanization remained the same as in 1911. Dalhousie recorded the highest increase of 52.02 per cent, followed by Shimla with 41.68 per cent. Against this, Dharmsala, a cantonment town, registered the highest decrease (–29.16 per cent), attributed to out-movement of troops and their families. The same applies to the decline of population in the cantonment towns of Sabathu, Dagshai and Bakloh. Nahan and Mandi, headquarters of the native states of Sirmaur and Mandi, also registered a decline in their population.

During the next decade (1921–31), urban population registered an absolute increase of only 7,134 persons against 7,325 persons in the previous decade, resulting in a marginal decline in decennial growth rate to 10.72 per cent from 12.37 per cent during 1911–21. The relative proportion of urban population registered only a marginal increase: from 3.46 per cent in 1921 to 3.69 per cent in 1931. On face, seven new/reclassified towns came up in 1931. These included Kasumpti, Jogindarnagar, Shamsherpur, Jutogh, Una, Bilaspur and Dalhousie cantonment. This reduced the number of the new/reclassified towns to 5 only. Only Jogindarnagar, which grew with implementation of the Barot hydel power project, was the new town added during this decade. Shimla town registered decline in its population for the first time. Exclusion of the population of Kasumpti and Jutogh towns from that of Shimla in 1931 was mainly responsible for the highest decline in the population of Shimla town during the decade. Against this, impressive increase in the population of the municipal towns of Nahan and Dalhousie was caused by the addition respectively of Shamsherpur and Dalhousie cantonments in their population. Nevertheless, the spatial pattern of urbanization remained almost unaltered during this decade also.

During 1931-41, urbanization registered further increase as the decadal growth stepped up to 16.90 per cent (rural population growth being 11.33 per cent) from 10.72 per cent during the previous decade. Three new 'towns' added in the Census of 1941 were the reclassified towns of Solan, Nalagarh and Rampur. This increased the number of towns to 22 in 1941. Of them the latter two were capital towns of the native states. With this the number of towns in the state again touched the 1901 level.

The growth of urban population varied widely. It varied from an increase of 64.35 per cent in the Sabathu cantonment town to a decline of 53.89 per cent in Jogindarnagar. An increase in the former case was associated with the induction of troops here while, a decrease in the latter case was due largely to a decline in construction activities at the hydel project site. Mandi, Dharmsala, Una, Bilaspur, Dalhousie, Bakloh and Jutogh registered an increase that was higher than the state average. Some development of tertiary services resulted in the growth of urban population in Chamba, Mandi, Nahan and Bilaspur towns. All were capital towns of the native states (Annexure 14.1). On the other hand, those registering decline other than Jogindarnagar included Dagshai, Kasauli and Sundarnagar.

The distribution pattern of towns in 1941 was a continuation of the pattern existing before 1931. The addition of reclassified towns did not bring any significant change in the pattern.

Post-Independence Period (1941–2001)

This period witnessed a reversal in urbanization trend in the state: from the previously sluggish growth to fast growth of urban centres. Of the total increase of 518,000 persons in the urban Himachal Pradesh during the century, 508,000 or more than 98.0 per cent took place during 1941–2001. Nearly one-third of this was added during the latest census decade of 1991–2001. As many as 24 out of the total of 57 urban centres in the state emerged during the last three decades since 1971. The spatial pattern of urbanization also changed considerably in favour of new locations. The urban centres are now located in ten districts of the state, as against in six districts during the pre-Independence period.

The decade 1941–51 was marked by important events on the Indian scene. The first half of this decade was spanned by continuation of the second world war and the later half was occupied by events like post-war industrial unrest, followed by partition of the subcontinent in 1947. The latter event had a direct bearing on urbanization in Himachal Pradesh, because one-half of the present territory of Himachal Pradesh was then a part of the East Punjab state. The displaced population from the newly born country, Pakistan, was settled in different districts of the present Himachal Pradesh. The displaced persons showed a distinct tendency of settling down in urban places. New towns came up and the old ones registered a sharp increase in their population. The net impact of all these developments was a boost to the process of urbanization in the state.

Urban population, registered a sharp increase during this decade from 3.80 per cent in 1941 to 6.38 per cent in 1951. In absolute terms, it amounted to 154,000 making a decadal increase of 78.7 per cent. This increase is attributed to: (i) reclassification of towns such as Kangra and Nurpur which stood declassified since 1911; (ii) emergence of 10 new towns namely Kullu, Yol, Nagrota, Paonta Sahib, Palampur, Dharampur, Kandaghat, Garkhal, Arki and Theog; and (iii) sharp increase in the population of the existing urban centres due to settling of displaced persons. The number of towns went up to 29 from 22 in 1941. In fact, with the addition of 10 new towns in 1951, the number should have been 32 but for declassification of Bakloh (Chamba district) and Kasumpti (Shimla district) towns and inclusion of Jutogh with Shimla town. With the exception of Yol, a spur town, all new/reclassified towns in 1951 were valley towns.

The reclassification of Kangra town and the emergence of four new towns of Yol, Nagrota, Palampur and Nurpur in Kangra district led to a three-fold increase in urban population in the district. A big army camp, with 13,520 personnel, was set up at Yol. On the other hand, declassification of cantonment towns of Bakloh and Dalhousie along with repatriation of Muslim population from other towns of the district to Pakistan were responsible for a negative change of 40.3 per cent in the urban population of Chamba district.

At town level, urban population in Sundarnagar increased by more than 200.0 per cent. Other towns experiencing very high increase include Shimla (151.5 per cent) and Solan (114.9 per cent). Merger of Jutogh with Shimla, coupled with the shift of the East Punjab capital to Shimla from Lahore caused this spurt in the case of Shimla. On the other hand, rapid growth in the population of Solan town was attributed to settling of displaced persons along with shift of the Panjab University offices to this place. Jogindarnagar continued to decline in this decade also. Three former capital towns of the native states of Mandi, Nalagarh and Rampur too declined under the changed circumstances.

The decade of 1941–51 can rightly be called a watershed in the history of urbanization in the state. For the first time, decadal increase in urban population in Himachal Pradesh was higher (78.7 per cent) than the national average (41.3 per cent). Moreover, as many as 12 new/reclassified towns emerged and urbanization entered new locations.

In the next decade of 1951-61, the urban population registered an impressive absolute increase of 24,448 persons though the proportion of urban population declined marginally to 6.34 per cent in 1961 from 6.38 per cent in 1951. This number was nearly thrice the total increase (8,767 persons) during the previous four decades (1901-41). Four towns of Dharampur, Garkhal, Kandaghat and Sanawar were declassified for not satisfying the new definition laid down in the 1961 census. However, emergence of 5 new/reclassified towns of Bakloh, Dalhousie, Jutogh, Nainadevi and Narkanda resulted in an increase of towns to 30 from 29 in 1951.

Locationally, all the five new/reclassified towns of Dalhousie, Bakloh, Jutogh, Nainadevi and Narkanda, emerging in 1961, were hill top towns (Annexure 14.1). This raised the number of hill top towns to 11 from 6 in 1951. The spatial pattern of urbanization remained almost the same as in 1951. The impact of post-Independence development programmes on population growth of several towns was quite evident by now. Paonta Sahib, a religious centre, attracted a lot of trade and industrial activities during the decade, resulting in rapid growth in its population. Impressive growth of Bilaspur, Mandi and Kullu towns was associated with expansion in administrative activities. On the other hand, decline in Shimla was due to the shift of Punjab's headquarters to Chandigarh, the newly constructed capital city.

Urbanization picked up further momentum during 1961–71 as the decadal increase in the state jumped to 35.7 per cent from about 16 per cent in the previous census decade. As many as 6 new towns of Hamirpur, Santokhgarh, Pandoh, Manali, Ghumarwin and Saharan emerged, taking the number of towns to 36. These contributed 19,166 persons or 7.9 per cent of the total urban population in Himachal

Pradesh in 1971. Of the new towns, Hamirpur and Ghamarwin were tahsil headquarters. Manali, an important tourist centre located on the left bank of the river Beas, enjoyed direct access to Shimla, Chandigarh and Delhi. Pandoh emerged as a class V town directly due to the hydel power project.

Urban growth varied widely at town level. Sundarnagar, a project township in Mandi district, registered the highest increase of 268.5 per cent, distantly followed by Paonta Sahib with 101.4 per cent and Kullu with 83.3 per cent. Against this, most of the cantonment towns declined due to the outward movement of troops.

The spatial disparity in the distribution of urban centres accentuated further during this period. The main concentration of towns was in Kangra valley and southern parts of the state adjoining the border with Haryana and Punjab. Together, the three districts of Kangra, Shimla and Solan accounted for about half of all the urban centres in the state. By contrast, Hamirpur, Una, Bilaspur and Kullu districts had fewer towns.

Half of the urban centres in the state were located in the valleys of the Beas and the Sutlej rivers. Earlier, in 1941, the number of such towns was more, exceeding three-fourths of the total towns in the state. Thus, more urban centres emerged away from the valleys. Nearly 60 per cent of urban centres were imparting administrative functions, as administrative headquarters at different levels. A large majority of towns (75.0 per cent) were small towns (having a population of less than 10,000 persons), accommodating more than two-thirds (68.3 per cent) of total urban population in the state.

The 1971–81 decade was full of new developments in Himachal Pradesh. The state got full statehood in 1971. This induced new zeal and enthusiasm among the masses, bureaucracy and the leadership in the state. Administrative and developmental activities expanded on a large scale. New centres emerged with the expansion of administrative activities. In absolute terms, the increase of 84,000 persons in urban centres during this decade was nearly the same as total urban population (86,000) in the state at 1941. As many as 11 new towns emerged, taking the number of towns to 47. Shimla, the largest town, was still in class II category of urban centres, pointing to the predominance of small towns in the state. At least 34 were very small in size, each having a population of less than 5,000 persons.

Among the new towns were religious centres such as Jwalamukhi

(Kangra district) and newly emerging industrial centres such as Parwanoo (Solan district) and Mehatpur Badsehra (Una district). The location of the airport at Bhuntar (providing air link to Kullu from Delhi) was mainly responsible for its emergence as a town. Some of the new towns were tahsil headquarters such as Rohru, Tira-Sujanpur and Nadaun. Other new centres included Dera Gopipur, Daulatpur, Chauri Khas and Gagret. New towns cumulatively added a population of 33,114 persons to the urban Himachal Pradesh, representing one-tenth of the total urban population in the state in 1981.

In 1991, the size of urban population in the state rose to 449,000 persons, registering an increase of 37.8 per cent during the decade 1981-91. The urban share in the total population also increased to 8.7 per cent from 7.6 per cent in 1981. Eleven new towns were added, taking the number of towns to 58 from 47 in 1981. With the exception of Chaupal and Narkanda all the new towns emerged in the valleys. 5 in Shimla district, followed by 20 in the Mandi district. Nearly three-fifths of the urban centres and more than half of the urban population in the state was thus concentrated in the four districts of Shimla, Solan, Mandi and Sirmaur.

Entrance of Shimla, the capital town, into class I category marked the significant development of the 1991 census decade. In the history of urbanization in the state, it was for the first time in 1991 that any town acquired the status of class I centre. Shimla city accounted for more than one-fifth of the total urban population in the state. Next in hierarchy were Mandi and Solan, categorized in class III (having population between 20 and 49.9 thousand). Obviously, there was no class II town in the state in 1991. All the newly emerged towns were in class VI (having population of less than 5,000 persons). Only 15 towns in the state namely, Shimla, Mandi, Nahan, Solan, Sundarnagar, Dharmsala, Chamba, Kullu, Paonta Sahib, Hamirpur, Una, Bilaspur, Kangra, Nurpur and Yol had populations higher than the average population size (7,745 persons) of a town in the state. The overwhelming majority of towns was, thus, small in size.

The latest census, conducted at the beginning of the new millennium, has enumerated 594,881 persons in 57 towns of Himachal Pradesh. During the decade 1991–2001, more than 150,000 persons have been added to urban population in the state. This was not only the largest ever-absolute increase in urban population but also was roughly equal to the size of total urban population in the state in the 1951 census. Nevertheless, the urban component in the population of the state has been less than one-tenth (or 9.80 per cent), and also the lowest of all the 35 states and union territories in India. At the same time, the decadal growth of urban population has slowed down to 32.4 per cent in comparison to 37.8 per cent in the previous decade 1981–91. The annual exponential growth rate has also come down to 3.24 per cent from 3.78 per cent during the same period. Though a national phenomenon, slowing down in the rate of growth of urban population in Himachal Pradesh may be empirically analysed thus.

While as many as 11 new towns were added during 1981–91, only two new towns emerged in the state during 1991–2001. On the other side of the scale, two towns were declassified and two were merged during 1991–2001, against none during 1981–91. Three of the 57 towns in the state, namely Garget (Una district), Bakloh (Chamba district) and Jubbal (Shimla district) recorded a negative growth and another four registered a decadal increase of less than 10 per cent population during 1991–2001. While new towns emerged in Kangra (Mant Khas town) and Solan (Baddi town) districts, declassified towns belonged to Sirmaur (Saharan town) and Mandi (Pandoh town) districts. Moreover, due to the difficult terrain several large sized central villages acted as service centres for the surroundings villages. The presence of a large number of small to very small sized rural settlements also failed to provide the threshold required for further growth of towns/cities, while the low level of industrial development negatively influenced the process of urbanization in the state.

Urban growth in the state has been quite uneven. Degree of urbanization, however, rose to 9.80 per cent in 2001 from 3.80 per cent in 1941, interestingly, though, it has been marked by inter-regional disparity. Table 14.1 reveals that the spatial disparity indexes (calculated to know inter-district disparity in urbanization) rose to 2.98 in 1951 from 1.62 in 1941. The index value declined again to 2.06 in 1961, with a decline in the degree of urbanization in the state. Again, the index value rose to 1.73 in 1991 and then to 2.30 in 2001 from only 1.36 in 1981. Increase in disparity index value corresponds with urban growth: from 7.61 per cent in 1981 to 8.70 per cent in 1991 and to 9.80 per cent in 2001. In this way, spurt in urban growth in the state finds marked association with intra-state disparities in urbanization. It seems that urbanization process in the state is favouring districts located in the Lower Himalayan zone, adjoining the Punjab and Haryana borders. The com-

Table 14.: Himachal Pradesh: Trends and Disparity in Urbanization, 1901–2001

(*Figures in percentage*)

State/District	1901	1911	1921	1931	1941	1951	1961	1971	1981	1991	2001
Himachal	4.03	3.12	3.45	3.63	3.80	6.45	6.34	6.99	7.61	8.70	9.79
Chamba	7.95	7.68	7.90	7.53	7.64	4.55	7.96	7.50	6.84	7.60	7.50
Kangra	3.38	1.47	1.04	1.28	1.71	6.79	5.84	4.32	4.93	4.81	5.39
Solan	7.49	7.08	5.93	5.70	9.76	11.42	10.89	10.08	10.75	12.74	18.26
Sirmaur	4.61	4.57	4.09	5.25	5.08	6.24	7.22	8.45	8.74	10.05	10.38
Hamirpur (1)	–	–	–	–	–	–	–	1.38	4.98	6.31	7.32
Una (2)	2.87	–	–	2.57	2.77	2.74	2.27	3.95	7.72	8.61	8.80
Bilaspur (2)	3.51	–	–	2.36	2.60	2.96	4.88	5.30	4.68	5.73	6.44
Mandi	4.51	3.34	3.93	5.98	4.44	5.20	5.60	9.35	7.33	7.30	6.77
Kullu (3)	–	–	–	–	–	2.53	3.19	5.59	7.09	7.02	7.92
Shimla	6.80	8.67	12.05	7.85	8.05	8.05	14.07	14.59	15.69	20.43	23.12
Lahul & Spiti (4) -	–	–	–	–	–	–	–	–	–	–	–
Kinnaur (4)	–	–	–	–	–	–	–	–	–	–	–
Spatial Disparity Index*	1.61	1.91	2.47	1.71	1.62	2.98	2.06	1.87	1.36	1.73	2.30

Notes: (1) Urban centre emerged in the 1971 census. (2) Urban centres remained declassified in 1911 and 1921. (3) Urban centre emerged in the 1951 census. (4) Wholly rural district.

* Disparity Index has been calculated by taking the range—Difference (i.e. maximum value - minimum value) divided by the Median value in the series.

bined share of the three districts of Solan, Sirmaur and Kangra in the total urban population of the state, has gone up to 64 per cent in 2001 from 58 per cent in 1971.

At district level, decadal growth of urban population varied from a high of 92.8 per cent in Solan to a low of only 9.3 per cent in Mandi during 1991–2001. The other districts experiencing urban growth higher than the state average (32.4 per cent) were Kullu and Hamirpur. The rest of the districts recorded a growth rate that was lower than the state's average. The districts of Lahul & Spiti and Kinnaur were yet to have an urban settlement. At town level, the tourist town of Manali registered the highest growth of 157.5 per cent. In contrast, Kangra (MC) recorded the lowest growth of 1.5 per cent. Besides Manali, other towns experiencing growth of more than 50 per cent included Solan, Sabathu and Ghumarwin. In another 24 towns, decadal growth was between 25 and 50 per cent. In the remaining 22 towns experiencing positive growth, it was less than 25 per cent. During 1991–2001, three towns recorded negative growth – Gagret (–25.3 per cent) in Una district, Bakloh (–9.1 per cent) in Chamba district, and Jubbal (–2.4 per cent) in Shimla district.

New towns of Baddi (Solan district) and Mant Khas (Kangra district) have appeared in class III and V category of towns, respectively. Among different sizes, class I category registered the highest (60.5 per cent) rate of growth and the class VI, the lowest (21.4 per cent). With the exception of class V towns, there has been a positive association between the size category of towns and their growth rate of population during 1991-2001 (Table 14.2).

Site of Towns

Locationally, there exists four types of towns in the state: valley towns; hill/ridge towns; spur towns; and gap towns (Map 14.1). Hill/ridge towns, numbering 13 out of a 57 towns in the state, came up mainly during the British period as hill resort towns. Valley towns, which are of indigenous origin, are quite old. They number 41, accounting for nearly 72.0 per cent of all towns in the state. Of the remaining 3 towns in the state, 2 are spur towns and the remaining one town is a gap town (Annexure 14.1). In this way, valley, followed by the hilltop, is the most favoured site for locating the towns in the state. Valley towns are nearly ubiquitous in their distribution while hilltop towns are mainly confined

Table 14.2: Association between Size and Growth Rate of Population

Size Category	Number of UA's/towns	Population size		Decadal increse (%)	Annual exponential growth (%)
		1991	2001		
Class I: (100,000 +)	1	88,592*	142,161	60.47	4.84
Class II: (50,000–99,999)	–	–	–	–	–
Class III: (20,000–49,999)	6	112,241	153,912	37.13	3.21
Class IV: (10,000–19,999)	7	89,735	113,376	26.35	2.37
Class V: (5,000–9999)	16	86,902	113,633	30.76	2.72
Class VI: (5000 or below)	26	59,135	71,799	21.42	1.96
All Classes	56	449,196	594,881	32.43	2.85

Notes: * To make population figures of class I towns comparable for 1991 and 2001 censuses, population of Dhalli (NAC), merged with Shimla (MC) in 2001 has been added in its 1991 population. The same procedure has been adopted in the case of two outgrowths of Jutog (CB), which were, earlier in 1991, treated as a part of Jutog (CB), now merged with Shimla city. For other categories of towns also, the 2001 Census has been taken as the base to compare with the 1991 population figures. Population figures for 1991 of the 'new towns' designated 2001 have been picked up from the village directory, available in District Census Handbooks of Himachal Pradesh.

** UA = Urban Agglomerate; NAC = Notified Area Committee; MC = Municipal Council; CB = Cantonment Board.

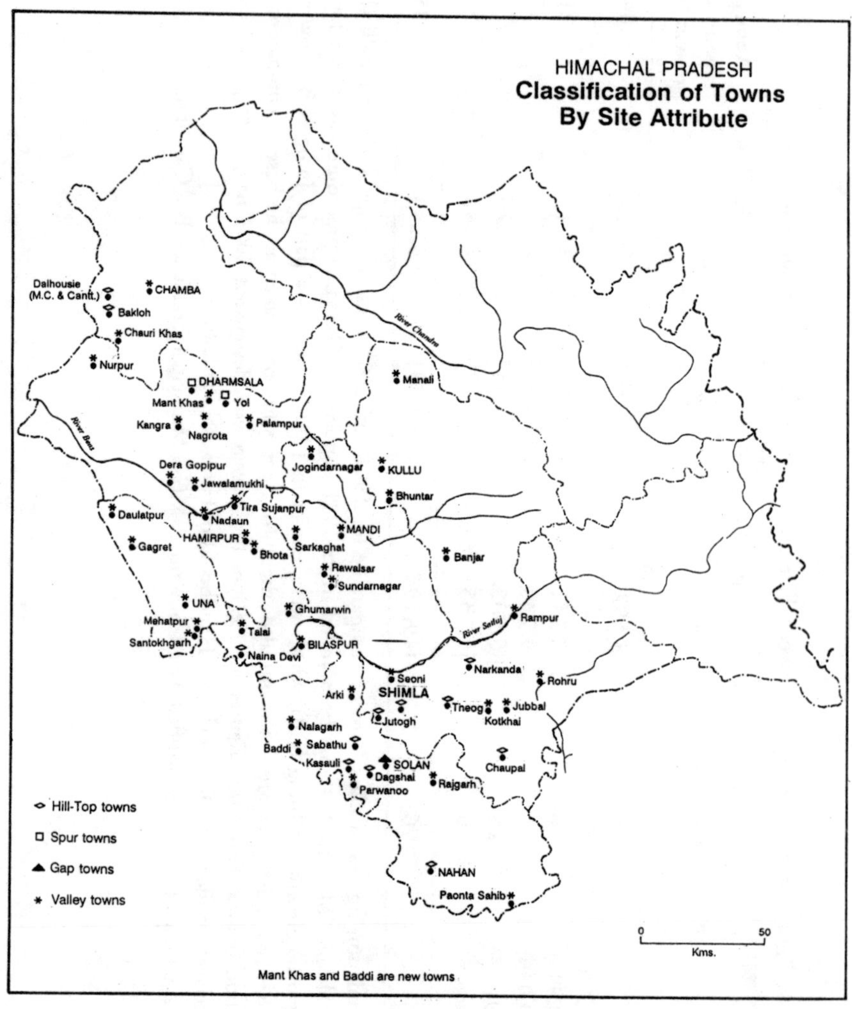

Map 14.1: Himachal Pradesh: Classification of Towns by Site Attribute

to three districts of Shimla, Solan and Sirmaur. Majority of hilltop towns are located along the Chandigarh-Shimla national highway. In terms of growth, gap towns were growing the fastest (57.1 per cent) against the slowest growth (11.2 per cent) of spur towns. However, there were wide variations in growth behaviour of hill towns at individual level. While Sabathu, Chaupal and Shimla were growing relatively fast (40 per cent), Bakloh, Narkanda, Dalhousie and Kasauli were growing slowly or even declining. In the light of wide variations in the demographic behaviour of towns based on site attributes, consideration of locational aspects of towns becomes quite significant for a meaningful urban development planning in the state.

ORIGIN OF TOWNS

Notwithstanding the long history of urbanization in the state, a large majority of towns emerged during the post-Independence era. Of the 57 towns in the state, 32 came up during this period only. Of the remaining, 11 towns emerged during the British period and only 14 of these towns existed in the pre-British period (Map 14.2).

With a few exceptions, post-Independence towns emerged in the valleys of Beas, Sutlej and Giri rivers. Important exceptions to this were Chaupal and Narkanda, located on the hilltops. Further, in their distribution nearly three-fourths of these towns fall in four districts of Una, Hamirpur, Kullu and Mandi. Their combined growth rate during 1991–2001 was 34.3 per cent. A large majority of these towns are small in size, and render administrative and trading services to their surrounding areas. With a population of 22,592 persons Baddi, an upcoming industrial centre, is the largest town in the group, and Narkanda, a resort town, with only 712 persons is the smallest, giving a ratio of about 1:32 between the two towns. Earlier in 1991, this ratio was 1:20. Scenic beauty, cold climate and defence were the major considerations for selection of hilltop locations by the British. Dharmsala, sited on the spur, is a major exception in this group. In their spatial distribution, these towns were confined to the districts of Shimla, Solan, Kangra and Chamba. No such town was in the districts of Hamirpur and Kullu. Shimla, the state capital, is not only the largest urban centre in this group but also the biggest in Himachal Pradesh. The ratio between the population of the largest (Shimla) and the smallest town (Seoni) of the

Map 14.2: Himachal Pradesh: Classification of Towns by Origin

group is of 1:93. Together, they registered a growth rate of 27.4 per cent during 1991–2001.

Fourteen towns of pre-British origin evolved as the headquarters of princely states. Though they present one-fourth of the total urban centres in the state, they account for more than two-fifths of the total urban population. Further, with the exception of Nahan and Solan, all other towns in the group are sited on riverbanks. The former is a hilltop town and the latter is a spur town. In this group, Solan, with 34,199 persons, is the largest town and Palampur, with only 3,706 persons, the smallest. The population of these two towns make a ratio only of about 1:8. They are growing at a slow pace. Their combined growth rate during 1991–2001 was 25.2 per cent against the state average of 34.2 per cent. Administration is the dominant function of all the towns of pre-British origin.

In brief, site differential was a marked feature of the evolutionary process of the towns in the state. A large majority of pre-British and post-Independence towns are sited in the river valleys while the British towns find their location on hilltops. Considerations of effective administration and water supply formed the major factors in the former case, whereas scenic beauty and defence guided the location in the latter case.

Functional Character of Towns

More than two-fifths of the towns in the state have administration as the dominant function, while in another one-third trade is the dominant function. Thus, overwhelming majority of towns in the state are either administrative or trade centres (Map 14.3). Most of such towns emerged either during the pre-British or in the post-Independence period. Of the remaining one-fourth towns, one-half have defence as the dominant function and all of them find their origin during the British period. In the rest of the 7 towns, 3 each are tourist and religious places and one an industrial centre is Parwanoo, located on the Haryana-Himachal border, the lone urban centre having industrial production as its dominant activity. Originated in the post-Independence period as a planned town, it has attracted lot of industries due to easy accessibility and attractive concessions offered by the Himachal government to industrialists. In other words, higher reaches of the hilly terrain restrict the expansion of the industrial base of towns.

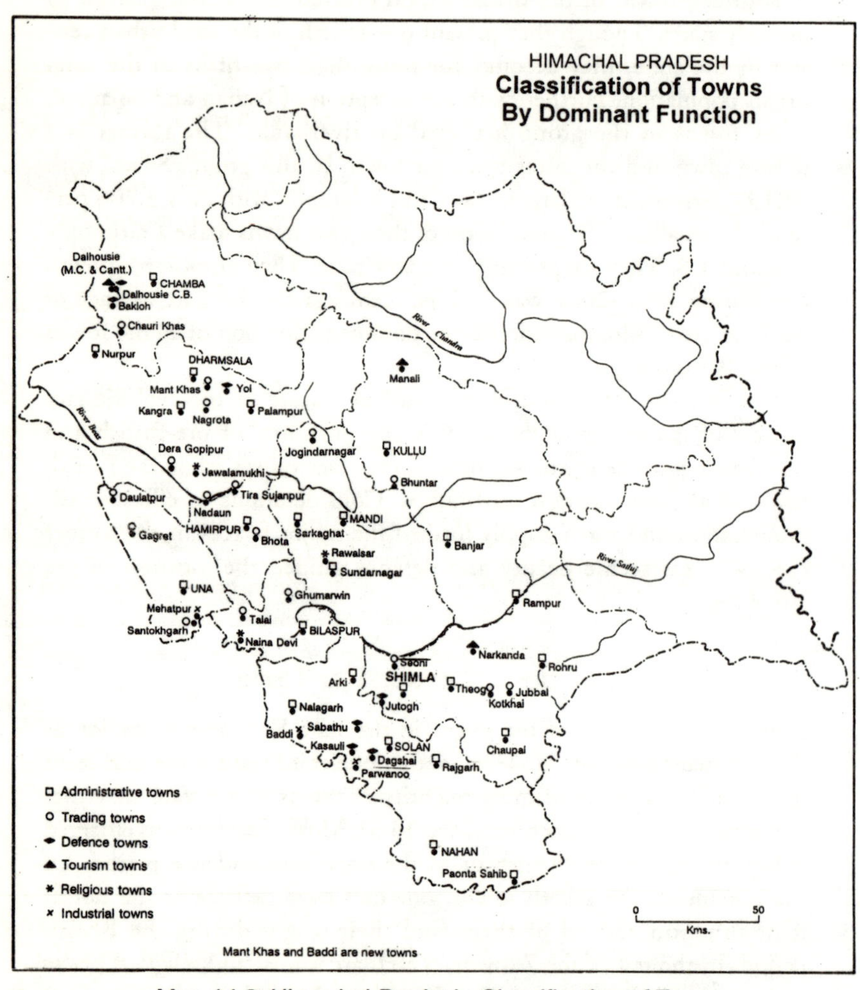

Map 14.3: Himachal Pradesh: Classification of Towns by Dominant Function

Mono-functionality is, in fact, the dominant characteristic of towns in the state. In 1991, as many as 30 towns were mono-functional. Another 20 were bi-functional and only 8 multi-functional.

Conclusion

Together, however, the three districts of Shimla, Kangra and Mandi take away more than a half of the urban population in the state. In contrast, Kinnaur and Lahul & Spiti districts are without any urban centre. Spurt in urban growth and regional disparities in urbanization find positive association with each other. A conscious policy of urban dispersal has to be followed. Rural-urban linkages are needed to be intensified. Simultaneously the rural service centres are to be provided with the requisite stimulus.

1. Shimla is the only city in Himachal Pradesh. It enjoys primacy, having more than four times the population of the second town (Solan) in the state. Forty-three out of a total of its 57 towns have a population size of less than 10,000 persons each; 27 among these have even less than 5,000 persons each. Eleven towns are distinctly small, each having a population of less than 2,000 persons. Narkanda, the smallest town in the state, has less than 1,000 persons. The ratio between the smallest and the largest urban centre in the state has increased over the century: 10:1 in 1901 to 196:1 in 2001. Site has been of great significance in determining the role and importance of towns in Himachal Pradesh. As many as 41 of its 57 towns are sited along the river valleys, 13 on the hill tops, one in gap and remaining 2 on spurs. Virtually all the valley towns are positioned on river terraces. Hilltop towns range in elevation from 2,000 to 2,500 metres. Gap and spur towns are in the altitude range of 600 to 2,000 metres.

2. Most of the towns, originating during the pre-British and post-Independence period, occupy valley sites. Many of the pre-British towns such as Mandi, Chamba, Kullu, Bilaspur and Rampur were the capitals of the former native states. On the other hand, majority of post-Independence towns such as Gagret, Daulatpur, Talai, and Nagrota are market towns.

3. As regards their distribution, practically all the towns are located in the southwestern part of the state. The northern and northeastern parts are devoid of any urban centres. Within the southern part also, the Shimla hills, the Kangra valley and Jaswan *dun* contain majority of

towns. These find their location mainly on the Kalka-Shimla, Nangal-Manali and Pathankot-Jogindarnagar road/rail routes. A string of towns on the side of the Himachal border with Punjab and Haryana is also emerging.

4. During the century under study, urban population of Himachal Pradesh recorded nearly eight-fold increase: from 77,332 in 1901 to 594,881 in 2001. This was concomitant with a rise in the number of towns from 21 to 57. The share of urban population in the total population moved up to 9.80 per cent from 4.03 per cent during this period. By comparison, India's urban population has grown by eleven times: from 26 million in 1901 to 286 million in 2001. All India propositions of urban population have moved to 27.8 per cent from 10.84 per cent during this period. As compared to India as a whole, the pace of urbanization has been slow in the state. Indeed, hill towns are not subject to strong rural-urban interactions. Their potential to offer employment is limited.

5. A large part of increase in the state's urban population is attributed to emergence of new towns. Contribution of net in-migration seems to be less important in urban growth in Himachal Pradesh. Higher order administrative centres such as district headquarters are growing fast due to considerable in-flow. By contrast, growth of cantonment towns has been slow because of their exceptionally low rate of natural increase.

6. Population size of towns find some positive association with their size and location. Valley towns are relatively large, the spur towns medium and the hilltop towns are small in size. Shimla is an exception to this. This hilltop urban centre has the privilege of being the state capital and a tourist centre of international repute. By and large, however, the size of a town and its growth have been related to the peculiar physical and socio-economic conditions prevailing in hill areas.

In short, hill areas have their own context of size hierarchy of settlements. Because of the geographical constraints, there is little chance of emergence of any big urban concentration. Numerically, small towns predominate which have their own virtue of being manageable units for intensive planning. In a developing country like India hill areas have been characterized by a low degree of urbanization. It is attributed mainly to their subsistence agricultural economy, meagre industrial base and modest scale of transport development. In such a situation, rural service centres have to share the obligations of towns. Their identification, planning and development have to be an integral part of any urbanization policy.

REFERENCES

Krishan, G. and N.R. Verma, 'Site Analysis of Hill Towns', *Transactions of the Institute of Indian Geographers*, vol. 2, no. 1, 1980, pp. 101–9.

Mitchell, Nora, *The Indian Hill Station: Kodaikanal*, Chicago, 1973.

Sharma, K.D., 'Patterns and Processes of Urbanisation in a Himalayan State: A Case Study of Himachal Pradesh (India) 1881–1981', *Transactions of the Institute of Indian Geographers*, vol. 14, no. 1, 1992, pp. 1–12.

ANNEXURE 14.1: Himachal Pradesh: Some Select Characteristics of Towns

Name of town	Site attribute	Period of evolution	Dominant function	Population in 2001	Rank in 1991
1. Shimla	Hilltop	British	Administrative	142,161	1
2. Solan	Gap	Pre-British	Administrative	34,199	4
3. Mandi	Valley	Pre-British	Administrative	26,858	2
4. Nahan	Hilltop	Pre-British	Administrative	25,972	3
5. Sundarnagar	Valley	Pre-British	Administrative	23,979	5
6. Baddi*	Valley	Post-Independence	Industrial	22,592	*
7. Chamba	Valley	Pre-British	Administrative	20,312	7
8. Paonta Sahib	Valley	Pre-British	Administrative	19,087	9
9. Dharmsala	Spur	British	Administrative	19,034	6
10. Kullu	Valley	Pre-British	Administrative	18,306	8
11. Hamirpur	Valley	Post-Independence	Administrative	17,219	10
12. Una	Valley	Pre-British	Administrative	15,900	11
13. Bilaspur	Valley	Pre-British	Administrative	13,058	12
14. Yol	Spur	British	Defence	10,772	13
15. Nalagarh	Valley	Pre-British	Administrative	9,433	16
16. Kangra	Valley	Pre-British	Administrative	9,155	14
17. Nurpur	Valley	Pre-British	Administrative	9,045	15
18. Mehatpur	Valley	Post-Independence	Trade	8,686	19
19. Parwanoo	Valley	Post-Independence	Industrial	8,609	20
20. Santokhgarh	Valley	Post-Independence	Trade	8,304	18

Name of town	Site attribute	Period of evolution	Dominant function	Population in 2001	Rank in 1991
21. Dalhousie M.C.	Hilltop	British	Tourism	7,419	17
22. Tira Sujanpur	Valley	Post-Independence	Trade	7,077	22
23. Rohru	Valley	Post-Independence	Administrative	6,606	35
24. Manali	Valley	Post-Independence	Tourism	6,265	40
25. Ghumarwin	Valley	Post-Independence	Trade	5,720	29
26. Sabathu	Hilltop	British	Defence	5,720	30
27. Nagrota	Valley	Post-Independence	Trade	5,655	24
28. Rampur	Valley	Pre-British	Administrative	5,653	26
29. Mant Khas*	Valley	Post-Independence	Trade	5,240	*
30. Jogindarnagar	Valley	British	Trade	5,046	23
31. Kasauli	Hilltop	British	Defence	4,994	25
32. Jawalamukhi	Valley	Post-Independence	Religion	4,931	28
33. Nadaun	Valley	Post-Independence	Trade	4,405	33
34. Dera Gopipur	Valley	Post-Independence	Trade	4,336	34
35. Bhuntar	Valley	Post-Independence	Trade	4,260	37
36. Palampur	Valley	Pre-British	Administrative	4,006	31
37. Theog	Hilltop	Post-Independence	Administrative	3,754	38
38. Sarkaghat	Valley	Post-Independence	Administrative	3,706	36
39. Daulatpur	Valley	Post-Independence	Trade	3,352	39
40. Garget	Valley	Post-Independence	Trade	3,180	27
41. Chauri Khas	Valley	Post-Independence	Trade	3,016	43
42. Arki	Valley	Post-Independence	Administrative	2,877	45

(contd.)

ANNEXURE 1 (contd.)

Name of town	Site attribute	Period of evolution	Dominant function	Population in 2001	Rank in 1991
43. Dagshai	Hilltop	British	Defence	2,751	42
44. Rajgarh	Valley	Post-Independence	Administrative	2,527	46
45. Jutogh	Hilltop	British	Defence	2,417	21
46. Talai	Valley	Post-Independence	Trade	2,010	48
47. Dalhousie C.B.	Hilltop	British	Defence	1,962	47
48. Bakloh	Hilltop	British	Defence	1,809	44
49. Seoni	Valley	Post-Independence	Trade	1,529	51
50. Chaupal	Hilltop	Post-Independence	Administrative	1,507	53
51. Bhota	Valley	Post-Independence	Trade	1,472	50
52. Rawalsar	Valley	Post-Independence	Religion	1,369	54
53. Jubbal	Valley	Post-Independence	Trade	1,346	49
54. Banjar	Valley	Post-Independence	Administrative	1,262	55
55. Naina Devi	Hilltop	Post-Independence	Religion	1,161	57
56. Kotkhai	Valley	Post-Independence	Trade	1,148	56
57. Narkanda	Hilltop	Post-Independence	Tourism	712	58

*New Towns.

15

Social Parameters of Punjab Urbanization since Independence

GOPAL KRISHAN

As a brief narrative of Punjab urbanization since Independence in 1947, this paper focuses on the social ambience of its urban places as evolving over time. The analysis is based on the data made available by the Census of India counts from 1951 to 2001. The discussion addresses itself firstly to the magnitude, growth rate, and morphology of urbanization, and secondly to the matters of population replacement, religious composition, caste characterization and slum habitation of urban population. Along with, changes in the physical layout of towns, formation of urban corridors, planning interventions by the government have also been taken into account.

Urban Demography

At the first post-Independence Census of India in 1951, Punjab recorded an urban population of 2 million against the total of 9.2 million (Table 15.1). With one-fifth of its population living in urban places, as compared with one-sixth in India, Punjab was a relatively more urbanized state of the country. Among its 110 towns at that time, 3 were large (population at least 100,000 each), 19 medium (population between 20,000 and 99,999 each), and 88 small (population less than 20,000 each). The urban population was shared almost equally by these three categories of towns. Here it would be pertinent to add that all urban places are termed as towns by the Census of India, and a town with a population of 100,000 and above is called a city.

By 2001, the size of urban population had grown to about 8.3 million while its total population was recorded at 24.4 million. During

Table 15.1: Punjab Urbanization, 1951–2001

Census year	Number of towns/urban agglomerations	Urban population (in millions)	Percentage of urban population	Decadal growth rate of urban population	Decadal change in percentage point
1951	110	1.99	21.72	–	–
1961	106	2.57	23.06	+29.06	+1.34
1971	106	3.22	23.73	+25.27	0.67
1981	134	4.65	27.68	44.51	3.65
1991	120	5.99	29.55	28.95	1.87
2001	157	8.25	33.92	37.58	4.37

Source: *Census of India, 1991, Punjab:* General Population Tables and Primary Census Abstracts, Part II A and Part II B, pp. 14, 19 and 99, and *Census of India, 2001, Punjab:* Final Population Totals, pp. 3 and 11.

1951–2001, the state's rural population increased by 2.3 times but its urban population multiplied by 4.2 times. The share of urban population in the total was now 34 per cent as compared with 27.8 per cent in India. There was a significant rise in the number of towns as well from 110 in 1951 to 157 in 2001. The share of large, medium and small towns in urban population was 58.4, 28.9 and 12.7 per cent respectively.

The mean distance between towns got reduced from 24 to 20 km; thereby further enhancing their proximity to rural areas. The state had witnessed the emergence of its first metropolitan city (population at least one million) of Ludhiana in 1991 and Amritsar acquired this status in 2001. Jalandhar may join this group in the next census of 2011. Urbanization morphology (distribution of urban population by size category of towns) was getting tilted in favour of large towns.

Urban-rural linkages are strong in Punjab. Many rural-urban commuters finally finish as rural-urban migrants. Ex-servicemen, with rural background, normally prefer to settle in a town after retirement. All such persons retain a regular link with their native villages. A class of people is emerging whose economic interests are partly rural and partly urban (Krishan, 1998: 162).

Population Replacement

Beyond this statistical background, the story of Punjab urbanization since Independence makes an interesting reading in terms of significant changes in its composition. The first tumultuous change took place as an aftermath of the partition of the subcontinent in 1947. Barring Malerkotla and Qadian, all other urban places experienced a virtual exodus of the Muslim population to Pakistan (Krishan 1998: 157). In their place, the non-Muslim population (mainly Hindus and Sikhs) displaced from Pakistan was settled. The displaced population accounted for one-third of the Punjab's urban population at that time; their proportion being significantly high in places like Ludhiana, Amritsar, Jalandhar and Patiala. As a part of the rehabilitation policy, displaced persons were resettled in *mohallas* or localities, which were earlier inhabited and eventually evacuated by the Muslims (Singh 1952). This brought in its wake a change not only in the religious composition of urban places but also in their cultural landscape associated with the places of worship, work premises, and life style of different religious communities.

In fact, the space vacated by the Muslims was far too inadequate to accommodate the entire influx of displaced persons. The Hindu and Sikh urban population had left behind 154,000 houses and 51,000 shops/business premises in West Punjab, whereas the Muslims in East Punjab vacated only 112,000 houses and 17,000 shop/business premises (Singh 1972: 132). Additional avenues had to be managed for the purpose.

One of the reasons for raising a completely planned new city of Chandigarh as the capital of Indian Punjab was to provide scope of work and residence for the displaced persons. Rajpura township, as an adjunct to the existing town, was also meant to accommodate them. Likewise, model towns were appended to the existing cities, such as Ludhiana, Amritsar, Jalandhar and Patiala, for the same reason. This process not only caused physical expansion of several towns but also rendered a dual character to their demographic scene, defined by the coexistence of original residents and displaced persons. Newly raised model towns offered better infrastructural facilities as compared with the main city but took time in evolving as coherent social communities, in general.

Planning Process

Despite such efforts at resettlement, much of the physical growth of towns was taking place in a haphazard manner. This caused a serious concern on the part of the government. As a response, the Department of Town and Country Planning was constituted in 1961. One of its first jobs was to prepare master plans for all the towns with a population of 20,000 and above. By that time, the completely planned city of Chandigarh had also assumed some visible form, and the idea of urban development on planned lines had taken roots. The impact was manifest in the layout and design of all newly built localities of Punjab towns.

During the Fourth Plan (1969–74), the cities of Ludhiana, Jalandhar and Amritsar were covered by the Integrated Urban Development programme of the Government of India, with a view to upgrading the level of infrastructure in cities. Subsequently, other towns also started receiving some attention under the Integrated Development of Small and Medium Towns programme, launched in the Sixth Plan (1980–5), again by the Government of India. Meanwhile, the Environmental Improvement of Urban Slums programme had been initiated in 1972. This was meant to ameliorate the unhygienic living conditions in slums. It continues till date. Whatever the degree of their success, these efforts did cause some change in the fabric of urban Punjab.

A lot of physical growth of towns was, however, distinctly haphazard in nature. This took the form of encroachments at the micro-level and emergence of unauthorized colonies at the city level. Ludhiana is the biggest money spinner in Punjab as the hosiery capital of the country, but the 50 per cent of its structures have been raised without any planning or regulation (Sandhu and Sandhu 2003: 79).

The most problematic has been the issue of slum proliferation. About one-fifth of the urban population was recorded as slum dwellers in Punjab towns, with a population of at least 50,000 each in 2001. The Census of India treated all those urban localities as slums which were notified or recognized as such by the state/local level government or which had poorly built, congested, unhygienic tenements, sheltering at least about 300 persons each. In their distribution, slum localities clustered near the industrial units, construction sites, drainage lines, and major transport routes and nodes, such as bus stands and railway stations. Notably, the urban slums in Punjab were not that worse off as in many other parts of the country. The very fact that only 5.8 per cent of Punjab's urban population was below poverty line as against 19.6 per cent in slums shows that over two-thirds of the slum population was above the poverty line. Literacy rate of the urban slum population at 73.8 per cent was only somewhat lower than that of non-slum population at 80.4 per cent. This is a welcome situation of relative equity.

To address the problems of urban planning and development in a comprehensive manner, the Punjab Regional and Town Planning and Development Act was enacted in 1995 (Gupta 2001: 26). In the same year, the Apartment and Property Ownership and Regulation Act was gone through to promote raising of (residential) colonies on planned lines, in partnership with the private sector. By now, under the Act, about 120 private colonizers have registered their proposals with the government. To what extent this step could stem the emergence of unauthorized colonies, only the future will tell. A greater hope can be pinned on the Constitution (Seventy-fourth Amendment), which stipulates regular elections to the urban local bodies, devolves planning and development functions to them, and reserves one-third of the elective seats for the women.

Redefining Territorial Jurisdiction

All such developments necessitated a redelimitation of the territorial jurisdiction of towns. The requisite data for the year 2001 is yet to be released, constraining a statement on the latest situation. Since Independence to 1991, as many as 93 towns out of 120 had experienced a change in their territorial limits. Among these, 85 experienced increase in area and 8 were cases of reduction. There were three main considerations underlying the extension of the limits of the physically expanding towns: to provide urban services to newly emerged colonies on their outer periphery, to make available additional land for development on planned lines, and to rope in enterprises which were evading payment of octroi by locating themselves outside the municipal limits. The 'decrease in area' cases were those, which were previously over bounded and had extensive agricultural land around the main settlement. Cantonment towns were not subjected to any area change.

On account of the above, but more because of the rise in the number of towns, the area under urban places increased phenomenally

Table 15.2: Punjab: Increase in Urban Areas, 1961–2001

Census year	Urban area (sq. km.)	Area per town (sq. km.)
1961	673	6.35
1971	692	6.53
1981	1,199	8.97
1991	1,441	12.01
2001	2,178	13.87

Source: *Census of India, 1991, Punjab:* General Population Tables and Primary Census Abstracts, Part II A and Part II B, pp. 99-103.

over the years. The process has been more pronounced since 1971, that is after the formation of Punjab in 1966. Urban area in Punjab, which was 692 sq. km. in 1971, increased to 1,441 sq. km. in 1991 and further to 2,178 sq. km. in 2000 (Table 15.2). As such, over 4 per cent of the state's area is under urban settlements as compared with 2 per cent in India. The average area per town in Punjab has more than doubled from 6.4 sq. km. in 1961 to 13.9 sq. km. in 2001. Urbanization does involve a cost in terms of the loss of agricultural land but then it also generates a variety of economic activities, offering employment and higher incomes to people.

Corridor Development

An outcome of such a tendency has been the corridor development along main trunk routes connecting big cities, such as Ludhiana, Jalandhar and Amritsar. Most prominent corridors may be listed as Ludhiana-Amritsar, Ludhiana-Rajpura, Ludhiana-Chandigarh, Ludhiana-Malerkotla, Chandigarh-Lalru and Amritsar-Pathankot. It is notable that 372 out of 620 medium and large scale industrial units in Punjab in 2001, that is 60 per cent of the total, were located in villages, mostly along such corridors. Several of these villages are towns of tomorrow. Industrialization is now creating a linear pattern of urbanization while agricultural development had earlier ensured a kind of uniform distribution. A tendency towards a gradual concentration of towns along the transport routes is now getting more manifest.

In some elaboration, the process of agricultural development which started picking up after Independence and took the form of the green revolution in mid 1960s, had a multifarious effect on Punjab urbanization. Agricultural market towns grew fast and strengthened rural-urban commuting (Gosal 1985: 76). Through the New Mandi Township Development and Regulation Act, 1960, Punjab upgraded the infrastructure in such towns and pre-empted the 'integrated development of small and medium towns' programme launched by the Government of India, under the Sixth Plan (Krishan 1996: 237). Other small and medium towns also displayed dynamism under a stimulus to their trade and service functions and agro-based industry. It is evident that agricultural development promotes rather than constrains the urbanization process.

The Difficult Decade

The 1980s take us to a different track in our understanding of the Punjab urbanization. It was a time when Punjab was undergoing a traumatic experience of militancy. The social milieu was highly disturbed, political institutions were non-functional, administrative capacity was feeble, and security considerations were paramount at all levels (Krishan 1994: 37). Situation was worse in rural areas. An explosive urban growth was expected in the wake of much talked about exodus from vulnerable villages to safer towns. This did not happen, at least on the scale it was envisaged.

The 1991 census data revealed that the decennial urban growth rate had dipped from 44.5 per cent during 1971–81 to 29.1 per cent during 1981–91. Over three-fourths of the addition to the urban population was simply because of natural increase or the difference between birth and death rates. Net in-migration contributed less than one-fourth. It seems that while there was considerable migration from villages to towns, several towns had also suffered sizeable out-migration to places outside the state. Meanwhile, migration from other states to Punjab towns had slowed down.

Taking a relatively long-range view of 1951–2001, the compound annual growth rate of Punjab's urban population was worked out as 2.9 per cent as compared with 1.6 of rural population. The rate of natural increase over this period is estimated as 1.9 per cent. On a rough count, one may infer that one-third of urban growth was due to rural-urban migration. There is discernible spatial pattern in growth behaviour of towns. A greater degree of dynamism was observed in the case of towns located south of the Sutlej *vis-à-vis* those located to its north. A sharper focus reveals that town growth was distinctly rapid

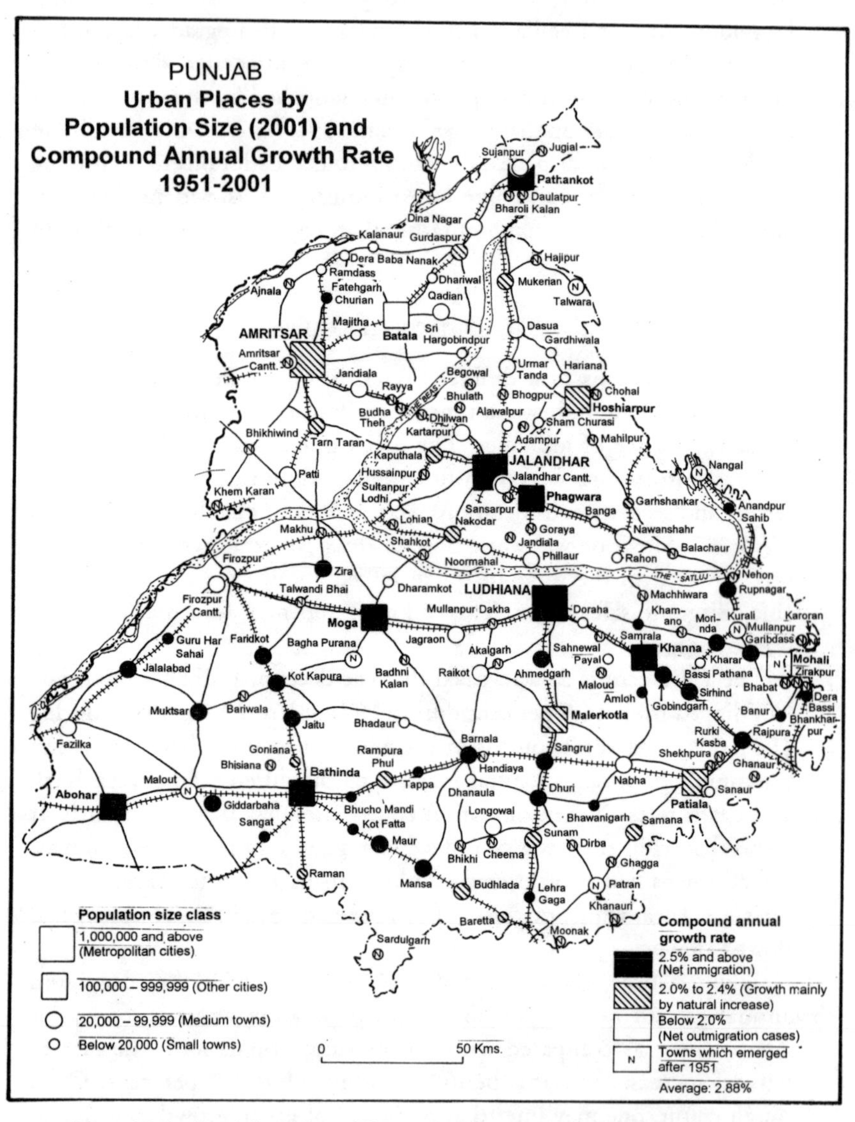

Map 15.1: Punjab: Urban Places by Population Size (2001) and Compound Annual Growth Rate 1951–2001

along the Ambala-Ludhiana rail route, in the proximity of the state capital of Chandigarh, and in the southwestern region focusing on Bhatinda. On the other hand, towns were generally marked by sluggish growth in the districts bordering with Pakistan and in the foothill region.

Religious Composition

Such a growth behavior of Punjab towns during 1981-91 was not without its implications for their religious composition. In 1981, the Hindu population in urban places made 64.1 per cent of the total and the share of the Sikh population was 33.2 per cent. By 1991, the percentage share of the Hindus had come down to 60.5 and that of the Sikhs had risen to 36.7. The growth rate of the Hindus in urban places at 21.5 per cent was virtually one half of that of the Sikhs at 42.5 per cent, during the decade. The two communities were recording differing tendencies of migration (Table 15.3).

A more detailed analysis of the data shows that as many as 44 towns out of 120 experienced net outflow of the Hindus against net inflow of the Sikhs. This feature was more typical of towns located in Amrtisar, Patiala and Bhatinda districts. In the case of Amritsar city, the Hindu population grew by only 9 per cent whereas the Sikh population increased by 33 per cent. From 16 towns, there was net outflow of both Hindus and Sikhs and such towns marked a greater frequency in Gurdaspur and Jalandhar districts. Several of these were small towns. Only 26 towns were noted for net in-migration of both the Hindu and Sikh populations. These had a greater frequency in Ludhiana, Rupnagar and Sangrur districts. In Ludhiana city, the Hindu population grew by 68 per cent and Sikh by 78 per cent. On the whole, a tendency toward a parity among the Hindus and the Sikhs in urban population was taking shape. Eventually, this will break the popular perception of the Hindus being predominantly urban and the Sikhs largely rural in Punjab. This will also mellow down the conflict between the urban and rural interests, as sometimes pegged on religious lines.

Scheduled Castes

A gradual urbanization of the scheduled caste population is a redeeming feature of the Punjab scene. In 1961, 12.9 per cent of urban population was recorded as scheduled caste; by 2001, this figure had risen to

Table 15.3: Punjab: Classification of Punjab Towns by Migration Behaviour of Hindus and Sikhs, 1981–91

State/ district	Number of towns characterized by					
	Hindu-out-migration and Sikh-in-migration	Hindu-in-migration and Sikh-out-migration	Hindu-out migration and Sikh-out-migration	Hindu-natural increase and Sikh-in-migration	Others (including new towns)	Total
Punjab	44	26	16	12	22	120
Gurdaspur	4	2	4	0	2	12
Amritsar	5	0	1	0	4	10
Firozpur	4	3	1	1	1	10
Ludhiana	5	4	0	0	1	10
Jalandhar	4	2	4	2	2	14
Kapurthala	2	1	0	0	0	3
Hoshiarpur	3	1	1	1	3	9
Rupnagar	1	3	0	1	3	8
Patiala	6	3	0	2	1	12
Sangrur	4	4	2	1	1	12
Bathinda	6	1	2	1	1	11
Faridkot	0	2	1	3	3	9

Notes: *Out migration denotes an increase rate below the rate of natural increase and immigration stands for an increase rate above the rate of natural increase.

**Hindu population in urban places of Punjab increased by 21.5 per cent and the Sikh population by 42.5 per cent during 1981–91.

***Rate of natural increase of Punjab's urban population, during 1981–91 was 23.7 per cent. See *Census of India, 1991, India*: Provisional Population Totals, Rural-Urban Distribution, p. 58.

Source: *Census of India, Punjab*: Religion, Part IV B (ii), and *Census of India, 1981, Punjab*: Religion, Paper 1 of 1984.

20.7 per cent. During 1961–2001, the compound annual growth rate of Punjab's scheduled caste population in urban places was 4.2 per cent as against 2.7 per cent of the non-scheduled caste population. This wide difference can be attributed partly to a higher rate of natural increase of the scheduled caste population but largely to a faster rate of their migration from rural areas to urban places. This is a development of critical significance. Urbanization is likely to prove as a more effective factor in raising the socio-economic status of this historically disadvantaged segment than all the social welfare measures taken by the government (Table 15.4).

As expected, this kind of transformation is of higher order in cities. The percentage share of the scheduled caste population in city population shows a significant rise during 1961–2001. This tendency was more marked in the case of those cities which are located in areas with high proportion of scheduled caste population in their rural hinterlands. One could infer short-run migration being more frequent on the part of this economically weak section.

Towards an Urban Majority Punjab

Punjab is popularly perceived as an agricultural–rural state in the light of the strides it made in agricultural development, eventually shaping itself into the green revolution. To visualize it as an urban majority state in not too distant a future may seem rather intriguing. With over one-third of the state's population already in urban places and urban growth rate pacing fast, the developments are already in that direction. International experience suggests that urbanization gets a momentum in regions after they become 30 per cent urban and simultaneously achieve a per capita income of U.S. $500 (Mohan: 1990: 5–6). Punjab had already met this description by 1991. On the basis of current trends, it can be safely projected that the state would become urban majority by 2030. The implication is that urban issues are going to gradually attract greater attention. A change in the thrust of the policy in favour of the urban areas is inevitable.

Where would most of this urban growth take place? Going by the prevailing tendencies, things could be projected on the following lines. First, a large segment of this urban growth will get concentrated along the corridors. These corridors are already studded with a number of large and medium industrial units, several of them located in the adjoining villages. These are the potential towns. Secondly, cities like

Table 15.4 (a): Punjab: Percentage of Scheduled Caste Population in Urban Population, 1961–2000

Census year	Percentage of Scheduled caste population in urban places	Increase in percentage points during the decade
1961	12.94	–
1971	15.36	2.42
1981	18.21	2.85
1991	19.76	1.55
2001	20.70	0.94

Table 15.4 (b): Punjab: City-wise Change in Percentage of Scheduled Caste Population, 1961–2001

City	Percentage of Scheduled caste population	
	1961	2001
Jalandhar	16.6	27.4
Phagwara	15.3	25.9
Khanna	16.2	24.4
Hoshiarpur	10.3	24.3
Batala	8.8	23.7
Bathinda	13.6	21.3
Abohar	15.6	20.8
Amritsar	9.5	20.0
Moga	14.5	19.9
Pathankot	12.2	16.8
Ludhiana	6.3	13.1
Patiala	4.8	10.6
SAS Nagar	–	6.9
Malerkotla	4.2	5.6

Source: *Census of India, 2001, Punjab*: Final Population Totals, *Census of India, 1991, Punjab*: General Population Tables and Primary Census Abstracts, Part II A and Part II B, pp. 99–103, and *Census of India, 1961, Punjab*: Primary Census Abstract (Special for Reorganized Punjab), pp. 86–113.

Ludhiana, Jalandhar, Amritsar and Patiala will continue growing fast with the emergence of planned urban estates and residential colonies, within or on the periphery. Finally, urbanization will be rapid in Punjab areas adjoining Chandigarh.

Some emerging patterns on the social horizon of the urban scene may also be indicated. First, the scheduled caste population is in the process of being gradually urbanized. Traditionally overwhelmingly rural, this section is marking a steady rise in its share of urban population. This represents an upward mobility through rural- urban migration on their part. A break from traditional vocations and rigid caste hierarchy is a natural consequence. Secondly, the share of the Sikhs in urban population, again through the process of rural-urban migration, will rise. This will be in greater conformity with their significant majority in total population. An additional factor to this effect would be the graduation of eligible villages to the town status, and such places are more likely to have a large segment of Sikh population. Finally, the proportion of the slum population will enlarge further in Punjab towns as a consequence of a boost to their industrial and construction activities. Employment opportunities therein will attract migrants not only from within the state but also from other parts of the country. This migrant labour, with a sizeable component of scheduled caste population, is likely to take shelter in slum localities.

Perspectives on urban development vary. Some express their preference for aesthetics of the city by way of its beautification in diverse ways. Another paradigm shifts in favour of healthy cities providing high quality services. Still another view cherishes cities as dynamic economic entities, attracting a variety of activities, generating employment and incomes and yielding revenues for their proper maintenance. A perspective for Punjab towns can be defined on similar lines: well designed in physical lay out, equipped with a delivery system of quality services, and providing ready employment (Krishan, 2002, p. 591).

REFERENCES

Gosal, G.S., 'Agricultural development and the urbanization process with special reference to Punjab', *Travause et Documents de Geographic Tropicale, Cegtet*, 1985, pp. 63–76.

Gupta, Jit, *Status Report on Urbanization of Punjab*, prepared for the Government of Punjab, Chandigarh, 2001.

Krishan, Gopal, 'Demographic Change', in J.S. Grewal and Indu Banga (eds.), *Punjab in Prosperity and Violence, 1947–1997*, Chandigarh: Institute of Punjab Studies, 1998, pp. 156–76.

——, 'The integrated development of small and medium towns in the Punjab', in Kulwant Singh, Florian Steinberg and Nanthaniel von Einsiedel (eds.), *Integrated Urban Infrastructure Development in Asia,* New Delhi: Oxford & IBD Publishing Co., 1996.

——, 'Major urbanization issues in the context of emerging Punjab situation', *Political Economy Journal of India,* 1994, 3, pp. 37–40.

——, 'Development Perspective', *Punjab Development Report,* New Delhi: Planning Commission, Government of India, 2002, pp. 582–600.

Mohan, Rakesh, *Issues in Urban Employment Planning,* Asian Regional Team for Employment Promotion, New Delhi: International Labour Organization, 1990.

Sandhu, R.S. and Jasmeet Sandhu, 'Urbanization in Punjab: pattern and development', in M.S. Gill (ed.), *Punjab Society: Perspectives and Challenges,* New Delhi: Concept Publishing Company, 2003.

Singh, Kripal, *The Partition of the Punjab,* Patiala: Punjabi University, 1972.

Singh, Tarlok, *Land Settlement Manual for Displaced Persons in Punjab and Pepsu,* Shimla: Controller of Printing and Stationery, Punjab, 1952.

16

Urbanization in Punjab: Problems and Prospects

J.K. GUPTA

India is passing through a phase of massive urbanization and Punjab is no exception. Urbanization has been considered as an index of development but in the case of developing countries like India, urbanization is not merely the outcome of the growth potential generated by urban settlements. The people-work relationship in rural areas is equally relevant. It is so critically balanced that any increase in population inevitably pushes people out of agriculture into non-agricultural occupations. The urban settlements can offer substantial non-agricultural employment and absorb persons moving out of an agricultural economy. If job opportunities in urban areas are productive and lead to gainful employment, urbanization becomes a catalyst for economic development. If, however, urbanization is merely a process of transfer of rural poverty to the urban environment, it only results in concentration of misery. Depending upon if urbanization is viewed and encouraged as a positive developmental process, it can be used to alleviate rural poverty.

The Context

In India, urbanization is largely emerging as a process involving transfer of rural poverty to urban areas and concentration of misery. It has resulted in malfunctioning of most of the urban centres, leading to the emergence of a number of imbalances and problems. Most of these settlements suffer from improper and haphazard development, absence of basic infrastructure and services, uncontrolled and unchecked growth of slums, high degree of visual and environmental pollution and uncontrolled and unregulated traffic. The cumulative effect of these factors is degradation of the quality of life, unsustainable growth and development requiring huge amount of subsidies. This is more evident in case of large cities, especially metros and super-metros.

It has been observed that contribution of urban India to net domestic product in 1950–1 was 29 per cent. It grew to 37 per cent by 1970–1 and 50 per cent in 1990–1. It increased to 55 per cent by 2001 when the urbanization level came to be of the order of 28 per cent. In other words, about 28 per cent of population living in urban India contributed 55 per cent of the national income. The economic well being of the country will largely depend upon the productivity of these urban centres. In order to enable these settlements to act as generators of wealth and prosperity it is necessary to ensure that there is appropriate input of planning, development and management so as to effectively channelize developmental forces.

The Punjab Scenario

In March 2001, the population of Punjab stood at 24,289,296, spread over an area of 50,362 sq. km. and housed in 157 urban settlements and 12,729 villages. The urban centres housed 8,245,566 persons, giving an urbanization level of 33.95 per cent. Rural areas accounted for the rest of 66.05 per cent population. This compares favourably with the national scenario in which every fourth person is an urbanite. Among the Indian states, Punjab ranks seventh in the level of urbanization, but 15th in terms of population. However, urban population recorded in the 2001 census was of a lower order than the figure of 35.8 per cent projected in 1984 by the Expert Committee on Population Projection, although the present level of urbanization is higher than that of 1991 (29.55 per cent).

It would be worthwhile to look at Punjab right from the beginning of the century so as to understand the trends of growth in urban population. Punjab's urban population recorded a decline of 13 per cent in 1901–11 due to the havoc caused by epidemics and famines. Thereafter it recorded a steady growth till 1941. In 1941–51, the growth rate of urban population once again recorded a decline due to large scale migration during partition. The rate slowed down to 25.27 per cent in 1961–71, but 1971–81 recorded an unprecedented growth of 44.51 per cent, the highest so far. The number of urban centres rose from 108 to

Table 16.1: Decadal Growth Rate of Punjab, 1901–2001
(Percentage of Decadal Variation)

Decade	Total	Rural	Urban
1901–11	-10.78	-10.46	-13.60
1911–21	+6.26	+6.17	+6.92
1921–31	+12.02	+8.92	+34.37
1931–41	+19.82	+16.06	+41.84
1941–51	-4.58	-9.71	+20.02
1951–61	+21.56	+19.47	+29.06
1961–71	+21.70	+20.63	+25.27
1971–81	+23.89	+17.48	+44.51
1981–91	+20.81	+16.69	+29.11
1991–2001	+19.76	+12.28	+37.58

134. The growth rate once again slowed down in 1981–91 to 29.11 per cent due to reduction in the number of urban centres from 134 in 1981 to 120 in 1991. However, growth rate again picked up in 1991–2001 when it was recorded as 37.58 per cent, with the number of urban centers increasing from 120 to 157.

As evident from the Census of 2001, in Punjab every third person is an urbanite as against the all India average of one out of 4 persons. The average population of a town in the state is 52,920 persons. A critical assessment of the various census figures and facts of urbanization reveals the following interesting points:

(i) During 1901–2001, the area covered by the present state of Punjab recorded more than nine-fold increase in its urban population.

(ii) Urban population in Punjab merely doubled in the first five decades whereas it increased more than four times in the last five decades.

(iii) Till 1931, there was only one class I city, i.e. Amritsar, In 1931 two more cities, i.e. Jalandhar and Ludhiana, were added to the list. The number of class I cities in 1991 was 10 and by 2001 it rose to 14.

(iv) At the beginning of the twentieth century, Amritsar was the largest city in the area, with a population of 162,429. Ludhiana was only one-third of the size of Amritsar. In the census of 2001, Ludhiana became one and a half times larger than Amritsar and two and a half times larger than Jalandhar.

(v) Ludhiana district is highly urbanized, with 55.80 per cent of population living in urban centres, whereas Nawanshahar district is the least urbanized, with only 13.80 per cent urban population.

(vi) Ludhiana, Amritsar, Jalandhar and Patiala are highly urbanized districts in the state. Three of these (Amritsar, Jalandhar, Ludhiana) are on the G.T. Road, indicating its influence and highlighting the area of concentration of population.

(vii) There is a polarization of population in fourteen class I cities of the state. Their share of population increased from 54.16 per cent in 1991 to 58.39 per cent in 2001. Thus, more than half of the state's urban population lives in these cities.

(viii) The share of nineteen class II towns in the urban population declined from 19.91 per cent to 16.45 per cent during 1991–2001.

(ix) Jointly, thirty-three class I cities and class II towns, held 74.84 per cent of population in 2001, showing a high degree of concentration in the large centres.

(x) The population of 124 towns in classes III–VI showed a slight decline from 25.72 per cent in 1991 to 25.16 per cent in 2001.

(xi) Ludhiana, with a population of 1,395,093 is the largest city in the state. In 1991, Ludhiana became the metropolitan centre. With Amritsar joining the rank in 2001, the state now has two metro centres out of 35 such centres in the country. Jalandhar is expected to join them by 2011.

(xii) Ludhiana, Amritsar and Jalandhar are three of the five corporation cities in the state and they jointly hold nearly two-fifths (37.25 per cent) of its total urban population.

(xiii) SAS Nagar (Mohali) emerged as a new centre of promise with the highest growth rate of 57.14 per cent among cities in the state. It also has the highest urban literacy rate of 92.5 per cent in Punjab.

(xiv) The slowest growth rate among class I cities was recorded by Phagwara (15.62 per cent).

(xv) In all, 2,252,341 people joined urban centres during 1991–2001 out of which 1,568,181 preferred class I cities and 163,215 class II towns. At the same time, 5,29,945 people came to classes III–VI.

(xvi) During 1991–2001, SAS Nagar, Malerkotla, Khanna and Phagwara became class I cities. It is expected that by 2011, class I status would be give to 9 more towns: Kapurthala, Mansa, Ferozepur, Barnala, Faridkot, Rajpura, Mukatsar, Kotkapura and Sangrur.

(xvii) Population pressure is comparatively less in the northern and southern part of the state. However, the central zone has high concentration of population.

(xviii) Certain urban corridors are fast emerging as nodal centres for concentration of industrial activity and population: Amritsar-Chhehrata, Amritsar-Jalandhar-Ludhiana-Rajpura along the G.T. Road, Ludhiana-Samrala, Chandigarh-Mohali-Kharar, Ropar-Balachaur, Banga-Nawanshahr, Ludhiana-Mullapur, Jagroan-Moga, Chandigarh-Rajpura, Chandigarh-Dera Bassi-Lalru, Hoshiarpur-Tanda-Mukherian, and Amritsar-Batala-Pathankot.

(xix) For the relative growth rate in each class, see Tables 16.2–16.7 at the end.

Future Projection

The economy of the state of Punjab draws its strength basically from agriculture, and agricultural production must continue to grow at a faster pace with the support and adoption of innovative technologies, changed cropping pattern and high-yield varieties. The future urbanization strategy for the state would be largely governed by this important parameter. With merely 1.53 per cent of the country's land, Punjab houses 2.37 per cent of the nation's population, indicating that land resource of the state is already under high stress. The population density of the state is 482 persons per sq. km. With the state population touching 30,500,000 by 2011 and 38,000,000 by 2021, it can well be seen that the available per capita land-man ratio will inevitably go down. The urban population is expected to increase from 82 lakh to 120 lakhs by 2011 and to 163 lakh by 2021. Already, large area of precious agricultural land is being utilized for non-agrarian purposes. If this trend continues, urbanization would adversely affect the state economy by considerably reducing agricultural production. Appropriate steps have to be taken by the state to confine growth only to urban areas. Taxing vacant land, curbing land speculation, minimizing extension of municipal limits, and evolving norms and standards for effective utilization of urban land could be considered as few options to achieve the objective.

Massive funds are likely to flow to the urban centres of the state as a result of the state of Punjab undertaking a massive programme of industrial growth and development, by involving entrepreneurs from within and outside India. Investment in the industrial sector is likely to give boost to economic activities in the state, resulting in increased rate of migration and concentration of population. This would lead to faster growth of urban areas, particularly the larger urban centres. Thus, effective steps to manage the growth and development of urban centres would be necessary in order to ensure their orderly development. Since urbanization has to be viewed not in isolation but as an essential and integral part of the ongoing socio-economic development process in the state, it would be desirable to ensure a balanced and dispersed growth. If the prevailing trends are any indication, unless the state effectively intervenes, urbanization would get localized in the larger urban centres and distort the state's urban and economic growth. Since the area adjoining the G.T. Road is highly urbanized, the future investment policy of the government must focus on the northern and the southern areas and declare these areas as incentive areas to attract private investment. Incentives should be localized in urban areas so that industries are established in the identified industrial zones. Disincentives for making investment should be a part of the strategy to minimize further concentration of population and economic activity in the central zone along the G.T. Road.

Till now, urban centres in the state have grown without much planning and developmental input. Only Improvement Trusts were created at a few places to promote planned development in pockets of urban centres for which schemes were framed. Over the years most of these Trusts have become defunct and urban centres are growing without any direction or control. A few state level agencies are undertaking development in urban areas. It is essential that appropriate strategies are framed for ensuring orderly growth of these areas. Attempt in this direction has been made by the state by enacting three comprehensive planning laws: 'The Punjab Regional and Town Planning and Development Act, 1995', 'The Punjab Apartment and Property Regulation Act, 1995', and 'The Punjab Apartment Ownership Act, 1995'. It is hoped that new planning regime brought in by these laws would provide necessary institutional and development inputs at the local and state level for urban centres to be planned and developed in a given framework. Under the Town Planning Act, the state has already created the Regional and Town Planning Board headed by the chief minister of the state. It is a high-powered body entrusted with the task of preparing policy and coordinating the activities of all the development agencies including the Punjab Urban Planning Development Authority (PUDA).

In the history of urbanization, it has been seen that state level agencies cannot ensure the orderly growth of all the human settlements. Only the local level agencies which are properly equipped with resources, both technical and financial, have shown desired performance. Accordingly, it would be appropriate to create local level agencies in the state and to declare municipalities as planning and development authorities. The municipalities will have to be strengthened by providing necessary technical input so as to enable them to discharge the difficult task of urban management. As per the 74th Constitutional Amendment, Ludhiana would require the creation of a Metropolitan Area Planning Committee for undertaking its planned development. All Improvement Trusts should be made an integral part of the municipalities and act as the technical arm for aiding, advising and assisting the municipalities in undertaking planned growth of these urban centres.

Large urban centres like Jalandhar, Ludhiana and Amritsar are facing an onslaught of unauthorized colonies, creating numerous developmental problems in the process. In the absence of appropriate infrastructures, these colonies are not providing appropriate quality of life to the residents. They have become liabilities for the municipalities which are already short of resources. Colonizers have made huge profits by unauthorizedly selling these plots. In order to eliminate this menace, law has already been enacted under which PUDA alone can sanction private colonies within the state. But even the colonies thus sanctioned do not have adequate social amenities. These colonies would emerge as planned slums in the years to come. It is necessary to ensure that all approved colonies contain appropriate level of basic infrastructure, services and provision for funding the city level facilities. The power to sanction colonies within urban areas should be vested in the municipalities so that funds raised by them are invested at the local level.

Slums are the shadows of urbanization. Their growth is due to various causes, ranging from the inability of migrants to provide themselves with appropriate shelter to the inability of the local agencies to provide adequate infrastructure. The slum population of the state was placed at 1,151,864 in 2001 which is 13.97 per cent of the state's total urban population. To deal with this problem, poverty alleviation programme, providing for a package to the urban poor, can be re-launched. A fund for income generating activities and provision of infrastructure for the urban poor can be created. Poverty alleviation fund can be established in every municipality. Shelter related programmes can be made community based to involve users in the programme. To ensure effective implementation, all the programmes should be monitored by state level agencies. Private sector and NGOs can also be involved in the programme. A close watch on the growth of slums needs to be maintained besides evolving appropriate strategies to minimize them.

Urbanization policy for the state needs to be evolved immediately which will help in an even spread of the forces of urbanization so that urban and rural settlements grow in tandem and not at the cost of one another. Efforts should be to make the growth and development of small and medium towns sustainable, more orderly and effective so as to enable these centres to play their vital role in the growth of the state. Regional and Town Planning and Development Board must be made to play its vital role in guiding and promoting the urbanization process in the state.

Settlement structure plan, indicating future urbanization pattern for the state, needs to be worked out for guiding and channelizing the forces of urbanization for its sustainable growth and development. Future urbanization pattern should be based on the premise that it will be people and community oriented and would involve the urban poor and informal sector as coparceners in the overall development process. Future growth strategies should aim at making all urban and rural areas environmentally sustainable. Human settlements should be planned on the basis of their holding capacity in terms of population, resources, economic activity and sustainability. Growth of over-sized and metro-cities should be discouraged. In short, the focus needs to be on the orderly growth and development of smaller settlements.

URBAN POPULATION PUNJAB—2001*

Table 16.2: Class I Cities (in descending order of population growth)

S. No.	Name of Town	Population 2001	% age Growth Rate (1991–2001)
	STATE'S AVERAGE	4,814,405	48.31
1.	SAS Nagar	123,284	57.14
2.	Khanna	103,059	43.16
3.	Batala	147,753	42.94
4.	Amritsar	1,011,327	37.65
5.	Jalandhar	709,255	37.63
6.	Bathinda	217,389	36.69
7.	Ludhiana	1,395,053	33.79
8.	Pathankot	168,275	31.26
9.	Patiala	323,309	27.43
10.	Moga	134,242	20.98
11.	Hoshiarpur	148,243	20.81
12.	Malerkotla	106,802	20.54
13.	Abohar	124,303	15.99
14.	Phagwara	102,111	15.62

Source: * Based on Tables 5(a)–10(a) in the author's Status Report on Urbanization of Punjab (forthcoming)

Table 16.3: Class II Towns (in descending order of population growth)

S. No.	Name of Town	Population (2001)	% age Growth Rate (1991–2001)
	STATE'S AVERAGE	1,356,386	13.68
1.	Sirhind-Fatehgarh Sahib	50,788	64.80
2.	Gobindgarh	60,672	44.24
3.	Sangrur	78,717	39.52
4.	Mansa	72,608	31.80
5.	Kapurthala	84,361	30.66
6.	Kotkapura	80,741	29.33
7.	Barnala	96,397	27.30
8.	Sunam	56,096	27.76
9.	Jagraon	60,106	26.88
10.	Mukatsar	83,099	25.18
11.	Malout	70,958	24.78
12.	Faridkot	73,042	24.59
13.	Gurdaspur	68,417	23.24
14.	Firozpur	95,451	21.23
15.	Taran Taran	55,587	16.95
16.	Rajpura	82,551	16.30
17.	Fazilka	67,424	16.19
18.	Nabha	61,953	13.84
19.	Firozpur Cantt.	57,418	8.14

Table 16.4: Class III Towns (in descending order of population growth)

S. No.	Name of Town	Population (2001)	% age Growth Rate (1991–2001)
	STATE'S AVERAGE	1,030,623	33.08
1.	Kharar	42,415	62.45
2.	Pattran	22,170	54.73
3.	Jalalabad	32,934	42.52
4.	Sujanpur	21,743	41.06
5.	Zira	31,778	33.96
6.	Dhuri	49,290	31.68
7.	Longowal	20,269	31.45
8.	Kurali	23,039	30.96
9.	Talwara	22,580	29.93
10.	Jalandhar Cantt	40,521	28.56
11.	Samana	46,509	27.23
12.	Rupnagar	48,165	26.76
13.	Dina Nagar	21,494	26.67
14.	Budhlada	23,499	25.55
15.	Morinda	21,788	25.07
16.	Bagha Purana	21,617	25.05
17.	Patti	34,432	23.96
18.	Jandiala	23,829	23.51
19.	Gidderbaha	36,593	22.52
20.	Rampura Phul	44,661	20.52
21.	Mukerian	21,379	20.02
22.	Kartarpur	25,152	19.24
23.	Urmar Tanda	22,115	17.72
24.	Raikot	24,738	17.46
25.	Jaitu	33,459	15.98
26.	Qadian	22,575	12.81
27.	Nakodar	31,422	10.34
28.	Dasua	20,118	9.63
29.	Ahmedgarh	28,007	9.57
30.	Maur	27,531	9.34
31.	Phillaur	22,228	6.07
32.	Nawanshahr	31,901	3.26
33.	Nangal	45,315	2.87
34.	Zirakpur	25,006	–
35.	Karoran	20,351	–

Table 16.5: Class IV Towns (in descending order of population growth)

S. No.	Name of Town	Population (2001)	% age Growth Rate (1991–2001)
	STATE'S AVERAGE	809,370	24.86
1.	Amritsar Cantt.	11,300	194.89
2.	Bhogpur	13,893	183.76
3.	Doraha	18,975	97.88
4.	Bhawanigarh	17,780	75.78
5.	Dera Bassi	15,690	63.40
6.	Banur	15,005	49.84
7.	Mullanpur Dakha	14,607	44.08
8.	Fatehgarh Churian	15,879	43.21
9.	Goraya	15,138	41.37
10.	Talwandi Bhai	14,570	39.27
11.	Rayya	12,620	38.35
12.	Guru Har Sahai	14,348	36.65
13.	Dharamkot M.C.	15,399	36.36
14.	Machhiwara	18,363	35.48
15.	Tappa	18,887	33.51
16.	Bhucho Mandi	13,183	31.75
17.	Dhariwal	18,706	31.60
18.	Majitha	13,006	31.21
19.	Anandpur Sahib	13,886	30.09
20.	Baretta	14,882	28.99
21.	Amloh	12,686	28.74
22.	Garhshanker	15,094	28.34
23.	Lahragaga	19,310	24.14
24.	Shahkot	12,631	23.28
25.	Samrala	17,610	23.26
26.	Goniana	12,812	23.01
27.	Sanaur	17,938	22.76
28.	Rajasansi	12,131	21.21
29.	Dhanaula	18,397	15.22
30.	Sultanpur	15,653	14.07
31.	Bhadaur	16,818	13.57
32.	Noor Mahal	12,630	13.28
33.	Raman	19,549	13.16
34.	Rahon	12,046	11.84
35.	Adampur	16,620	8.41

(contd.)

Table 16.5 (contd.)

S. No.	Name of Town	Population (2001)	% age Growth Rate (1991–2001)
36.	Banga	18,892	6.61
37.	Bassi Pathana	18,547	2.25
38.	Bhikhiwind	10,269	-14.12
39.	Ajnala	18,602	–
40.	Balachaur	18,106	–
41.	Sahnewal	17,248	–
42.	Jugial	16,664	–
43.	Sardulgarh	16,315	–
44.	Hussainpur	15,343	–
45.	Bhikhi	15,078	–
46.	Moonak	14,928	–
47.	Dirba	13,073	–
48.	Kalanaur	12,915	–
49.	Makhu	12,173	–
50.	Khem Karan	11,938	–
51.	Khanauri	10,977	–
52.	Nehon	10,158	–
53.	Bhulath	10,079	–
54.	Mahilpur	10,019	–

Table 16.6: Class V Towns (in descending order of population growth)

S. No.	Name of Town	Population (2001)	% age Growth Rate (1991–2001)
	STATE'S AVERAGE	207,891	101.94
1.	Sangat	5,396	97.58
2.	Payal	7,267	24.18
3.	Ramdass	5,790	21.51
4.	Gardhiwala	6,263	21.40
5.	Hariana	7,813	20.70
6.	Akalgarh	6,600	18.62
7.	Kot Fatta	6,493	15.72
8.	Alawalpur	7,172	10.88
9.	Dera Baba Nanak	7,493	1.53
10.	Badhni Kalan	6,373	-25.65
11.	Handiaya	9,725	–
12.	Begowal	9,612	–
13.	Cheema	9,347	–
14.	Bhankharpur	9,118	–
15.	Khamanon	8,876	–
16.	Budha Theh	8,730	–
17.	Lohian Khas	8,546	–
18.	Ghagga	8,212	–
19.	Rurki Kasba	8,186	–
20.	Dhilwan	7,980	–
21.	Jandiala	7,704	–
22.	Bariwala	7,545	–
23.	Chohal	7,433	–
24.	Malout	7,160	–
25.	Mullanpur-Garibdas	6,143	–
26.	Bhabat	5,794	–
27.	Ghanaur	5,754	–
28.	Hajipur	5,366	–

Table 16.7: Class VI Centres (in descending order of population growth)

S. No.	Name of Town	Population (2001)	% age Growth Rate (1991–2001)
	STATE'S AVERAGE	26,895	-4.63
1.	Sri Hargobindpur	3,993	15.37
2.	Shamchaurasi	4,221	13.74
3.	Bhisiana	4,775	–
4.	Daulatpur	4,544	–
5.	Sansarpur	4,061	–
6.	Bharoli Kalan	3,369	–
7.	Shekhpura	1,932	–

Index

Foreign Friends of the Institute

Canada

Harmohinder Singh Bains, Lakhwinder Singh Bains, Manga Bassi, Jugraj Bath, Sarbjit Singh Bathal, Sadhu Binning, Piara Singh Beesla, Bachan Singh Buttar, Harcharan Singh Daliwal, Paramjit Singh Dhaliwal, Pritpal Singh Dhaliwal, Ujjal Dev Singh Dosanjh, Niranjan Singh Gill, Paramjit Singh Gill, Sarwan Singh Gill, Zora Singh Gill, Hardial Singh Grewal, Harnek Singh Grewal, Rajinder Singh Hans, Sukhwant Hundal, Jaswant Singh, Kulwant Singh Khatra, Raghbir Singh Mangat, Sohan Punni, Gurmail Ria, Gurpal Singh Sahota, Jasbir Singh Sahota, Ranbir Singh Sahota, Harbhajan Singh Sandhu, Surjit Singh Sandhu, K.S. Sekhon, Dharampal Sharma, Amrik Sull and Gulzar Singh Willing, Vedic Hindu Society of British Columbia.

United Kingdom

Hardev Singh Brar, Hari Singh Chahal, Tejinder Singh Dhaliwal, Gurcharan Singh Grewal, Gurdev Singh Grewal, Hardeep Singh Grewal, Jagdev Singh Grewal and Malkiat Singh Grewal.

United State of America

Karam Singh Burn, Bhupinder Singh Gill, Rahuldeep Gill, Harjit Singh Mangat and Jasbir Kaur Saluja.